Groundcrew Boys

Aeronautics was neither an industry nor a science. It was a miracle.
IGOR SIKORSKY

GROUNDCREW BOYS

True Engineering
Stories from the
Cold War Front Line

DAVID GLEDHILL

with SIMON JAKUBOWSKI

GRUB STREET • LONDON

This book is dedicated to the generations of groundcrew
who loaned their precious machines to the aircrew who flew them.

Published by
Grub Street
4 Rainham Close
London SW11 6SS

A CIP record for this title is available from the British library

ISBN-13: 978-1-911667-02-5

Typeset by Francesca Mangiaracina

Printed and bound by Finidir, Czech Republic

Contents

In memoriam

This book is dedicated to Andrew 'Wardy' Ward.
Wardy served as an armourer in the Royal Air Force from 1987
to 2006. Working on the Tornado F3 and, later, the Typhoon,
he was universally admired by those who served alongside him.
He passed away in February 2020 and will be fondly
remembered by his friends and family.

Foreword

AIR COMMODORE GEORGE C. MARTIN MSc, CEng, FRAeS

I am immensely humbled to have been asked to contribute a foreword to *Groundcrew Boys* and hope that my own words and those of the authors will help to embrace the *esprit de corps*, the kudos and unique standing of the roles, the opportunities, the skills, the characters, the tenacity, the resourcefulness and, ultimately, the professionalism of groundcrew across all our services.

In my own case, although now retired from the RAF, I look back with great pride at the near 40 years I spent working in and around the support and operation of aircraft while managing the men and women who served as groundcrew. I cannot believe how fortunate I was to undertake so many fascinating roles and meet so many outstanding characters in my career as both an airman and an officer within the engineering trade of the RAF; all of which satisfied my thirst to support and maintain aircraft. I know I am not alone when I say my desire to work on, support, manage, design, certify and indeed fly aircraft of all shapes and sizes, in most corners of the world, was both a passion and a privilege.

Having read the tales in this book, I am drawn to just how many common themes they all contain. While there may be variations of aircraft, location and indeed service, beneath all of them are real-life stories that all of us, fortunate enough to have been in and around aircraft and the characters that support and operate them, can relate to. I, like most, have way too many tales to offer of humorous, exciting, sad, frightening and proud memories, however, on reflection, I am drawn to my first tour straight out of training to highlight two memories that I cherish and which I believe reflect the underlying beauty of the stories in this book to help define groundcrew colleagues past and present.

Having spent three years training as an apprentice (a Brat) at RAF Halton in the late 1970s/early 1980s, l was very fortunate that my first tour was on an operational, fast-jet squadron—No. 54 Squadron—operating Jaguars and based at the time, at RAF Coltishall, Norfolk. I was a sponge for the initial part of my tour and soaked everything up … the crewroom banter which was fierce, the characters, the laughs, the humour and the wisdom of my colleagues.

I was only 20 years of age and working on a front-line squadron and recall thinking there was no better job in the world, especially when I was put under the watchful eye for nearly a month, of one of the squadron flight line mechanics (FLMs pronounced 'flem'). Although 'my' FLM was really old, probably 25 at the time, he was a king in my eyes since he had, on reflection, an encyclopaedic knowledge of the aircraft. He was one of eight FLMs on the squadron and all of them were 'go-to' members of staff especially for the aircrew since, unbelievably, there was virtually nothing they didn't know about the aircraft. They did not pretend to be something they were not; they did not profess to be academically gifted, although many were; they did not profess to wish for themselves a full career ahead of them; they were happy remaining as some of the most junior ranks on the squadron and they were happy to remain and continue to do 'the magic' they did. That said, to a man, they taught me so much and I have remained indebted for the sheer professionalism I saw from such a small band. Problems with fault diagnostics on the line? Call in the FLM; first port of call for the aircrew after a difficult flight? Call in the FLM; going on detachment and debating what equipment to load? Call in the FLM; want a 'special' Christmas function organised? Yip, call in a FLM. Moral of the tale never, never judge the book by the cover!

The other individual who shone for me at that time on No. 54 Squadron was the squadron warrant officer, who was, no less, a formidable character. They all were/are but who I, on reflection again, owe so much to. It was he who, upon hearing the news that my mother had died unexpectedly while I was working on a night shift, brought me into his office the following morning, arranged a call with my father and on hearing it was going to take close to ten hours to get home by train, spoke to the squadron boss and negotiated a flight in the back of a Jaguar straight into a civilian airfield, to allow me to be with my family that afternoon, a gesture I still to this day cannot forget. It was he who, when he saw the paperwork with my offer of a commission, *told me* I was to sign it; my choices being a commission or going for three months on a Red Flag exercise in Las Vegas. Moral of the tale? As a manager your role is an absolute privilege so grab it with both hands and … manage!

I look back in awe at these characters and say they were giants in my life who, without question, influenced how I behaved throughout my career regarding looking after colleagues. I can absolutely guarantee and I am not alone in saying, that the pedigree of groundcrew that all three services have enjoyed for many years, and withstood the operational challenges in many campaigns and conflicts, has been drawn and developed from, at its core, good education and training and the opportunity to have exposure to such a wealth of talent.

Enjoy what are some fascinating, and in the most part humorous, ground-crew tales which all help to open the door, across a mixture of services, ranks and experience levels, on the truly unique and fascinating life of groundcrew. They are totally professional personalities privileged to do, in my eyes, the best job in the world.

Following a three-year apprenticeship at RAF Halton, George Martin served as groundcrew on No. 54 Squadron at RAF Coltishall working on Jaguar aircraft. On successful selection for commission, he graduated as an engineering officer on No. 60 Initial Officers Course at RAF Cranwell in July 1982. During an extensive career supporting air operations he served on F-4 Phantoms at RAF Leuchars before then enjoying overseas tours in Hong Kong and Brunei. His tours of duty included being a weapons trials officer on Buccaneer, Tornado and Harrier; as the integrated project team leader for E-3D Sentry; as OC Engineering Wing at RAF Lyneham for C-130J/K and wing commander integrated logistics support for the Airbus A400M project at Abbey Wood. Promoted to group captain, he became the RAF director within the Post-Graduate Division for the Defence Academy. Returning to the procurement arena he was the operations manager responsible for the testing, build and acceptance into RAF service of the Nimrod MRA4 aircraft. He was the first chief air engineer appointed within 22 (Training) Group overseeing the introduction to service of the Hawk T Mk 2 advanced trainer at RAF Valley. His last tour of duty was as head of programmes in the MoD Saudi Projects Team, based in Riyadh, Saudi Arabia supporting the programmes for Royal Saudi Air Force Typhoon, Tornado, Hawk and PC9/21 operations. He retired in 2016 and is now working for a leading UK defence contractor.

Introduction

I must start by thanking Simon Jakubowski, without whom this book would never have appeared. It was his inspiration that set the project running which has resulted in what you see here. Simon is an avid aviation book enthusiast who runs the Aviation Enthusiasts Book Club Facebook group inspiring others to share their passion for aviation writing.

I wasn't groundcrew because, as many of my former squadron colleagues often reminded me, I wasn't smart enough! Nevertheless, as you read the stories in the book you will realise that many of us received our 'trade' training on the job.

A squadron is a complex beast and is, without doubt, the sum of its constituent parts. It has been said that the aircrew receive the accolades but the groundcrew are the beating heart and this is a fact. The way a squadron operated was dictated by the daily flying programme and the need to be able to meet NATO generation targets. At any time of the day or night, a simple message might require a unit to generate all of its declared aircraft. These aircraft had to be made serviceable and, if necessary, armed, within strict time limits. At least 50 per cent, and then 70 per cent, had to be declared as available to fly within a few hours. To fail to do so affected careers in a detrimental way.

As a young aircrew member, the 'troops' were an unruly mob who 'chest poked' at the regular 'all ranks' get-togethers. The banter was irreverent and brutal and no one was safe—apart from, maybe, the senior engineering officer and the boss—maybe! They often spoke a different language, speculating on the health of the LRU 5A2 and whether it was communicating with the MCS. I understood the problem. Often the failure I had seen in the air could not be reproduced on the ground and when the system failed on the next sortie, it was easy to accuse the technician of a lack of diligence. What I often missed was that I would not spend that night in the hangar trying to reproduce a tenuous or intermittent fault, trying to coax a reluctant system back to life. I just expected the system to work when I took to the air.

It was only when elevated to the role of squadron programmer that the reality became clear. The flying task was dictated by higher headquarters and was sacrosanct. That there might not be enough airframes to meet the task was irrelevant to 'their airships' and the system was 'can do'. Success was expected at all levels but hard to achieve with limited resources. The burden fell on the engineers.

Although a squadron might be allocated ten airframes, at least one of those would be in deep servicing and maybe another grounded with significant technical problems. Another might be sitting on QRA (quick reaction alert) and another might be awaiting spares. For that reason, it was almost impossible to generate every aircraft theoretically on the squadron's books. As a programmer, I would often schedule eight into six into four, a total of 18 sorties from six airframes. With modern complex aircraft this was often unlikely. To do so, the engineering team had to produce the maximum number of aircraft and to keep them serviceable. As a flight commander and then boss, the full extent of the groundcrew contribution was clear. I might rue the fact that I was sitting on QRA quick reaction alert for my 24-hour stint but, whenever I was shackled to the telebrief, there was a dedicated team of groundcrew down the corridor and a rectification team working in the hangar. Without them the jets simply could not fly. I have on many occasions walked into the dispersal in the wee small hours, knowing that I would re-emerge in the dark, feeling sorry for myself, but I would probably pass the night shift just going home, having achieved miracles.

I can say without fear of contradiction that I served with some of the most capable, motivated and professional engineers in the world. We naturally think of those on the flight line and in the hangars but there is a myriad of support roles and they know who they are. To keep our aircraft flying, we needed safety equipment fitters, air traffic controllers and suppliers to name but a few of the supporting trades. Every single person contributed to keeping the aircraft in the air. I may even admit to some of them being amongst my best friends—well that may be going a little too far! You will take it from this that banter was mandatory.

I was delighted to be asked to compile this compendium of tales as it compliments my other aviation works. On this occasion, however, I cannot boast at having authored the stories. I hope, like me, you'll be fascinated at the wealth and breadth of the experiences, not only of the line engineers but also the band of enthusiasts who preserve our aviation heritage. The tales are funny, thought provoking and absorbing in equal measure.

The 'Groundcrew Boys' were, and are, without doubt, unsung heroes.

My thanks go to all our contributors of both stories and images. It is my intention to donate all the profits from this book to military charities to support their invaluable work.

DAVID GLEDHILL

David Gledhill joined the Royal Air Force as a navigator in 1973. After training, he flew the F-4 Phantom on squadrons in the UK and West Germany. He was one of the first aircrew to fly the F2 and F3 air defence variant of the Tornado on its acceptance into service and served for many years as an instructor on the operational conversion units of both the Phantom and the Tornado. He commanded the Tornado Fighter Flight in the Falkland Islands, the Electronic Warfare Tactics and Countermeasures Wing, the Special Projects team and was wing commander operations at the Air Warfare Centre. After working extensively with the armed forces of most NATO nations, including serving as the senior operations officer at the Balkans Combined Air Operations Centre, the exchange officer at the Joint Command and Control Warfare Centre in Texas and as the UK liaison officer at the USAF Warfare Centre at Nellis Air Force Base, he retired in 2010. He has published a number of factual books on aviation topics and novels in the Phantom Air Combat *series set during the Cold War.*

DAVID GLEDHILL   SIMON JAKUBOWSKI

The Squadron Hierarchy

VIC WINWRIGHT

At the top of the engineering tree on any squadron was the senior engineering officer (SEngO), a squadron leader. They would have the overall responsibility for engineering practices on the squadron and would be supported by a flight lieutenant, the junior engineering officer (JEngO). On some outfits there may be a third engineering officer, a first tourist straight from training who was known as BEngO; the 'baby engineering officer'. Next down the line would be the warrant officer engineering who would have the responsibility for the day-to-day running of all things engineering and its manpower. Two shifts would cover flying operations and beyond; a day shift and the evening or night shift. With limited manpower, a swing shift might bridge the gap between a true day or night shift. Although in peacetime, aircraft would normally land by midnight, often the night shift would extend into the early morning hours in order to meet readiness states for NATO.

Each aircraft was managed by an aircraft servicing chief (ASC) whose responsibility was to progress his aircraft's serviceability state to make it available for flying. To achieve this, he would be supported by the trade managers and their tradesmen for each specialisation. Each shift was run by either a senior ASC or, in some cases, by a flight sergeant.

The servicing trades changed over the years but were, traditionally, referred to as two groups: 'heavies' and 'fairies'. The heavies comprised the airframe trade, the propulsion or engine trade and the armourers. The fairies were made up of the radar trades, the wireless or radio trades and the instrument trades. Another trade did not quite fit into either group, namely the electricians or 'lekkies'. In later years the trades were changed so that a tradesman might be a combination of engine, airframe and armourer or all of the 'fairy' trades combined. Where the lekkies fitted in was often a mystery. When introduced, these combined tradesmen were called 'split brains' or 'splitties'. Whilst on the subject of nicknames, engine tradesmen were 'sooties' which originated when they would get black from going down the jet pipes of early jet engines. Airframe tradesmen were 'riggers' which stems from the First World War when aircraft had wire rigging. Armourers were called 'plumbers' but why is a mystery and set in legend. Fairies were so called because they were assumed to be delicate things yet always available when a 'gash' job needed doing.

Starting at the very bottom of the rank structure, an aircraftman emerged from training, soon promoted to leading aircraftman (LAC) and then senior aircraftman (SAC). These were the mechanics. The way up 'the slippery slope' was by passing trade examinations and from time on the job. The next stage was a major step forward by becoming a fitter which attracted the rank of junior technician (J/T) in later years. The qualification was achieved by selection for an advanced course in trade, at a training school. Next was the first level of supervisory rank as a corporal, again achieved by passing an exam after sufficient time as a J/T. Next came sergeant through to chief technician, also attained by assessment and time. The senior non-commissioned officers on a squadron were the flight sergeants and the squadron warrant officer. With progress through the ranks, the job became more supervisory in nature and individuals became less of a producer.

There was only ever one warrant officer on a squadron!

CHAPTER 1

The Tornado with the Purple Heart

Allen Vernon joined the RAF in 1984 as a direct entry airframe technician. He was first posted to the airframe bays at Lossiemouth, followed by a tour doing Category 3 level airframe repairs on No. 431 Maintenance Unit at Brüggen followed by a posting to Repair and Salvage Squadron at Abingdon. These tours were working on anything, from Spitfires to Harriers. For his remaining time in the RAF, Al worked on Jaguars, at Coltishall and Coningsby, Harriers at Cottesmore and Tornados at Marham. On retirement, he was awarded a licensed aircraft engineering ticket and works for a regional airline as a line engineer. He was in Basra during the worst days of 2008 and at the time of the death of the last RAF serviceman in Iraq. The last ceremonial Jaguar paint scheme bears his name as the designer and he is also known for restoring the only running SEPECAT Jaguar outside India.

It's the morning of 2 August 1990 and I am a young, rigger corporal on his third tour of duty in the big wide world. I have joined the world of structural repairs since emerging from the direct entrant technicians course—I can hear the banter from the ex-flight line mechanics as I write. I'm on leave and moonlighting for my father's business to earn some extra cash for the imminent holiday when my mother, who is also involved in the business, mentions to me that Iraq has invaded Kuwait that morning. I had not heard this on the way to work as my Opel Manta only played cassette tapes. Is this event going to affect my life I ask myself? As I am only six months into a programme, replacing useless American-designed closure ribs on Harrier GR5 tail planes at Wittering, I doubt it.

Come 12 December 1990, I am in the control office of the Aircraft Repair Flight (ARF) of Repair and Salvage Squadron (RSS), based in C Hangar at RAF Abingdon, known to the locals as 'Abo'. There have been many changes since August and several RAF squadrons are already deployed to the Gulf. I have been working in No. 3 Hangar at RAF Coltishall for four months making repairs to four Jaguar fighter-bombers that have been declared Category 3 needing bird strike repairs. The work party consists of 20 other Abingdon-based guys. No. 6 Squadron, that live in the hangar, have already gone east and there are not enough station personnel left to repair the broken 'Cats'. I am back at Abo for a routine RSS training course but there are plans brewing for a war role, to form aircraft battle damage repair (ABDR) teams, although the people who have been picked seem to be the 'unfavourites'. My name has not been pulled out of the hat yet, however, the very same day, one guy pulls the 'family issue'. As I am lurking in the office, the controller asks me if I would fill the vacant post. I'm single, no ties so why the hell not?

The following week I find myself back at Abingdon, but now on an ABDR techniques course. For those who think that ABDR means to cover a hole with speed tape, rest assured it does not; it does, however, involve restoring the structural strength of the airframe following a combat incident. This does not mean restoring the finite life of the airframe nor does it protect against environmental issues such as corrosion. The modern term 'expedient repair' is a far better descriptive term, but I digress. I was there to learn the techniques, the Cold War way and there would be nothing in my way to stop me throwing a patch on here or a slab on there. We start with a Cold War Buccaneer ABDR training video, then move on to a Harrier GR3 fuselage repair. I failed that straight away as Harrier complex curves are a challenge in peacetime. Next, we are given a Tornado wing, still wearing its desert pink paint scheme. It was part of the most recently scrapped airframe in the RAF that has just been sent back from Saudi Arabia. It was even more challenging to get to grips with that technique. Then, it's a look into the various battle damage manuals for each aircraft type, including the infamous ABDR rivet-pitch formula. Eventually, we are all qualified to carry out wartime repairs and wait for the call to arms which is not long in coming.

I'm at Riyadh Airport, Saudi Arabia and it's 2130 (Zulu or Greenwich Mean Time) on 21 January 1991. I am still in the back of a No. 216 Squadron Tristar with 54 other helpless souls, trying to rip open the packaging around my nuclear, biological and chemical protective suit (NBC) but wearing a respirator—a gas mask to the uninitiated. To say the last 30 hours had been hectic is an understatement. Christmas 1990 had seen the first deployment from the Abingdon ABDR unit, to set up a base in the new theatre of operations. The manufacture of ABDR kits had been accelerated, to support the huge increase in RAF units being deployed for the inevitable war that is going to kick off between Saddam Hussein and the rest of the world.

The Gulf War started on the night of 16/17 January, with the boys waiting to deploy working at Wittering but my poor mate Mark would never see his beloved Sheffield Wednesday play in the Milk Cup that night. They never aired his game as when the commercial break ended, ITV went straight to CNN coverage of cruise missiles striking Baghdad.

The 'call to war' for me came direct from the commanding officer of the ABDR section at Abo, when the telephone rang at lunchtime at my parents' house, the following Saturday. "Be at Abo at 0430 tomorrow, ready to go to Innsworth," he said. A mad rush followed in an effort to get things sorted before I left. In order: watch England win at Cardiff Arms Park for the first time in my lifetime, see my hometown footy team win, then get my arse back to Abingdon.

There was just enough time to get a few pints in town and disconnect the battery on the Manta before I was due to leave. I had heard of the stories of the squadron guys having to call out the breakdown services when they got back to Coltishall because they had left everything hooked up. I wasn't going to make the same mistake.

The rest of the time was spent at RAF Innsworth or on an RAF bus shuttling between there and Abo. It took two hours to kit out each person with the equipment we needed to go to war. I was allowed one bag of 'civvies' and two 'sausage bags' containing my 'tropical greens'—and not forgetting being issued with my personal self-loading rifle. It was a mad rush to put my webbing together, get changed and get back on the bus to RAF Brize Norton from where the flight would depart. I decided to leave a present, as the training canister that was on my S10 respirator seemed somewhat surplus to requirements. I would need real ones from now on.

Arriving at Brize, we were fed the inevitable meal in 'Gateway House', the transit accommodation, before being shipped to the departure terminal. We were loaded on board a dual-role No. 216 Squadron Tristar which, bar the rear pallet of seats, was full of equipment. Then it was off to Saudi, smoking by the toilets in the back of the 'Timmy', as the Tristar was known, during a long, monotonous flight.

By the time the aircraft made its approach into Riyadh at 2100, an emergency had been declared on the ground, and the captain let us know over the passenger address system that we would be held off. After another ten minutes, the Timmy was allowed in and we landed. As we taxied onto the stand and stopped, the usual hive of activity was lacking. It was not what you would expect to see with an airliner arriving. What was going on, I asked myself?

I was sitting in an aisle seat, away from the window, watching a chief technician called Pete who was peering out. "They're launching fireworks," he said. "They're f***** Patriots," he said. Yes, our introduction to our new theatre of operations was to land in the middle of a Scud attack! Sonic booms and explosions rattled the airframe as we desperately tried to don our protective gear. Adopting 'NBC Category Black' in the confines of the cabin was daunting. Then we waited …

One of our group was known as Manny and had an Arab surname. He was getting a little irate that we were sitting in a tin can with weapons landing around us, sent by a guy with the same surname. The loadmaster's advice was offered but not taken up.

"Well, you can jump mate," he said, "but it's a 16-foot drop from here!"

Finally, the all-clear was sounded, the ramp handlers appeared, and we got off still suited up in our NBC kit but, thankfully, without gas masks. We were bussed to the military terminal. The floor underneath was a military hospital and one of my mates from back home, who had been pulled back into the army medical reserves, was based there. I try to find him, but he was off-shift. We were met by the RSS ABDR warrant officer who took us on to the ABDR compound on the outskirts of Riyadh where we are allocated to teams, given a villa and hit the sack.

A couple of hours later I heard a car horn going off in the background making a regular beat. I woke the others in the room:

"Is that an air raid warning?"

"Yes, it is!"

I masked up and knocked on the door of the senior non-commissioned officer's (SNCO) room next door. The occupants saw my head sticking through the gap wearing a gas mask, just as more explosions and sonic booms were heard, signalling the next attack on Riyadh. The rest of the team kitted up and there was a tense wait for the all-clear signal.

The incident got me the nickname 'Radar'—from the television series

M*A*S*H—and it stuck for the rest of the deployment. It seemed that I could hear 'incoming' enemy missiles fired at us, way before anyone else.

The next few days were hectic as we bumped into our fellow colleagues from Abingdon who had already been deployed since Christmas and had been the first members of the ABDR empire. I met the other members of the team to which I had been assigned and, within 24 hours, we were onboard a C-130 Hercules shuttle, flying to our respective airbases. The three deployed teams would be based at Tabuk, Dhahran and Bahrain. I was on the Dhahran team with five other colleagues. Our boss, Pete, was an electrician, with the airframe guys Bernie and 'Baldrick' from the Western Repair Flight, whom I had not known beforehand. The electrical/avionics guys were Tornado qualified which helped. Barry, who hadn't the slightest interest in being out there, was the chief gliding instructor for the RAF Gliding and Soaring Association at Halton and hadn't touched a 'Tonka', as the Tornado was known, in eons.

After dropping people off in Bahrain, passing the Jaguars on the flight line, that I had seen being modified and painted during my time at Coltishall, we flew on to Dhahran, landing in darkness. Even though it was dark, we were introduced to the largest airbase I had ever seen in my life, and it was jam packed with more aircraft types than I have ever seen in one place. Even the air fetes at the huge American base at Mildenhall were nothing compared to this. There were rows of Kuwaiti A-4s, alongside RAF Tornados, American F-16s, and enough US Army choppers to film *Apocalypse Now*, not to mention most of USAF Military Airlift Command, including five C-5 Galaxy parked together.

Once we were off the 'Herc', we bumped into two of the SNCOs from the Germany-based No. 431 Maintenance Unit (MU), ABDR team, who had been asked to greet us. 'Chalky', I had known from my own time on No. 431 MU. Also, present was one of the more famous RAF groundcrew characters from the Tornado world, 'Charlie'. He was wearing a bandana made from his scrim scarf and carrying a holstered machete. Not to let him off lightly I said: "Flipping hell mate, why in God's name are you carrying that ridiculous blade? You're a rigger, not Rambo!" Our accommodation that night was the fantastic *Rivatza* flats, home for the resident RAF Regiment Rapier squadron.

Next morning, the team was picked up and taken to our assigned accommodation, an ex-Patriot compound in Al Khobar where many of the non-formed unit personnel were based. We were billeted two to a room, with access to a kitchen and a lounge with TV, showing continuous Saudi war propaganda videos, interspersed with Saudi news bulletins and the calls to prayer.

The first task was to hitch a lift to the airbase, pick up security passes and travel to the squadron operating line where the ABDR set-up was based, in a Portakabin, next to the RAF field kitchen. Immediately we found out that one of the Tornados had been damaged on a raid the night before but had got back safely. It would be straight into the war role then.

An eight-ship Tornado formation from No. 31 Squadron had been assigned to carry out a medium-level attack on the Ar Rumaylah airbase, on the night of 24 January 1991, using 1,000-lb bombs. The first four aircraft carried variable timing (VT) fused weapons, set to air burst. This meant the bombs would explode above the target scattering shrapnel and was the ideal weapon for suppression of anti-aircraft artillery (AAA), or 'triple A'. The second formation carried ground impact, fused bombs to attack the south-western hardened aircraft shelter (HAS) complex. After two ground aborts and an airborne abort due to an electronic countermeasures pod failure, the senior formation leaders returned to base leaving the junior pilots to complete the attack. As the remaining members of the first formation released their stores, ZA403 and ZD843 were damaged after premature detonation of the weapons, leaving ZA403 so badly damaged, that she had to be abandoned. ZD843 was peppered with high-velocity fragments from her failed bomb but fortunately, the airframe was still responding and handling well enough—even with system malfunctions—to make a safe recovery to Dhahran. It had been the fifth operational mission for ZD843, notably the first Tornado to use the JP233 airfield denial weapon during Operation Desert Storm, flown that night by the commanding officer of No. 31 Squadron, Jerry Witt.

By the evening of 25 January, the ABDR teams were looking at ZD843, 'Delta Hotel', in the maintenance hangar, but it was a sorry sight. Both tailerons—the all-moving tail plane on the Tornado—were shredded. It was the same for the engine doors and the engine nozzles which had suffered damage to the petals which had been blown away. There were holes in the left-hand flaps, the wing structure and the spoilers and pieces of shrapnel had punctured the fin. One fragment had punched a hole into the triangular panel at the top and another had pierced the torsion box. Damn, that was bad because that was a fuel tank as well. Up front, there was a hole in the fuselage behind the folding nose, known as the maxi skirt, and a hole in the left gun bay door. When we opened the door, our finest piece of British cast-steel shrapnel had not only burst a composite door, but cut through a steel forging that formed the mount for the left-hand Mauser cannon. If that was not enough, it had gone through the cockpit floor as well.

Well, where does one start?

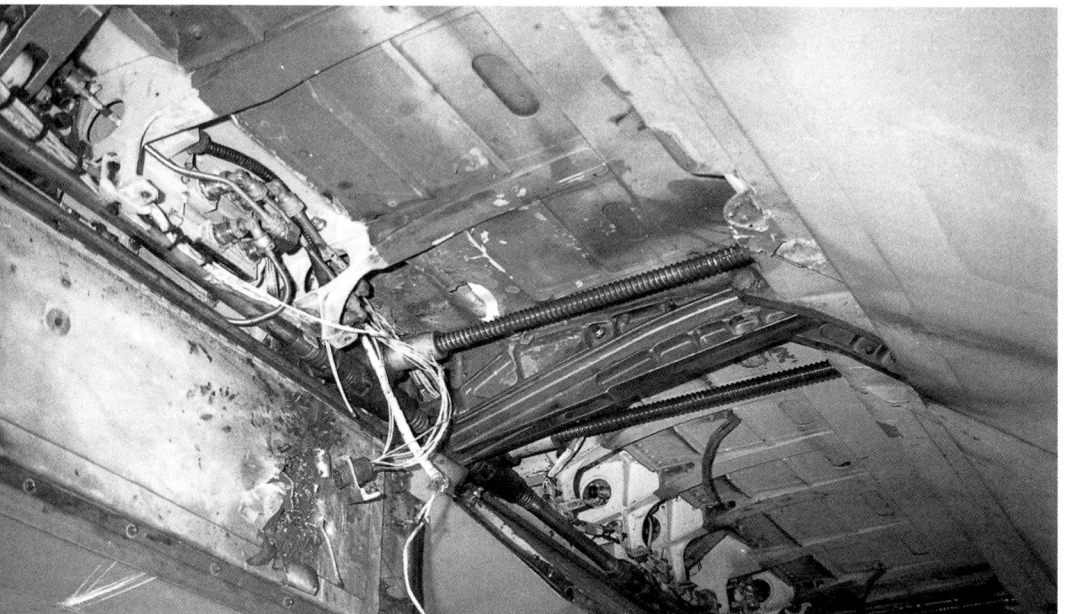

A CLOSE-UP IMAGE OF THE TORNADO GR1 SPOILERS. (ALLEN VERNON)

Les Hendy was the senior engineering officer of No. 31 Squadron and, in-the-atre, was the judge of what we could and couldn't do. He asked for an assessment of how long it would take to carry out repairs to peacetime standards. The senior NCOs were uncompromising. Their assessment was that using normal repair schemes and acquiring the spares to repair the airframe, to do the job would take about a year. Using ABDR techniques; less than two weeks was the general consensus. Consent was given for us to start the process. The MU boys, being Tornado qualified in their respective trades, would attack the areas where replacing components was the quickest solution, such as the flying controls and the doors. The squadron engineers would carry out the propulsion, armament and avionics equipment exchanges, leaving my own team—most of whom were not Tornado qualified—to do the repairs. The day shift went back to their digs while we looked at what we could begin that night. Starting with assessments of the damage and removing components for access, we began the massive task.

By the time we returned the following evening, the day shift and the squadron guys had gutted the back end of the aircraft, removed the damaged equipment, and had removed the avionics rack from the front fuselage where Bernie was going to repair the hole in that area. Being the junior member of the team, I had 'last shout' on being given a task until I saw Steve's idea to repair the cockpit floor. I explained that the plan was not going to work and offered to take it on. Bernie agreed so I ended up with the most complex job of all.

The main damage was to the cockpit which is, of course, a pressurised structure. It became apparent that the side structure was not made from sheet plate, having started life as a piece of aluminium, machined to form pockets to save weight. The pockets were inside the cockpit, just where I had planned to put a plate and there were components bolted directly onto the base where the repair was going to be made. The structure was built from 3-mm alloy and, in the bible of battle damage repair, we could use steel of half the thickness. A repair scheme was slowly being drawn up in my head and the practice repair on the Tornado wing a few months earlier, was going to be replicated. The rivet formula, that we had been taught in school, was as good as useless in this situation so I decided to use standard rigger trade practice for the rivets that I would use. The first problem: the rivets I had in the kit were not countersunk and that was going to be an issue. The gun bay door came off for access, along with the

damaged gun support foot and I cleaned the damage, establishing datums to work to. There would be no Cengar or Bahco saws involved as those are brutal ABDR tools but there would be some chain drilling and rotary file action. Another Scud attack interfered with the night's proceedings but, by then, it was a regular occurrence; usually at 2230 when we were having supper.

The following days saw the work progress. There was a nice insert repair on the front fuselage, only spoilt by the huge 3/16" Avdel mono-bolt rivets, those being the only fasteners in our kit. With a boiler plate repair to the wing and the spoiler replaced, this left the day shift to change the tailerons and to refit items that had been shipped out from the UK. The hole in the fin fuel tank was dressed out, removing the swarf and bomb-case fragments and a patch was riveted in place, sealing the tank with a fuel-proof polysulphide sealant.

My own repair was progressing well and I had produced an attachment angle, a filler plate and repair

THE FIN OF TORNADO GR1 ZD843. (ALLEN VERNON)

plates which had been fabricated and drilled, waiting to fit. I still had a problem finding suitable fasteners to hold it all together. In the background, we had found out that the British Aerospace Systems support organisation for the Saudi Tornados, had built a structural repair bay. Bernie and I paid a visit, bumping into an ex-RSS guy called Al. We explained that we were working on the dead 'Tonka' in the F-15 hangar and that we needed suitable rivets to finish the job. He offered 'cherry max rivets' which were ideal.

Al allowed me to raid their stores rack and loaned us the equipment required to install the parts but as I was raiding the store, Al continued his trade training with a very young Saudi maintenance engineer. He was explaining the different types of metal cutting files: "This is a bastard file. Bastard is a naughty word in English and so is this file!" The Saudi looked totally confused …

Bernie also experienced pronunciation issues when a Saudi tradesman approached him as we worked on ZD843.

"You s**t metalworker? I s**t metalworker!"

Bernie retorted in typical RAF style: "You probably are mate!"

Day six and my repair was nearing completion. A patch repair was fitted using PR1422 sealant to make it gas tight. A replacement cannon mounting foot had arrived from the UK but our lads had already restored the damaged foot and decided that it was going back in. In fact once the repaired cannon mounting was back in place, it was possible that the armourers might even be able to harmonise the cannon to fire accurately. Unfortunately, we could not guarantee that our repairs would take the shock loads. Operationally, the need to fire a Mauser 27-mm cannon when flying at 18,000 feet was not often required, so the left-hand cannon would be 'lim'd', and marked as inoperable. Even so, it would be refitted for centre of gravity reasons as the Tornado would not have flown properly without it.

By then, the team had repaired the gun bay door, underwing drop-down panel and the fin triangular panel using composite repair techniques, such as expanding foam to replace the smashed honeycomb internal structure. There was wire damage in the front equipment bay as well as the wing and Barry and Pete had crimped a number of cables that had been damaged to various degrees.

Towards the end of the recovery, the squadron personnel took over to carry out the long list of low-power and high-power engine runs to prove the new engines that had been installed and to complete operational tests of all the systems that had been disturbed. I hope they did a pressure test on my repair.

Pink Alkaline Removable Temporary Finish (PART) paint was applied to every area that had been repaired and a purple heart was applied to denote the status of 'war wounded'. I applied a silhouette on the gun bay door, in the form of a cat with a three-shaped tail, this being the RSS unofficial motif and tying into my unit's peacetime repair role. Unfortunately, the squadron guys began putting increasingly offensive graffiti on the airframe and SEngO was having none of that and took a hard line. Eventually, the purple heart was the only graffiti that survived.

The team had finished ZD843 and she was back on stream. The seniors had sorted out the paperwork and SEngO signed off the limitation on the left-hand gun. The mass of acceptable deferred faults (ADFs) that our work had produced had been recorded. Only a dent on the upper skin of the right engine bay survived our attention but it was only spotted on the last night of our work. In the scheme of things, I decided it best not mentioned, as it was not going to stop ZD843 returning to service.

On the night of 2 February, we heard that ZD843 had passed an air test that morning, was serviceable and had been selected to fly that night on a raid. Baldrick and I wandered over to see the wave launch. ZD843 growled and prowled out that night to do her task.

That was the last action we saw. With medium-level operations taking over, there was virtually no more battle damage, although I had other jobs to keep me busy as the war progressed. The squadron guys pitched up with a fragment of a Scud body that had been 'disturbed by Patriot high-velocity action'. They wanted small pieces but it proved to be Scud 1, Cengar saw 0. A junior engineering officer asked me to make up a component for an urgent operational modification which meant a return to the British Aerospace Systems workshop to use their kit. For all we knew, it was to be used in air-burst bombs, but the reason was never revealed. The job was done in two hours.

Daytime operations continued and we were asked to help with nitrogen charging of the fin fuel/air purging system but, not being trained on type, made us more of a hindrance than a help. Another team pitched up from Abingdon but saw no trade action at all but such is life. Their rather obnoxious sergeant, who complained about everything and pushed his weight about was quickly nicknamed 'Vic' after the vapour rub that would get up your nose.

The last week of the war saw me nobbled for guard duty at the main entry point for Dhahran. With 24 hours on and 24 hours off, it was an awful shift pattern, however, I was on the main gate on the morning that the land war started. Seeing the RAF Force commander into the base that day and checking his ID, I said:

"It's a great day today sir!" "Why?" the group captain asked. "Because we'll be going home soon, sir," was my response. The retort was curt.

The day after, having finished the guard shift, I was back in the compound, returning to the accommodation after dinner when the air raid sirens went off. We hadn't seen a Scud in flight up to that point so I looked up to see if I could see one as it was a clear night. I didn't see the Scud but soon heard the impact and sonic boom of it landing nearby. I masked up and ran back to the accommodation but heard later that, about three miles away, 28 US military personnel were dead as their accommodation had been destroyed. The missile could have landed anywhere within a ten-mile radius. That is war. By 28 February, the Iraqis had been forced out of Kuwait and a ceasefire was called. It was the end of Operation Desert Storm.

War is a serious thing but there are light-hearted moments. Returning from a Saturday day shift with the Ireland versus England rugby match on Grandstand— yes we had the BBC broadcast via satellite in the mess hall—the Irish were leading. A Welshman was the cheerleader for the Welsh in the room. Underwood scored the decider. The English cheered but the satellite went down! Who had won? I went to the phone box to find out from my mother who had won. We had she said. The satellite came back on line to show the French scoring two tries against the 'Troggs' in the highlights match, with Wales heading for their biggest ever defeat in Paris. The Welshman had his head in his hands as the English returned the favour.

We had no contact with the other ABDR teams in-theatre who had also found that the change to medium-level ops had reduced the chances of battle damage massively. The Brits suffered badly at first, as did the French with their only low-level raid using Jaguars. However, there were other incidents that required the skills of the RSS boys. A C-130 Hercules at Riyadh suffered wingtip damage in a collision with a helicopter on the ground, that required the lads to carry out repairs so it could be flown out. It was a much larger structural repair than anything on ZD843 and proved impressive.

With the end of the war, everything was to be returned to either the UK or Germany and we flew home to the UK on 13 March. I was met by my parents at Brize Norton and they took me back to Abingdon where, I am glad to say, after reconnecting the battery, the Manta started straight away.

So, that chronicles the role of the Repair and Salvage Squadron and of the No. 431 Maintenance Unit boys in the liberation of Kuwait. I would hear of ZD843 some 15 years later when I was attending an expedient repair assessors course with two other guys from No. 6 Squadron. The story of ZD843 had been used as an overview of how such repair processes would occur in the 21st century. The drill would be that we would assess the damage, manufacturer design teams would come up with a repair scheme and the Cat 3 boys would do the repair. My response was "Bull", similar to that of Val Kilmer in the movie *Top Gun*.

ZD843 flew ten more missions after its repair without a single operational abort before a cracked canopy hinge saw it returned to RAF Brüggen in Germany. The formal Cat 3 repairs took somewhat longer than we had estimated back in January 1991; it was more like two years. It seemed that the force of the weapon exploding, had twisted one of the mounts for the tailerons and had made it difficult to trim the controls in flight. The jet was not flying straight but the problem only emerged much later. It was fixed using another RSS repair scheme. Sadly the aircraft had a sad end and was 'reduced to produce' in 2016.

It was the end of the 'Tornado with the Purple Heart'.

CHAPTER 2

Life in the Persian Gulf

Trevor Bailey joined the RAF in September 1967 and after his apprentice-ship at RAF Halton, he trained as an airframe weapons fitter. He first ex-perienced the administrators' sense of humour when asking for a posting to Hong Kong, Singapore or Cyprus. He was moved from East Camp to West Camp at St Athan where he served in the seat bay, fitting and re-moving seats in V-bombers and Canberras. The early 1970s saw tours at RAF Muharraq in the station armoury with detachments to Masirah and Sharjah. Further tours in the UK followed including RAF St Mawgan, RAF Coningsby and RAF Wattisham. He left the RAF in 1976 and moved to Saudi Arabia with a defence contractor before finishing his time as a 'liney' on a Sultan of Oman's Air Force Hunter squadron at Thumrait.

During the conflict in the Gulf, names like Bahrain and Oman became familiar, as bases for military operations against Iraq. What may be less well known is that, after the Second World War, the Royal Air Force had bases in many Arab countries. The stations I mention in this story, RAF Sharjah in Oman and RAF Muharraq in Bahrain, were elements of the Near East Air Force and home to squadrons of Hunter fighters and Argosy transport aircraft.

Watching a video clip online the other day, I saw a man do a cracking job of blowing up his lawn and it brought to mind an incident back in the 1970s. At the time I was stationed at RAF Muharraq and my normal duties as an armourer had me working in the station armoury. This was the place on base where things such as guns, ammunition and anything that went bang, were stored.

HUNTER FGA9, XF519 OF NO. 208 SQUADRON AT RAF MUHARRAQ, BAHRAIN IN 1970.
(RAY DEACON COLLECTION)

There were two resident squadrons at Muharraq, Nos. 8 and 208 Squadrons, operating Hawker Hunter fighters. It was usual, when either of the squadrons needed to practise air-to-air gunnery, they would deploy to RAF Sharjah in Oman for a few months. This was known as an armament practice camp (APC). As the squadrons had a limited number of armourers, it was customary for station armoury personnel to accompany the squadron to boost the numbers. Once deployed, the augmentees would assist the gun pack teams and would help to service the guns and rearm the aircraft ready for the gunnery sorties.

So there I was, on the aircraft servicing platform (ASP) at Sharjah, the temperature hot enough to melt the fillings from your teeth. I was with my mate at the time, Dave Barbierato, who later served as best man at my wedding, and I am still in touch after 50 years. He is like a brother to me. Given the heat, my duty roster wasn't too onerous and was split between day and night shifts. On day shift, we would arrive at 0600, working until 1200 and on nights, it was from 1200 until cease flying. This meant a morning on duty, followed by a day off, then a night shift and a morning off.

Sharjah, although set on the coast, looked like a desert and the local terrain away from the base was known as the 'bundu'. This was a term in regular use among RAF personnel, coined from South African slang. It was a lot different to the English countryside. For days we had been plagued by huge fire ants that were almost as big as the local dogs. Rex, the 'bundu' dog, was a character. My mate and I used to take him to the local bar at night and buy him a pie. Despite his improved diet, how he hated Ringo the barman and, any time the poor bloke emerged, Rex would chase him back behind the bar. It was so bad that one night we were on our way to the cinema and Ringo came past. Rex was off like a scalded cat, ran up the wall next to the cinema and dived onto Ringo, bowling him off his moped. They were not big friends.

Back to the fire ants. They were mean, aggressive and could give a nasty bite that would spoil your whole day. Dave and I had already changed five or six gun packs that morning and, while we were waiting for the next pair of Hunters to land, we found ourselves with some spare time on our hands. This was dangerous for a pair of armourers on detachment.

"Let's have a look round and see if we can find that f***ing ants' nest," I said.

"OK, but what are we going to do if we find it?" Dave replied, the look of concern pretty obvious.

"Don't worry, I'll think of something. Trust me. I'm a J/T!"

After checking the 'bundu' at the edge of the ASP, we came across a suspicious-looking hole in the sand.

"This looks like it," said Dave, the ants flooding from the hole being a big clue. "So, now what?"

"Hang on while I give it some thought," I replied but I already had a cunning plan forming and it involved flammable materials. After a short while, in true J/T fashion, I came up with a plan. "Let's bumble over to the hangar, see the 'sooties', and ask if we can borrow a gallon of Avpin."

Now, for the unenlightened amongst you, Avpin is a liquid explosive, highly volatile even in small amounts, and was used to start some types of jet engines. It is very much akin to rocket fuel, it is highly combustible in an explosive manner and the exhaust gases if mixed with enough air, will reignite. Anyone who has heard an Avpin starter will never forget the sound. Anyone who has fuelled an Avpin starter will never forget the experience. Remember this, reader.

After a short while, Dave returned with the aforementioned, duly acquired, gallon of Avpin. I should, perhaps, also point out at this stage, that the outside air temperature was probably on the high side at 120°F. Taking the Avpin, I began to pour it, gingerly, into the ants' nest. I had always been a safety conscious armourer but, for want of a fuse, I decided to, carefully, lay a trail of Avpin as a substitute. It stretched for some distance from the nest.

"Give us yer lighter Dave, and I'll light this b****r up."

"I've left me lighter in the line hut," Dave replied. Always helpful was Dave.

"Well saunter off over there, and get it."

And saunter he did, his lack of urgency, probably, as a result of my impressive preparation. It would be, perhaps wise, to give you a little more information about my selected combustible. Avpin has a specific property, being a colourless liquid much like nitro glycerine, which gives off a heavier-than-air vapour. Of course, during the long wait for my best mate to retrieve his lighter, the vapour from the Avpin had filtered down through every gallery of the entire ants' nest; and I mean every gallery.

"Stand back. This should be fun." I declared.

It would be, almost, famous last words. I lit the trail of Avpin that I had, delicately, laid and we stepped back to watch the fun. An unspectacular, blue flame slowly meandered across the ground, and vanished down the hole.

Nothing.

"Well, that was a bit of a let-down," says I.

At that instant, with an almighty whoosh, about 90 cubic yards of Sharjah desert suddenly became airborne! Not only were we peppered with sand, there were ants everywhere and they were not happy. There were ants in the line hut, in the offices, in the aircraft cockpits, in tool bags, in spare gun packs. There were even ants in the pilots' ready room. They were everywhere! The explosion left a crater in the desert at the side of the ASP which was about 12 feet deep. It was a bit difficult to miss.

"Time we made ourselves scarce Dave," I said, as we beat a hasty retreat to hide behind the NAAFI wagon, which had just arrived on the line. Perhaps it was lucky that the Hunters had not yet arrived back or we may have made an even bigger impression; in more ways than one. In fact, it seemed like a really good idea to make ourselves scarce for the rest of the day. Given that this event happened in 1970, and that Dave and I are somewhat older and wiser, I hope we can now admit to it. I sincerely hope that there is a 'statute of limitations' on these events.

One of the less onerous duties in the armoury, but one that had potential advantages, was that we held the Very pistols for air traffic control. The pistols were issued to the local and runway controllers and the latter took them to the caravan at the end of the runway when flying operations were underway. If a pilot was feeling particularly bright and forgot to lower the undercarriage on final approach, the controller would fire off a red signal flare to warn of the mistake. Red flares saved many an unwary pilot from embarrassment.

Of course, the pistols needed to be tested occasionally and the job fell to us as the station armourers. We never had problems getting clearance from the local controller because we were checking out their kit. It always seemed like a good idea to test them in an area at the end of the runway. We often had a few extra flares that had reached the end of their life and it was easier to fire them off than to have them destroyed. With pilots who happened to be in the air warned of our task, we began to set off a series of flares into the air. Sadly, whoever worked out the flare burn time versus the time of flight, had got their sums a little off. After a spectacular firework display of reds and greens, we had to ask for help from the Fire Section to put out the 'bundu' fires that were the result of a few errant flares landing in the tinder-dry grass. There is no truth in the rumour that the runway had to be closed, temporarily, because it was blotted out by the smoke plume.

There was another pleasant spin-off which was a direct result of our duty. Muharraq was served by a commercial airlift that brought personnel and families from the UK, operated by British Overseas Airways Corporation using Boeing 707s and VC-10s. Naturally, the crews included some lovely air hostesses, who were in short supply in our desert paradise. It just seemed fortunate that the routine servicing of the Very pistols, that were fortuitously held in air traffic control, always seemed to coincide with the visit of the airliners. I suspect that the ATC pistols were the cleanest in the Persian Gulf.

We had to be careful when heading out into the local desert, normally venturing forth in a four-tonner. On one occasion, we had pulled up to have a break at Kahn Creek, a local landmark, when I noticed a chicken in a hole. Not so odd you might think. It didn't seem well and, on closer inspection, it was obvious it had gone to meet its maker. For some reason I decided to try to find out why and, having retrieved a spade from the truck, I began to dig down, being accused of trying to escape to Australia. After some time and none the wiser as to why the chicken had met its end, I decided to give the hole a final check before giving up. The expletives that followed were entirely due to the attention from a crab that had taken residence down the hole and had decided to take a piece out of my hand and seemed unwilling to let go. I guess it goes without saying that my mates were of little help, were completely unsympathetic and fell about laughing

AN AERIAL SHOT OF THE MODERN-DAY AIRFIELD AT BAHRAIN, THE FORMER RAF MUHARRAQ.
(DAVID GLEDHILL)

as I tried to get rid of the unwanted native. My lesson? Let a dead chicken lie.

Anyone who has been a part of the armed forces knows only too well that drinking was not only part of the experience but an essential 'wind-down' tool. The 'Pig's Bar' at Muharraq was also known as the 'Chippies Arms'. It would have to be because it had been built by the station carpenters. Like many unofficial bars around the world, it was a room in the NAAFI that had been converted in an Old English theme, complete with fake oak beams and the whole works. It was where the plumbers drank beer but no other trade would dare to venture within unless it was by invitation. After one night enjoying a few jars, we fell out of the bar, 'pissed as parrots' and were heading back for some well-deserved shut-eye. En route, we were intercepted by the padre, a rugby player, who grabbed us as he needed a choir for midnight mass in the church. I can only guess how we all sounded that night, although I hope it was melodic.

I returned to the UK in 1971 and was posted back to RAF St Mawgan, at the start of the holiday season. After a year in the Middle East, it was like all my Christmases had come at once. As to my thoughts on RAF Muharraq? I was London born and bred and, to me, an overseas holiday was a day out at Canvey

Island. Here I was, 19 years of age, on the other side of the world, in a land that I had only ever read about. I can honestly say with hand on heart, that it was one of my life's greatest experiences and showed me that there was more to life than jellied eels and fish and chips.

CHAPTER 3

Building the Impossible

John Kendal joined the RAF in July 1976 as a direct entry fitter and spent nine months training as an aircraft technician (propulsion). He served on No. 29 Squadron and in Aircraft Servicing Flight at RAF Coningsby on the Phantom, before a tour at Brüggen in the station engine bay on the modification recovery team working on Jaguars. Back in the UK he worked on VC-10s at Brize Norton and the Aircraft Operating Squadron at Brawdy on Hawks. Taking redundancy in 1994 he continued working on the Hawk for Airwork Ltd in the United Arab Emirates. Since his return to the UK, his skills have been exercised in diverse areas, including time as a stairlift fitter and as a roller coaster engineer. He now actively participates as a volunteer on vintage and light aircraft projects including a major service on a Dutch Hawker Hunter.

The Phantom was the mainstay of the air defence force during the Cold War. Although under the terms of the Treaty on Conventional Armed Forces in Europe the airframes were supposed to be dismantled, many survived. When the type retired from service in 1992, a notable example, and perhaps one of the best maintained, was 'Black Mike'. Painted in a commemorative gloss black paint scheme by No. 111 (F) Squadron in the late 1980s and carrying their distinctive squadron colours, XV582 had a unique history of its own. The paint scheme was a tribute to the historic formations flown by the squadron during

the Hunter 'Black Arrows' era. It also has a heritage that gives it a rare prove-
nance. It was first to pass 5,000 flying hours and it was also the aircraft which
completed the record-breaking Land's End to John o'Groats run on 1 April
1988, in just 46 minutes 44 seconds. The flight averaged over 757 mph for the
590-mile distance and was flown by No. 43 (Fighter) Squadron's commanding
officer Wing Commander John Brady with his navigator Squadron Leader
Mike Pugh.

It remained hidden at RAF Leuchars for many years, acting as a ground
instructional airframe, emerging only occasionally at the annual air show.
Eventually, it was sold to a private buyer for preservation. Before it arrived at
its final home at the South Wales Aviation Museum at St Athan, it starred in
the RAF 100th commemorative display at RAF Cosford. To do so, it had to be
dismantled, loaded on a flat bed and moved across the length of the country.

My association began in November 2016, when my mundane life was disrupt-
ed as I volunteered to join the British Phantom Aviation Group team (BPAG)
travelling to Scotland to prepare Black Mike for its wing removal before transportation to Bruntingthorpe. I had not been chosen for the first trip as I was
an engine specialist by trade and the team was looking for airframe fitters. At
this stage the idea was to dismantle the airframe but leave the engines installed.
From my previous experience, I knew this would be impossible.

It had been 36 years since I had last
worked on a Phantom having left RAF
Coningsby in 1980. The first task was
trying to remember the sequence for
gaining access to the engines but it's
surprising how quickly the memories come flooding back. Rear missile
launchers were removed, engine
doors dropped, drains disconnected
and access gained to the engines that
hadn't been seen for over 25 years.
With the help of Tom Lear, and using
only a plumb line made from a piece
of string with a spanner tied to the
end, we took some very basic measurements of the engine mounts and
the key distances. At the finish of the

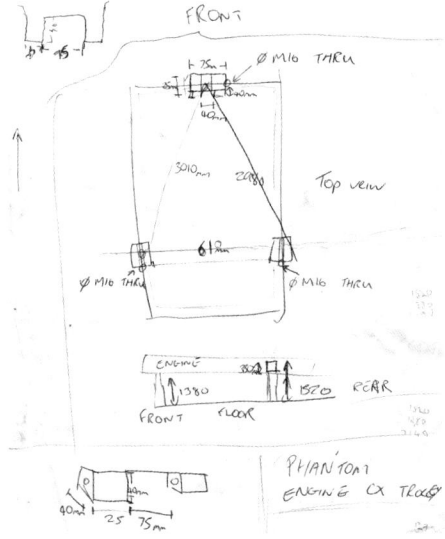

JOHN KENDAL'S ORIGINAL CONCEPT FOR THE
ENGINE STAND. (JOHN KENDAL)

THE ENGINE STAND TAKES FORM. (JOHN KENDAL)

week, I headed back home to deepest, darkest Wales with no inkling of what lay ahead.

Previous searches by salvage companies around the country had failed to find a Spey removal kit but, with further investigation and a rigorous search through many books on the development of the Phantom, I made progress. I found pictures of a trial to install Spey engines using a specially adapted frame, fitted to a stand designed for use on the J79-equipped Phantom. Some were still around in this country so I decided to have a go at reproducing this frame, originally developed by Rolls-Royce, which had been used during the development programme. I hoped that we would be able to borrow or purchase a stand to use with the original frame design. I spent time converting my 'fag-packet' measurements into accurate dimensions to build the adapters and framework that would, in turn, attach to the engine. With the donation of some box steel, a trailer axle, trailer jacks and various brackets, I was set to go.

The rear beam was built from the trailer axle, two pieces of scaffolding bar and an assortment of roofing brackets and bolts. For the attachments to the engine, a friend welded thick steel to the heads of two 5/8" bolts, and by flattening the top ends of the scaffolding bars and cutting a slot for the attaching bolts, drilling a hole through the scaffolding bar and adding a side bolt and locking pin, we had the first section finished. The next step was to produce a front beam with attachments. This was a bit more complicated as the beam had to swivel on each axis. After two or three attempts, the front mount was manufactured from a block of steel, a welded bracket and a piece of hefty threaded bar.

After a break for Christmas and despite more searching and enquiries by other members of the group, an engine stand suitable for a Rolls-Royce Spey or J79 could not be found. The only stands that might be adapted to fit were a couple of old Conway transportation stands which had at some time been used to service VC-10 engines. The stands, kindly donated by GJD Services, were located a considerable distance away from my home, so Paul Wright, another member of the group, was dispatched to take photographs and to measure the frame to see if they might be suitable. Once I had looked at the dimensions, it seemed that we might be able to make use of them.

By now I knew that I would have to work out how I would lower the engines from the bays in the aircraft to the ground. Another internet trawl determined that all potential solutions were too costly and without workshop facilities or the time to reproduce the original pillar and winch system used on the Spey stand, I realised that I would need a radical alternative. I decided that by using the original trailer jacks that had been donated, I could work around the problem. With a static lifting capacity of 3,000 kg each, by combining the lifting power of three jacks we would be more than able to cope with the weight of a 1.8-metric-ton Spey jet engine. The only drawback was that the jacks had a very limited distance of travel and a closed height of 650 mm. Out came my old school drawing board, a calculator and pencils—I am from an age before computer-aided design—and the sums showed that it could be done.

The first hurdle was that the Conway stand is a rather large piece of kit with a massive vibration frame mounted underneath. This would have to be removed first leaving just the smaller mounting stand. For better mobility, the stand itself would need to be mounted on castors. My sums showed that with the maximum height of the trailer jacks and the lowering capacity of the stand, there was little margin for error. Being at the opposite end of the country with no access to Black Mike, there would be a lot of hopeful guesswork.

When I first began, I had no idea that I would be building a complete Rolls-Royce Spey removal kit. The rough calculations now had to be converted into an accurate scale diagram of the Conway stand complete with jacks and lifting frame. I sat down with pencil and paper and began in earnest. The first big hurdle was that the engines did not sit level in the airframe with the front sitting much higher than the rear. The trailer jacks could only lower the engine by 250 mm which would be fine for the rear of the assembly, but the front would need to come down twice that distance, if not more. I had thought of this at the early stages which is why I had incorporated a threaded bar into the front mount. By extending the threaded bar by 300 mm, combined with the height of the jack, I would have a working height of 550 mm. All well and good, but as I completed my first scale drawing, I realised that the heights were all wrong as the beams on the stand were too high.

There was no way around the problem but to take more very accurate measurements of the Conway stand and of a real Spey engine. With Paul Wright despatched back to Bruntingthorpe, he measured every single part of the stand. With a further visit to Coventry Aviation Museum, where the trustees kindly allowed him access to their Spey engine, he collected more vital dimensions and took photographs which would prove invaluable as we progressed.

It was at this point that I heard about the schedule for the next planned trip to RAF Leuchars, at which time the team hoped to begin dismantling the Phantom. This gave me only three weeks to turn all the ideas in my head into a solid fully functional piece of precision ground equipment.

After looking through the new information, I realised there was an error in the overall length of the Conway stand and that my idea of using three jacks, similar to the original kit, was impossible as the stand was far too short. It seemed that I had reached an impossible hurdle which I could not overcome. This was a low point for me and I almost gave up on the whole idea. A time out was required to reassess the situation.

Inspiration came in an unusual way. Two hours later, during a shopping trip with my dear wife and sitting outside the ladies changing rooms in Debenhams, deep in thought, I had worked out how to change my design to adapt to the shorter stand. On returning home it was back to the drawing board. My idea for a single front jack was quickly changed to a double arrangement with a cross beam to support the original frame. More calculations and a further scale drawing followed and another issue emerged. The two jacks could not simply sit on the frame of the engine stand as I would still not have the lowering capacity I required. Also, with the jacks fully extended, there was a possibility that they would be too high to clear the fuselage and engine doors. With so many unknowns to deal with, it meant that there would be a lot of luck involved. Looking at photographs, it was apparent that I could bolt an extra, lower beam to the rear of the Conway stand giving me the lowering capacity I required, yet keeping the front jacks as low as possible.

I spent the rest of that day completing an accurate scale drawing of the whole design and, with this drawing complete, I could finally see the overall height and lowering capacity of my kit. Even so, I calculated that at full extent, the rear-lifting beam would still be 50 mm short, so would not be capable of taking the weight of the engine and I would need to find a way to make up this short-fall. Despite that I was ready to go, knew what I needed to build, so it was off to the workshop.

I had enough steel for the job and set to building the front-lifting beam. There was a lot of guess work involved as I could not determine how far the front of the engine needed to be lowered. To give me as much flexibility as possible I manufactured a basic cross-beam support which could quite easily be adapted on site, once we had access to the real aircraft. That was the least of my problems as everything would have to be able to fit in the back of a car, in order to transport it to Leuchars.

It was by now obvious that the front and rear beams would be of different heights but that they would still need to be joined together by welding up some box-steel sections on the bottom of the rear beam. I also had to bear in mind that this beam would need to be low enough to clear the gear boxes and ancillary kit on the bottom of the engine, yet be able to position the cradle in order to lower the Speys.

Two weeks passed by in an instant and, with only four days to go, I had made all the components I needed to build the complete engine stand. I began to assemble the other items I would need on site. I collected spare steel sections, bolts, nuts and any other parts I might possibly need, along with steel wire strops that might be useful once we began to lift the engine off the cradle. With two engines to remove I would also need an engine stand to free up the cradle. The front section was manufactured from a car brake disc welded to a piece of box steel. The rear section was simply steel channel fixed to a box section.

The simple part should have been transportation but with everything assembled it was clear that there was no way that all the gear would fit into my car along with my tool kits and luggage. Salvation was on hand. There was a truckload of kit travelling up from Bruntingthorpe to Scotland and I could take advantage of the opportunity. I had a family weekend booked in Northampton en route, so I persuaded my wife to borrow my daughter's car so that we could transport everything as far as Northampton. With all the heavy kit in one car I drove it over to Bruntingthorpe to be transferred into the lorry for the journey to RAF Leuchars. Back in Northampton, everything else was packed into my car leaving my wife free to drive home after the weekend. I think she

THE PHANTOM TEAM. (JOHN KENDAL)

was glad to see the back of it. With the load in my own car lightened, the journey up to Scotland was much more relaxed but I still arrived in Dundee on the Sunday evening, feeling a little nervous, not knowing how effective my kit would be.

When Monday morning dawned at Leuchars, a team of budding engineers turned up at the hardened aircraft shelter not knowing what to expect. The team consisted of Paul Wright, an ex-RAF airframe/engine tech, John Bell, another airframe/engine tech, Mike Davey, a plumber with a passion for the Phantom, Tom Lear, a student doing an engineering degree, and me, an engine tech/roller coaster fitter. We set to unloading tools and kit from our cars. Paul had power tools and a vital length of box steel required to complete my kit and Mike Davey had his arc welder; also vital. Once the truck turned up and everything was unloaded, we began the task in hand.

The first job was to unbolt the Conway engine stand and to remove the vibration plate. The components of my design were collected together and laid out on the floor next to the stand. Everyone looked at the pile of scrap metal and heads were scratched. It was a daunting task.

Next the four strong castors needed to be attached to the stand. Brackets and bolts were fitted after drilling holes to fix them in position. Meanwhile Paul and I did the first trial fit of the lifting adapters and frame, attaching them to the underside of the engine. Once the frame was fitted, the jacks were put in place underneath, supported on blocks of wood, checking their position once fitted onto the stand. With great relief, it seemed that most of my calculations had been correct. The now mobile stand was wheeled around into a side annex of the HAS for final assembly.

A piece of 50-mm U-section steel was welded onto the front cross beam of the Conway stand and the two rear-lifting jacks were welded on top of this. The difficult part proved to be the forward-lifting jacks. To give me the maximum lowering capacity at the front of the engine, the jacks could not sit on top of the Conway stand frame. So, using more U-section steel and some brackets, a new part was cut and bolted between the two sides of the rear of the stand as low down as possible. The feet of the jacks were cut off to fit into the channel and holes were drilled to bolt them into place on the cross beam. The front-lifting beam was then cut precisely to length to fit between the two jacks. The components were assembled and bolted together. Voila! One purpose-made, engine-lifting stand. With the frame in place under the engine, we wheeled the lifting stand into place to check that it matched up. Everything fitted perfectly.

On Tuesday afternoon it was time to check if we could actually take the weight of the engines and we wound up the jacks, taking the strain. The rear beam was no problem but we were lacking a bit of height on the front mounting. With more head scratching and a frantic discussion, Paul suggested we put a block of steel underneath the front part of the lifting frame, which would both take the weight and span the gap. Once more we tried to take the weight of the engine at the front but the box steel which had been used to join the sections, was not sufficiently rigid and began to bend. Fortunately, Paul had brought a spare piece of box steel which came to the rescue. The lifting beam was removed and the two pieces of box steel were tack welded together, providing a stronger frame. Once reassembled, it was clear that the front beam was now capable of taking the weight of the engine.

By 1700 on Tuesday evening, we were in a position to attempt to remove the first engine and, being time critical, it was a team decision to push on and try to get the first engine out. Tom was sent down the intake to watch from the inside and check clearances on the top of the bay. A fun job! Paul and John took up position on the forward winches, leaving Mike and me to operate the rear winches. We winched up the rear, just as we had in the old days until the inboard links of the engine were free to move. With the bolts removed and the links moved out of the way, Paul jumped up on to the wing and the front winches were adjusted until we had sufficient weight to remove the outboard link.

This was it. Months of planning were about to meet the test. Almost two tons of Spey engine were balanced on something out of *Scrapheap Challenge*!

The most serious test was yet to come. A willing volunteer was needed to go under the engine to undo the jaws of the main engine bearer. The only way to do this was to sit in the middle of the stand with a socket, a long extension and a ratchet. Paul volunteered being the leading member of the team, and undid the two nuts, locking them up and out of the way. The engine stayed put and, fortunately, did not drop into Paul's lap. Just as we would have done had we been lucky enough to have the proper kit, the engine was slowly winched down and rearwards out of the bay avoiding the many obstacles on the way. Unlike our experiences of the past, the process was finished a lot more sedately.

Two-and-a-half hours later, after much shouting and swearing, the first engine finally departed company with the airframe. The only damage was a few bent finger seals at the rear of the engine bay. My improvised engine stand had just replicated what the original Rolls-Royce kit used to do.

There was relief all round. Everyone shook my hand, Paul came out with the legendary words: "Everyone said it couldn't be done without the proper kit and when I saw the pile of scrap on the floor yesterday, I still thought it couldn't be done." I'm just glad he kept that to himself and that we carried on with my hair-brained scheme. Returning to the hotel that evening, there was a big sense of relief, followed by a celebratory trip to the pub and much merriment.

The following morning was spent trying to produce a suitable lifting sling from the remaining pieces of angle iron and the steel strops that I had brought with me. The first engine was set aside on the hangar floor so that the frame could be used for the second engine. Confidence in the kit was rising so the second engine was removed in about 45 minutes which was comparable with the kit we had used in service.

Since then the Conway stand has been reassembled, and along with a second example, modified to transport the two Speys to a new home. The project continued during the following months culminating with the successful removal of the wing by the middle of September. We had met the challenge.

Black Mike now sits in the hangar at its new home in the South Wales Aviation Museum at RAF St Athan. The engines await their fate, hopefully to be refurbished and refitted back into the airframe at a future date but that will be another story. When visitors see the aircraft, I doubt they will even consider how it was able to make its way from Scotland to Wales where it now provides enjoyment to a new generation of 'Phantom Phans'.

CHAPTER 4

Life in the V-Force

Vic Winwright joined the RAF in February 1960, originally signing on for only nine years. He wanted to be an armourer working on aircraft but was selected for training in the air radar trade on the navigation and bombing systems fitted to the V-bombers. His early years were with the V-Force at Wittering, Scampton and Marham, servicing Valiants, Victors and Vulcans. He then moved to the RAF unit at Goose Bay in Canada which handled Vulcans and Victors on North American ranger flights. Back in the UK, he was posted to Coningsby and was trained on the missile control system; the radar and weapons system fitted to the Phantom. Taking redundancy in 1988, Vic moved to RAF Cranwell and took a civilian job in the aircraft handling and rectification hangar, looking after Jet Provost Mark 5As and the Shorts Tucano. A spell with the Joint Elementary Flying Training School followed and he, finally, retired in March 2003 aged 63, having worked on aircraft for 42 years.

When I was posted to RAF Yatesbury in Wiltshire, to do my first trade training course, I had little idea where it would lead me. As it turned out, I would serve for over ten years on the V-Force and be involved in servicing all three types.

I found out quite soon that, along with two others, I was to be part of an experiment in putting airmen straight onto a fitters course instead of doing a mechanics course first. The rate of learning was too high for people who had no knowledge of electronics, so it didn't work. My course mates were mechanics who had been in the RAF for a couple of years and, prior to the fitters course, had done a two-week lead-in to prepare them for the electronics subjects. After five weeks we were way behind so the decision was made to transfer us to an alternative course with the promise of preferential placement on a fitters course in the future.

I passed out and was awarded the signals/communication trade badge to wear on my uniform sleeve. Posted to RAF Wittering, I finally arrived in the real Royal Air Force, joining No. 49 Squadron who were, at that time, equipped with the Valiant bomber. So began my association with the V-Force. No. 49 Squadron had recently taken part in Operation Grapple which was the dropping of live nuclear weapons off Christmas Island and most of those involved were still on the squadron.

My introduction was not pleasant as Wittering had a unique system. As an airman, on arrival you did a couple of weeks on the station warrant officer's (SWO) working party known as 'the SWO's marines'. The Valiants had not been with the unit long when an aircraft was lost shortly after take-off with the loss of the crew. A crash guard was mounted to protect the wreckage and the SWO's marines were an obvious choice for the task. We were warned by the guard commander about what to do if we came across anything unpleasant; and unpleasant it proved to be.

With my first grim task out of the way, I was able to join No. 49 Squadron proper and start working on aircraft. At last. The squadron was split into two flights of four aircraft each. We lived at the end of the airfield and I think I was on 'B' Flight. There were two levels of servicing on the squadron. The first was handling the aircraft and preparing it for flight, known as a pre-flight check. Next came the starting phase when the aircrew arrived, before seeing it off the dispersal to go flying. This was all done under the control of the crew chief. When the aircraft landed it was seen back into dispersal where it would be refuelled and after-flight checks would be carried out. The aircrew would be formally debriefed by the crew chief and each trade manager, to learn the nature of any faults that may have developed during the sortie. Each fault would then be fixed by the appropriate tradesman.

As a newcomer you would first learn your way around the aircraft. Where were the component parts of your particular piece of equipment located and how would you apply electrical power to the aircraft? As you became more familiar with the ropes, you would be given more responsibility and, eventually, be allowed loose to prepare the aircraft for flight as part of the team. Finally, we carried out fault finding.

My equipment was the main 'piece of kit' in the avionics suite, the navigation and bombing system (NBS). The title was self-explanatory as the aircraft was designed to drop bombs and the NBS was the means by which it was achieved. In its day it was, probably, the most complicated avionic system fitted to any aircraft and, for that reason, there was a dedicated operator, the navigator (radar). The NBS was, in fact, an early computer but was entirely analogue; digital systems did not exist and the way it was engineered had to be seen to be believed. Its accuracy in the hands of a good operator was amazing considering that we were talking about delivering free-fall bombs. As a result, the V-Force performed well against the USAF in many bombing competitions.

It was not all work and no play and the social side of life in the RAF wasn't bad. The food was reasonable. There was the NAAFI club, of course, and Wittering also had a Malcolm Club, which was unusual, as they were usually found only on overseas bases. Our accommodation was very good as we had the new type of barrack block that had four-man rooms on two floors, with a few single-man rooms for senior corporals. Until arriving at Wittering I had been used to wooden barracks with up to 24 in a room.

In those days, however, domestic life was challenging. My wife and son lived west of Slough with her parents but we had absolutely no chance of being allocated a married quarter on station given my lowly rank. Getting home at weekends was quite easy as I could often get a lift to London or catch a bus or train to Slough. For that reason, I made it home most weekends unless I was on 'duty crew' when you were confined to camp in case there was an alert and the squadron was required to generate aircraft, ready to fly. Money was tight as RAF pay was not very good but, as I was married, I got marriage allowance which was paid direct to my wife. Even so, I didn't have much spare cash to enjoy so I spent time helping out in the Wittering radio station to keep me busy.

In 1961, No. 49 Squadron was transferred from RAF Wittering to become the third Valiant squadron at RAF Marham in Norfolk. Assigned to NATO under the control of the Supreme Allied Commander Europe, it joined two other squadrons Nos. 149 and 207 but there was a fourth Valiant squadron at Marham— No. 214—one of the RAF's in-flight refuelling squadrons. There were now three aircraft, one from each squadron, on permanent QRA; ready to fly at a moment's notice. The QRA compound was on the south side of the airfield and could hold four aircraft of which three were on QRA leaving a dispersal for use when aircraft were changed over. The site had accommodation for both aircrew and ground-crew within yards of the aircraft and was manned 24/7 throughout the year. The aircraft were loaded with two nuclear weapons supplied by the USA. This meant a USAF presence which was somewhat restrictive and, in the event of a practice alert, the aircrew were not allowed to start engines. Each aircraft was guarded by two USAF guards plus an RAF policeman, all armed. The major difference being that the USAF guard's pistols were loaded. The primary USAF guard was the weapons custodian and he had to be the first to enter the cockpit where he would sit in the navigator's seat with his loaded .45 Colt semi-automatic pistol pointing at the door. It could be very awkward when you were trying to do the daily servicing.

A VALIANT BOMBER SIMILAR TO THE ONE WORKED ON BY VIC WINWRIGHT ON HIS FIRST SQUADRON. (DAVID GLEDHILL)

Food was supplied by the messes and delivered to the QRA site in heated containers on wheels, on a converted bomb trolley, towed behind a truck. The containers for the aircrew were retrieved by a steward and one of the groundcrew collected ours. Although plugged in to keep warm, having been driven across the airfield, the food in the containers survived badly. You may well find custard and beef for a main meal and soup and apple pie for pudding.

One evening I retrieved our trolley and plugged it in and the smell was rather good. A quick look and I discovered that it was some kind of a poultry casserole. I told the rest of the lads and very soon, we were tucking into a very nice meal. At this point the QRA commander, who happened to be the officer in charge of the QRA complex, appeared and announced that the aircrew had received congealed fried egg and chips for their evening meal. He presumed that we had enjoyed pheasant casserole. It turned out that the aircrew steward had taken the wrong trolley from the transport and left us with the casserole. The squadron leader asked if our food was always that bad and was told in no uncertain terms that it was. Did things change? No, they didn't.

The dispersal for normal operations was close to the officers' married quarters and its size meant a major change to our set-up as we had been operating as two flights on separate dispersals at Wittering. With the arrival of additional administrative manpower, it meant we had the luxury of being able to operate all eight aircraft from one dispersal.

We were pleased to be given a new barrack block of the same type that we had at Wittering which annoyed some of the resident sections as they thought they would get the new building. It was not all good because proud of the new rooms, we were a target for visiting dignitaries who were being shown how nice they were. That generated a mass of bull***t. With still no sign of a married quarter on the horizon, I continued to travel to and from Slough at weekends. Our second son soon arrived but at least this time I was at 'home' for his birth.

Work on the squadron continued as normal until the first of three weekend visits by the Campaign for Nuclear Disarmament (CND) whose stated aim was to dig up Marham's runway. They, obviously, knew nothing about airfield construction. Each section 'defended' its own bit of the perimeter so we were guarding the fence next to the married quarters. Split into groups of six under the control of an RAF policeman, we had instructions to let the campaigners climb the fence, then detain them and hand them over to the civvie police who would arrest them. By the third successive weekend tempers were somewhat frayed as all leave had been stopped. The offending protesters were no longer treated gently when they were apprehended. They were thrown back over the fence to the police.

There was a bit of drama one day when a Valiant caught fire. The aircraft came back early from a trip with a suspected fuel leak and, having landed, it returned to the dispersal. As it turned into its parking slot, fuel leaking out of the port wing, ran down the undercarriage leg onto the hot brakes and ignited. The crew chief quickly plugged a headset into the aircraft and advised the crew of the situation. It took very little time to vacate the aircraft. The groundcrew meanwhile, were fighting the fire with the extinguishers available on the pan while other groundcrew rushed up with more extinguishers. The fire trucks arrived and quickly put out the fire using foam.

At a subsequent inquiry it was decided that had the groundcrew not been so quick fighting the fire, the aircraft may have been lost. The undercarriage leg was made of magnesium alloy which burns fiercely and the prompt action by the groundcrew had kept the temperature down giving the fire crew time to respond. Those involved received 'Good Show' awards. In hindsight, I thought it unusual that the fire trucks had not followed the aircraft back to dispersal when it landed as it had declared a suspected fuel leak.

In early 1962 I was selected for a fitters course to start in May, again at Yatesbury, for 14 months this time. The course ended in July 1963 and, having passed, we were all duly promoted to the rank of junior technician. I was posted back to Marham and given a couple of weeks leave. We had found a caravan site on the edge of King's Lynn and moved the caravan. I bought a motorbike and sidecar for transport and reported back for duty, only to find that I was no longer on No. 49 Squadron. I now worked in the NBS servicing bay, working on black boxes that had been removed from the aircraft to be repaired. I was to service the radar antennas that were normally mounted in the nose of the aircraft.

I soon discovered that I much preferred working on real aircraft but I was stuck with the servicing bay until I completed another course before I could go back to aircraft work. This did not happen until May 1964 but completed my knowledge of the NBS equipment and gave in-depth knowledge of the equipment as fitted to an aircraft. This made no sense as it was exactly what I had been doing as a mechanic. But it was part of the route to my next promotion.

The course would offer up some much-appreciated flying when we were dispatched to RAF Lindholme, where the V-bomber navigators did their hands-on training in a Hastings fitted with NBS. We did some target study and made map overlays which were designed to help you identify a target on the radar screen and then flew in a Hastings twice. On the first trip we navigated using the radar to take fixes and on the next trip practised bombing runs on a target. My first trip in the Hastings proved more exciting than planned when an

THE HASTINGS TRAINING AIRCRAFT
EQUIPPED WITH THE NBS SYSTEM.
(DAVID GLEDHILL)

THE NAVIGATOR'S STATION IN
A HASTINGS SHOWING THE NBS DISPLAYS.
(DAVID GLEDHILL)

engine problem required it to be shut down, meaning an early return to base. Despite an emergency call, Lindholme was the nearest airfield so that's exactly where we headed. Over the North Sea, we trainees were made to don life jackets and strap in by the exit door but despite doing abandonment drills, the Hastings was very lightly laden and we recovered to Lindholme on three engines, without further worry.

I arrived back at Marham NBS servicing bay in September 1964 newly qualified and, out of the blue, I was offered a married quarter at Bircham Newton near Sandringham. We sold the caravan and put the money towards our first car a Vauxhall Velox and I enjoyed married life for the first time.

Later in the year, the Valiant hit problems when metal fatigue was discovered in the wing spars. The aircraft were soon grounded, although the QRA commitment continued. I was on QRA when we heard the news on TV before it was even announced, officially, to the station commander. He came to QRA to tell us shortly afterwards. Even as we made the aircraft safe, the USAF guards wanted to unload the bombs but they were told to come back the next morning.

By early 1965, the Valiant was scrapped. Apart from stripping usable components from the airframes, suddenly, there were a whole lot of people at Marham with nothing to do. The camp went onto a three-day week and we submitted bids for new postings. I was sent to Scampton, the home of the Vulcan and the Blue Steel stand-off bomb.

My new role was to carry out a modification programme on the electronic countermeasures (ECM) equipment fitted to the Vulcan but, since this was classed as wireless equipment, I was misemployed so I would only be involved for six months. With six of us working shifts we made sure we had uninterrupted time on the equipment, finishing the mod programme in four months. With the early finish, and despite congratulations all round from the engineering executives on station, I was concerned for my future employment. Luckily, an opening appeared in the NBS servicing bay just down the corridor and, although I didn't like bay work, I could get stuck into my corporal's promotion exam that was looming.

I was put to work servicing one of the critical black boxes in the NBS equipment called the 'Calculator 5'. It was a mechanical, analogue, right-angle triangle solver—say that after a beer—that determined the range of the aircraft to the target along the ground. The equipment was fed with the height of the aircraft, which positioned the vertical side of the triangle, and the slant range of the aircraft to target, which positioned the hypotenuse of the triangle. With this information, the triangle was solved producing the true range to the target. This was essential information that was used by the navigator to calculate when to drop the bomb.

The risks involved in flying were demonstrated soon after arriving when I witnessed a crash. Looking out of a window onto the airfield, I was having a smoke watching a Vulcan doing practice roller landings. It came to light that it was practising asymmetric landings during which the crew simulated coping with an engine failure. The Vulcan was about to flare onto the threshold but was left wing low and hit the runway heavily on the left-hand main undercarriage leg which collapsed. The left wing hit the ground and the aircraft left the runway and travelled across the grass. Slowly rotating about the left wingtip, it headed for the control tower, disappearing behind the building. As it reappeared going backwards, the left wingtip clipped the corner of the building and the aircraft slid to a halt in the adjacent car park writing-off several cars. The aircrew vacated the aircraft and, thankfully, there was no fire, although the fire section based in the same building, were on hand. I was rendered speechless as at one time, the aircraft looked as though it was heading for me. The aircraft was eventually removed to a hangar and written off.

By now promoted, I looked for a way to get away from Scampton as I couldn't stand the place. My chance came when a co-worker, a corporal with the same qualifications, was posted to Marham to No. 57 Squadron, one of the new Victor tanker squadrons. An exchange scheme allowed those posted to somewhere they did not want to go, to swap. Almost instantly it was approved and I was posted to Victor tankers. It was back to Marham as a corporal and I would become acquainted with the third of the V-bombers.

The new tankers were operating out of Honington in Suffolk, temporarily, while the runway at Marham was resurfaced so I reported to the squadron at Honington. I was interviewed by the warrant officer and discovered that the dispersal at Marham was the same one that had housed our Valiants. He said that I was the obvious choice to send to Marham to prepare the site for the arrival of the squadron; and so it came to pass. Our small team arrived the next day with an introduction letter to explain our role. We collected the keys to the dispersal, booked out a Land Rover for transport, and headed out. The buildings were still full of old Valiant kit, including spare parts and technical publications. The biggest surprise was a half-built, half-scale First World War fighter; an SE5A. Word got around that we had arrived so the SE5A was soon collected, the publications burned and the spares returned to technical stores. We cleaned the place up, made sure all the telephones worked and got a load of telephone directories. The warrant officer arrived and sorted out the respective offices and other accommodation. Most importantly, we sorted out where the tea bar and crewroom would be located. Priorities first. The aircraft soon returned and No. 57 Squadron was re-installed at Marham. Two additional squadrons arrived, Nos. 55 and 214 Squadrons plus Tanker Training Flight was formed.

The Victor as a tanker was in its final work-up phase and was soon operational, giving a huge improvement in capability. With the Valiant, the RAF could only muster one tanker squadron but now there were three. My squadron still had a Victor bomber on strength which was used for a while as a crew trainer, still painted in an anti-flash white colour scheme.

There were no opportunities for groundcrew to travel abroad during the Valiant days but the tankers were expected to deploy overseas regularly. It was something to look forward to, although it would mean spending time away from my family again but that was the name of the game. To quote that well-known RAF saying: "If you can't take a joke, you shouldn't have joined."

As it turned out there were not as many deployments for groundcrew as forecast and I only did three in my time on the squadron. Two of them proved to be lengthy deploying Lightnings to Singapore and back, to show that we could, should the need arise. For the outbound trip we deployed to Gan, an island in the Maldives in the Indian Ocean. For long-distance exercises, one tanker would refuel another before returning to its original base, leaving the other to proceed down route with full tanks. This procedure was used during the Falklands conflict on Operation Black Buck when a Vulcan bombed the runway at Port Stanley.

Gan was a year-long, unaccompanied posting meaning families remained at home. For all that, it wasn't as bad as others of its type with good swimming and a semblance of a social life. Landing on Gan was an experience with the runway ending at the beach and at the other end, extending into the ocean. Landing as a passenger, as the aircraft descended towards the threshold, all you could see from the window was the sea getting closer and closer until you touched down.

The forward party set up on Gan and the first Lightnings arrived soon afterwards, beating up the airfield and scaring the daylights out of the locals. The aircraft stayed remarkably serviceable so there was time for socialising between us and the Lightning groundcrew and aircrew. With the Lightnings dispatched successfully, we had only to see the Victors back from Singapore and we were off home, via Akrotiri in Cyprus. It was a very successful deployment lasting only three weeks. The squadron was to deploy to Singapore later to give the Lightnings more tanking practice. Unfortunately, I missed that one as I was 'poorly sick', which was a shame, as my brother and family were there at the time.

It soon became time for the Lightnings to come home so the plan began in reverse. This time we would deploy to Masirah Island. This one didn't go quite so smoothly. Masirah was not the best place to be, with little off-duty activity. Apparently, the indigenous Arabs were banished to the island many years previously for massacring the crew of a ship that had landed. The food in the

LIGHTNINGS OF NO. 74 SQUADRON BASED IN THE FAR EAST. (JIM MASON)

messes was rather boring with limited supplies so the fresh fruit and vegetables that we had brought along in the back hatches of the Victor tankers were very welcome. Guess who got the job of distributing it to the messes?

With the Lightnings once more dispatched and heading back to the UK, the main body of groundcrew were on the way home. We remained to see off the final Victor and then would climb aboard the Britannia and be away. The tanker took off but hit trouble straight away as its main undercarriage would not retract. With three greens to land—meaning the landing gear was safely locked down—it returned to the pan. There was always massive pressure under such circumstances but, even with the aircraft jacked up, the fault could not be reproduced. There was only one thing to do. It took off again but this time, the gear retracted. Feeling confident and with the 'wheels in the well', the pilot decided to fly past at low level with all three hoses trailed behind. Unfortunately, on retraction, the centreline hose would not play. We were not a happy bunch …

With an imminent mutiny, both onboard and on the ground, the decision was made to jettison the hose and carry on to Akrotiri. Simple it would seem?

The plan was to jettison the hose on the beach instead of fouling the runway so the tanker carried out a low pass over the beach and successfully jettisoned the centreline hose. As the aircraft climbed away bound for Cyprus, we watched the hose come down, ready in a Land Rover to go collect it. Given clearance to cross the runway we headed for the beach but of the hose and drogue there was no sign. We could see where it had hit the beach and slid along for some yards but the hose was missing. ATC confirmed that we were looking in the right place but still nothing. We assumed that the indigenous population of Masirah was now worshipping a big black snake with a conical head that fell from the sky one day. There was nothing for it but to climb aboard our Britannia and head for Cyprus.

There were happy memories of Masirah, even though swimming in the sea was discouraged because of the anti-social sea life. There was still a plentiful supply of barracuda steaks and crayfish tails which could be bought from the locals and stowed in the hold of our Britannia for the return trip. Even so, it's hard to believe that Masirah is now a budding holiday resort.

The offending tanker turned around at Akrotiri but on taking-off, the main gear once again failed to retract and the decision was made to fly the aircraft home with the gear down. The technical investigation discovered a fault with the detection circuit that reports the wheels as fully extended. With the fault present, the gear would not retract.

Tankers were often deployed to give the Cyprus-based Lightnings tanking practice. Custom was for one aircraft with a crew chief to detach but his work-load was high without groundcrew support, especially if the aircrew were less than cooperative with helping out on the turnrounds, as they should do. On one occasion, a team of groundcrew was dispatched for support so I found myself on a trip that was supposed to last for four days, including transit time. We flew from Lyneham in a Britannia on a routine flight called the 'East Med Run'. Akrotiri was closed for runway repairs so Nicosia was being used for all flying operations. Landing in the early morning, we were directed to a building to be allocated accommodation and to arrange transport. We were met by a flight lieutenant whom I recognised as a rugby-playing British Lion from my time at RAF Yatesbury. He recognised me and I introduced him to our flight sergeant shift boss who was desperately short of accommodation. Could our new friend arrange for us to stay in a hotel in Nicosia as a thank-you for my efforts in supporting the Yatesbury rugby team? It's not what you know, it's who you know, and we were treated royally by the hotel owner who offered excellent food and a bottle of wine for each of us at the evening meal.

The tanking exercise went well allowing the tanker to head home and it was our turn next. Our boss contacted the movements staff at Nicosia, only to be told that the earliest flight home was in five days' time and that we should report at 0001 hours on the appointed day. We stayed in the hotel for the rest of the time and hired a minibus to see the sights, including the Turkish, northern side of the island. On our last night in the hotel, we were given a farewell meal and two bottles of wine each to take home. Reporting to the airport for our flight to Lyneham, we were told that our seats had been taken by the army. Our boss complained, but the movements guy pointed at a group asleep in a corner telling us that they had taken our seats. They were a scruffy-looking bunch but turned out to be from the Special Air Service who were returning from business in the desert somewhere; they won! We were promised a flight later that morning but there were two seats on a Britannia leaving in 30 minutes. Two of us immediately said we would go and were shoved into a Land Rover and taken directly to the aircraft but it proved to be full of freight. As the only passengers, we were looked after well by the female air quartermaster. Landing at Lyneham, we were issued with rail warrants, taken to Swindon station and arrived back at Marham that evening. That was my kind of detachment.

There would be a sting in the tail just before my posting came to an end when we came close to disaster on our dispersal at Marham. Two USAF F-100 Super Sabres were in the circuit around the airfield when one of them had an engine fire. The pilot ejected but the aircraft carried on flying straight-and-level. Our dispersal was fully occupied at the time with a couple of aircraft crewing in ready to go flying. The F-100 turned slightly to the right and began to descend, heading straight for our dispersal. It hit the ground between two of the hard standings, which thankfully, were empty, before coming to a halt against the perimeter fence. If it had stayed a little higher, the F-100 would have crashed into the officers' married quarters. The fire section was quickly on the scene to put out the fire but it left us somewhat shocked by the near miss. Very soon the station dignitaries were on the scene and staff from the USAF base in Suffolk arrived. To say they were shocked when they saw how close the aircraft had come to the houses was an understatement. The wreckage was soon cleared, nobody was injured and the pilot landed safely on the airfield.

Shortly afterwards, I heard that I was being posted to RAF Goose Bay in Labrador, Canada for a year. Although I was familiar with the base as our Victors often visited, the bad news was that it was another unaccompanied posting. My wife was less than amused but there was no way out. Even playing the 'essential duty card'—the squadron was desperately short of NBS fitters—failed to work. So ended ten years with the V-Force and, after my tour in Canada, I would begin 11 years with the Phantom.

CHAPTER 5

Is this the RAF's idea of a Mystery Tour?

Eric 'Geordie' Dunn joined the RAF in 1955 as an apprentice and trained as a navigation instruments specialist. He served at home in the UK, including Kinloss, Finningley and Sealand and overseas in Kenya, West Germany, Singapore, Gibraltar and the United States before retiring in 1995. He is now a volunteer guide with the Battle of Britain Memorial Flight.

An ex-Halton Brat, I left RAF Halton newly qualified as an instrument fitter (navigation) in July 1958, and was posted to RAF Kinloss. If you are a member of the Flat Earth Society, that is about as far north as you can go without falling off the end of the world, and an interesting prospect for anyone who is used to living south of the border.

Kinloss was home to the Maritime Operational Training Unit (MOTU) operating the Shackleton maritime patrol aircraft. It was a fine old aeroplane and you could trace its history back to the Lancaster bomber of the Second World War and, in fact, it had a very similar configuration. Also a product of the Avro aviation company, with its four Rolls-Royce Griffon piston engines, twin tails and tail wheel, it looked very similar to its illustrious predecessor. Only the nose-mounted radome on the early versions diverged from its heritage. High technology it wasn't but noisy it was. With its contra-rotating propellers, the

A SHACKLETON AEW2 WITH A HUNTER FLYING IN CLOSE FORMATION.
(PHOTOGRAPH COURTESY OF THE OLIVER FAMILY)

Shackleton was described by one wit as 'a million rivets in close formation'.

In those days you were expected to work on all the instruments not just the navigation stuff, and on all types of aircraft, not just the 'Shack'. At Kinloss we had a Station Flight consisting of a de Havilland Chipmunk, an Avro Anson and a Gloster Meteor T4 so I had plenty of variety.

We were paid cash back in those days. I had no such thing as a bank account and pay parade was always on a Thursday. I had just been promoted to corporal, and, at one particular pay parade in November 1958, I was told by the warrant officer to get my things, pick up the spares to fix a cylinder head temperature problem on a Shackleton that had diverted to an airbase in Norway, and to report to air traffic control at 1330 hours prompt. I had never been overseas in my life and was still very wet behind the ears so the prospect was exciting. Straight after lunch and armed with my RAF-issued side pack, my tool bag with spares and a few personal items stuffed in a bag, I duly arrived at the tower along with another corporal, Joe, a rigger.

Eventually, a Royal Norwegian Air Force Neptune maritime patrol aircraft arrived to take us to Norway. A twin-engined piston aeroplane built by the Americans, the Neptune was quite similar to a Shackleton. Up to that time, the only flying I had experienced was in the back of a Chipmunk; oh and a quick

THE ROLLS-ROYCE GRIFFON ENGINE ON A SHACKLETON MR3
AT NEWARK AIR MUSEUM. (DAVID GLEDHILL)

ride in an Anson while I was still at Halton, so this was very new and exciting for me.

We were met on arrival by the flight engineer from the Shackleton crew and immediately taken to the unserviceable aircraft. The cowlings were already open with ladders in place, so with no fanfare, it was straight on with the job. The crew had diverted with an apparent overheat on one of the engines and it might have been a serious engine problem but I was hoping for a quick fix. Sure enough, a change of the bulb that monitored the engine temperatures seemed to fix the problem. To make sure I needed an engine ground run to check that all was well. I asked the flight engineer to run the engine only to be told that it would be done the next morning on departure. All this came as a big surprise.

My quick trip to Norway had just turned into an overnight stay. Expecting to be back at Kinloss that evening, my hastily assembled bag of 'essentials' was now looking a little meagre. This was a big learning curve for me, never having been away from base before. The first thing was to borrow a few items of clothing as I had flown out in my RAF uniform, which was still of the 'hairy blue' variety much loved by many post-war recruits. The crew managed to cobble together a shirt and a pair of trousers which would see me through the evening and, fortunately, my fellow rigger Joe who had arrived on the Neptune from

Kinloss with me, was on hand. He had been to Norway before and knew the ropes about getting hold of accommodation.

Arriving at our temporary lodgings we found out that we would have to pay for our food; a not insignificant sum in Norway, but by a stroke of fortune, we had been paid that morning. I only relaxed when Joe told me that we could claim back expenses when we got back to Kinloss. We had a nice night in the land of the fjords, drank a little and ate a little, courtesy of Her Majesty.

The next morning at 0700 hours prompt, we arrived at the aircraft, to help with the flight checks and to wait for the engine ground run. Eventually, the aircrew arrived and we all climbed on board. I was told to sit next to the navigator, with the flight engineer at his station behind me. He indicated he was starting the engines and, as they ran up, he signalled that the indications were fine. Problem solved!

I signed the Form 700, the aircraft logbook, for the work I had carried out and assumed that the job was done. Only then did I find out that the next stop was Malta, not Kinloss as I had assumed. All I had was an overnight bag with a razor, toothbrush, and underclothes from the day before. I made some quick negotiations to hang onto the clothes I had borrowed overnight. It would have to do. Malta it was then!

The flight down the Mediterranean was not short. The Shackleton had many attributes but speed was not listed among them. At about 180 knots the flight took many hours during which my horizons were widened. I was introduced to in-flight ration boxes which kept many a Shackleton crew happy over the years. As a newly qualified avionics fitter it was interesting sitting next to the navigator and seeing the equipment that I had been trained on, in its real environment and working. For the first time I saw the ADRIS, the automatic dead-reckoning indicator system, the kit I was responsible for, actually being operated. There is no such thing as a free ride and, true to form, I was co-opted to fix an autopilot snag en route. The Mark 9 autopilot was fitted in the Shack Mark 1, so glass valves were the order of the day and you always kept spares in your tool bag, as they were not very reliable. It was a quick valve change and the kit was working again leaving a very happy pilot.

Finally arriving in Malta, Joe and I were taken to the transit accommodation but then left to fend for ourselves. We found our way to the mess and the NAAFI but Kinloss was still not yet on the flight plan. It turned out that we were to spend two nights in Malta, one night in Gibraltar, one night in St Mawgan, and if all went well, finally back to Kinloss. By now we were struggling. Joe was in the same boat as me with a distinct lack of clean clothes, having been given the same information. As always, he came up trumps. He found clothing stores, and, after a sob story to the duty storeman, we managed to persuade him to part with a spare shirt, socks and underclothes for each of us—of course as long as we signed for them.

All went well for the rest of the trip back to Kinloss. The warrant officer welcomed me back, and apologised for the lack of advanced information. He introduced me to the Form 1771, the expenses claim sheet, showing me how to fill out my travel claim. I was amazed at how much I got back.

All in all, I learned a lot on that trip. RAF Halton taught us a lot in the three years we were there about our trade but not that much about how the RAF operated. But for a small failure of a temperature bulb, I may have waited many years for a similar experience. As it was, it would not be long before I served overseas again.

A SHACKLETON AEW2 AIRBORNE. THE MARK 1 WAS SIMILAR
IN CONFIGURATION TO ITS LATER BROTHER
WITH A NOSE RADOME AND TAIL WHEEL CONFIGURATION.
(TONY DIXON)

CHAPTER 6

Ice Station Lossiemouth

*Allen Vernon joined the RAF in 1984 as a direct entry airframe techni-
cian. He was first posted to the airframe bays at Lossiemouth, followed
by a tour doing Category 3 level airframe repairs on No. 431 Maintenance
Unit at Brüggen followed by a posting to Repair and Salvage Squadron at
Abingdon. See page 16 for a full biography.*

It was 15 February 1985 and we were into the last few weeks of our direct entry
airframe technicians' course at RAF Halton. Friday lunchtime and I am walking back from the Maitland Mess to the barrack block. We are all on tenterhooks and still waiting for our first-tour postings but I have hedged my bets.

My first choice is Binbrook as I want to work on Lightnings; second is
Chivenor as I have heard good things about the station and my third choice is
Leuchars and 'Tooms'. No tight cluster of bases for me. As I arrived at the block,
our three Scottish course members are laughing. So I asked what was funny? 'JJ',
the youngest, lets the secret out of the bag: "Lossiemouth, for you!"

Lossiemouth? Buccaneers. Damn, not in the plan and there was worse to
come. I was not even posted to a squadron. ME(A)S? What's that? Nevermind,
off to Preston with a mate for the weekend.

By 4 March 1985 I'm standing outside Elgin train station with Griff, another guy from my course who
has been posted to Lossie,
although he's going onto
the Shackleton with No. 8
Squadron. His journey was
less adventurous than mine
as he stayed in the Bridge of
Don Barracks at Aberdeen
overnight.

Leaving Elgin, every building in this town seemed grey
as the taxi headed for 'Lossie'

A FAMILIAR SIGHT FOR NEW
ARRIVALS AT RAF LOSSIEMOUTH.
(ALLEN VERNON)

THE BARRACK BLOCKS AT RAF LOSSIEMOUTH.
(ALLEN VERNON)

which seems massive. Arriving at the main gate, this looks like no other RAF base I have ever seen. The domestic site comprises five huge blocks, a downgrade from the four-man rooms we had enjoyed at Halton. The naval heritage is soon evident with names like the Fulmer Club (the NAAFI) and the Fulmar Bowl, harking back to its former life as a Fleet Air Arm base. Personnel Services Flight is only open part-time so we are stuck into the transit floor of the airmen's block. The first night's explorations prove that this is not what we expected.

It takes three days to trudge around the station collecting arrival signatures before we finally arrive on our new sections. Griff will live on the other side of the airfield with the squadron whereas I will be in the airframe bay. I meet my

A HUNTER T7 UNDERGOES MAINTENANCE. (CRAIG SLUMAN)

chief Norman who sounds Australian but is from Norfolk. For the 'newbie', the pecking order says that I am confined to the tyre bay where I meet Al, my senior NCO boss and Paddy, my corporal. The 'old sweat' SACs are Gerry and Dave who show me the ropes. Our bread and butter are Buccaneer wheels as there are two squadrons of 'Buccs' plus the operational conversion unit (OCU). With no two-seat trainer, Hunter T7s provide the capability which means different wheels. There are Jaguar wheels for the Jaguar OCU, wheels for the Sea Kings of No. 202 Squadron and of course, the huge main wheels for the Shackleton. The work is dirty and it is years before health and safety would demand protective gloves.

The Buccaneer main wheels are seriously heavy with built-in brake units. Most are returned with tyres worn to limits but, occasionally, worn brake units or a locked-up wheel mean that the rim is damaged and is scrapped. We strip them, clean the components, test for damage using non-destructive test sets, rebuild with new tyres and seals before re-inflating with nitrogen. After final checks, they are signed off and reissued to the squadrons. The only flying I see is from the window, where formations of Buccaneers launch, fuel venting from the airframe as they select full power and start to roll.

I have joined the Mechanical Components Servicing Flight (MCSF) which includes the airframe and propulsion bays. The engine men live in D Hangar where the Spey and Adour engines are serviced. The annexes house the airframe component bays which spill into the main hangar that is also used by the Visiting Aircraft Servicing Section (VASS). With Lossiemouth designated as a master emergency diversion airfield (MEDA), VASS is manned 24/7 and has a control desk and living accommodation. Our busy flight also services Buccaneer in-flight refuelling pods, runs the liquid oxygen charging facility, filling the Buccaneer and Jaguar LOX pots and services the oxygen equipment.

The first few months of my tour sees me working on trade ability tests which are vital when entering the real world. Academics are interspersed with Mineval and Maxeval exercises as the station builds up to its annual Tactical Evaluation (Taceval). The weather is very Scottish and the snow lasts well into April. Without a green weapons handling chit—the station was way behind in general defence training—the station commander had ordered that anyone without a valid green card could not even book leave. For the first exercises I would be armed with a pickaxe handle!

It would be four months before I could attend the weapons course meaning no days off. With Lossiemouth being so remote, it became apparent that there wasn't the bomb burst of escapees at weekends, typical of stations further south. Scotland's licensing laws were less restrictive than England, although Lossie and Elgin didn't have a nightclub so everything shut at midnight on Friday and Saturday. Thank goodness that the Saturday discos on base were open until 2 a.m. Life, however, was not boring and the six-man rooms generated plenty of banter, finding myself in a room of young armourers, most of whom had also passed

THE UNCONVENTIONAL BUCCANEER UNDERCARRIAGE SHOWING
THE LARGE MAIN WHEELS. (CRAIG SLUMAN)

out as direct entrants. Some of the local pubs took the RAF in with open arms, however, fisherman's pubs did not, with The Harbour and Steamboat being off limits for 'crabs'—the navy term for the RAF. The locals who drank there were not fans and we were not welcome.

With Taceval looming the squadrons were flying late on a Friday evening. It was the day after my 19th birthday and we were well into our beers in the Clifton pub when a rumour began to circulate that a 12 Squadron Buccaneer had crashed on the airfield and the station crash plan had come into effect. The older 'sweats' knew to keep their heads down or they would be standing crash guard. It seemed that an input rod in the tailplane actuator had disconnected on final approach to land—a known design flaw in a locking bolt—causing a runaway, uncommanded, control movement. While the pilot warned the navigator to eject in time, he could not get out before the aircraft crashed into the undershoot of the main runway and he was killed. With two runways and a Cold War ethos, Taceval continued as planned, flying from the supplementary runway, while crash recovery and investigation began.

With my tyre bay induction complete I moved into the structural component repair bay where we were trying to rebuild the fairing panels for the Buccaneer radar altimeter. The original Blackburn spares had long since been used up so it was make do and mend, but there were more important events to come. The major event on the Lossie social calendar was the Lossie Raft Race.

Charlie lived in the Buccaneer hydraulic bay and took on the project to build the riggers' raft. After a raid on the station workshops, a supply of pine, ply, speed tape and signal red paint was liberated. A name for the beast? 'Crafty Crabs'. An eight-man beast emerged and sea trials began with young Junior Tech Vernon nominated for man-overboard training. The river was freezing and young Al emerged from the water as fast as a Polaris missile. With a creditable third place in the race, our raft beat the Armament Engineering Flight effort that was classed as favourite—mainly for its design and waste of public money—which sank after being sabotaged by an armourer with a drill. Marquis of Queensbury rules it was not! With our newfound fame, we looked at other races on the Scottish raft-racing calendar and entered an open raft race on the Cromarty Firth. Our small craft was no match for the semi-professional teams from southern Scotland fielding rafts and crews that would give the Oxford and Cambridge boat race crews a good race for their money. We were well and truly trounced and lapped.

The winter of 1985 in Scotland was like winters of old, and I got my first chance to ski up at the Lecht in the Cairngorms. Alas, my sporting skills didn't match my ambition and my spectacular crashes kept the experienced skiers entertained.

Back at Lossiemouth, snow meant 'Blacktop' duties with the snow and ice clearance team being nobbled to operate the equipment to keep the runways clear. My first duty was memorable as I missed the call out and narrowly avoided a charge. Being required back at Lossie on 2 January, and with no trains running in Scotland for the first two days of the new year, I enjoyed a lovely coach ride from London to Aberdeen before a bus ride on the A96 to Elgin losing 18 hours of my life. Lossie was remote.

If our work was a little mundane, VASS often had dramas. After an emergency landing, a Dutch F-16 taxied to a remote location to be met by the see-in crew. The pilot, however, waved them frantically away as he had operated the emergency power unit that used the chemical hydrazine. After a strong dose of fumes and a trip to the station medical centre for a check-up, the boys were much wiser.

There was a liney on VASS; a good lad, cocky, a treat for the ladies but the unluckiest man in NATO. During a trial by the Tornado Operational Evaluation Unit, he noticed that the ejector release safety pin had not been removed from a pylon. The aircraft had already started when he saw the offending pin and removed it. He then took it towards the front of the aircraft to show the crew. Alas he had forgotten about the auxiliary air intake doors and in holding up the pin, he offered something to the greedy RB199 engine, a little more solid than the air it expected. With foreign object damage to the engine, he struck up his first black mark.

Worse was to follow when a visiting Andover was assigned a parking slot on the pan outside D Hangar. With VASS busy with other movements, two of us from the bays were nominated by the flight sergeant to handle the arrival. Fortunately, VASS arrived as the Andover was taxiing in and we were relieved, unceremoniously, by the shift corporal. This proved to be a good thing as the infamous liney positioned the Andover perfectly so that its left wing hit a lamp post on the edge of the pan. Although not totally his fault, a speedy return to the bays followed.

The start of 1986 saw me escaping to support two Buccaneer squadrons on a Joint Maritime Course exercise at the RAF station at St Mawgan in Cornwall to coincide with their Taceval. That meant more war games. Before deploying I spent a week in the bay learning how to charge a LOX pot which provided the Buccaneer crews with oxygen in the cockpit. Whilst hearing Steve Wright on Radio One I listened to the launch of the Space Shuttle Challenger which

exploded on take-off. A salutary lesson when playing with liquid oxygen.

One of the advantages of our remoteness was that we deployed with No. 208 Squadron aboard a Hercules to St Mawgan. It was an unaccustomed luxury to fly on a UK detachment especially as we learned that we would be accommodated in hotels in Newquay. A family run establishment in a backstreet called 'The Beach Buoys' was our abode for three weeks, sharing with the squadron engineers.

Of course, as non-squadron personnel we were known as 'Klingons' with different work patterns. Two of us worked in the station tyre bay keeping the stocks of serviceable wheels refreshed, while others charged the LOX pots for the next day's flying. The Buccaneer could carry a mobile LOX pot cradle in its bomb bay along with some with spare pots. Our new home was a 12 x 12 tent on the dispersal which would house the cradle. Now the fun part. The tent needed pegging down into the ground but the 'elf and safety fun officer' wouldn't let us place the tent on soil due to the risk of liquid oxygen and grass combusting, as could oxygen and the canvas of the tent. As we were not officers, who were we to argue? The tent was positioned on a patch of concrete with sandbags weighting it down. All was well until the evening when the first engine ground run by a Buccaneer saw the tent, the cradle and six full LOX pots take to the air. The tent suffered badly but, fortunately, the LOX pots and the cradle, miraculously, survived without significant damage.

The detachment was not incident free as a Buccaneer landed with the nose-landing gear still stuck in its bay. The crew were recovering to St Mawgan when, after lowering the undercarriage, they realised that only two green lights had illuminated for the main wheels, the nosewheel being stubbornly reluctant to extend. Following the flight reference card drills, the crew tried to extend the nose gear to no avail. With fuel getting low, the crew flew out to sea and jettisoned the external fuel tanks and the canopy, before making a main-wheel only landing. Quite a sight. Deputising the St Mawgan volleyball players, the aircraft was lifted and the reason for the nose gear jam was found. A faulty steering motor had allowed the nosewheel to rotate and jam in the bay. It did not take long to release and drop the nose gear but damage to the nose of the airframe was extensive. With the abrasion of the concrete runway surface, the radome, the folding nose section, and the front fuselage had been ground through the bottom skins, exposing the frames beneath. Finally back on its undercarriage, the Buccaneer was towed to the Nimrod maintenance hangar for assessment.

There was no let up as the exercise continued into a third week culminating in the Taceval. I was nobbled to act as a sector guard with my main role being to open the sector gates to let aircraft in and out. The poor squadron leader who I persuaded to lay on the ground was less than thrilled as his fake ID card wasn't fake at all. I now know that an officer's service number has a letter at the end of the numbers unlike ours.

After more time in 'NBC black' conditions, in whiteout snow showers, the exercise drew to a close. Although No. 208 Squadron returned to Lossie, No. 12 Squadron continued for more flying on the JMC exercise and I was left behind to support the commitment. Although the squadron was in on-base transit accommodation, we were allowed a few days' grace at The Beach Buoys along with the No. 208 Squadron riggers who were patching up the damaged Buccaneer. A new nose-landing gear, radome, folding nose and canopy had been fitted and a thick sheet of aluminium cut in a semicircle and rolled out to cover the hole on the forward fuselage lower skin. Attached with huge jo bolts (battleship repairs), the kite was a patchwork quilt of colour. After a parting gift of a charged LOX pot, we were dropped off at our final accommodation.

Those who have stayed in the transit blocks at St Mawgan will know that they date from the 1940s, comprising eight wooden huts, joined to the washrooms by an unheated corridor. The morning ritual of a sprint to the showers in the sub-zero temperatures was quickly established. The saving grace was the airmen's mess but the NAAFI was dead and we had exhausted the hospitality of Newquay in the last three weeks. Even if we hadn't, we had no transport to escape the station. It would be quiet nights for us for the rest of the detachment and the lure of Lossiemouth was strong as there was more fun up there than in Cornwall in winter. We happily flew back to Lossie after five weeks away.

Back at Lossie I found out I had been seconded to Buccaneer Aircraft Servicing Flight for a couple of weeks to help their propulsion team trace a leak in one of the fuselage fuel tanks. The tank had been caked with sealant to the point that I had never seen a tank like it and never will again. We dug a possible track where we thought the leak was and resealed it with hope. It seemed to work.

Imagine my surprise when I found out almost immediately, that I was to attend an airframe Q course on the Buccaneer. I didn't know why this was necessary as I didn't work on them. But by day three of the course, it all became apparent; I was being posted to Brüggen in West Germany in midsummer.

On my return, Lossie still had a few surprises to throw. It was a Friday and our glorious flight sergeant had a brainstorm and decided that he wanted the Argosy moved to the burning area. There had been an Argosy hulk sitting on the grass near the lighthouse for eons. As we were enjoying typical spring weather—horizontal rain for three days—the ground was a quagmire. Wiser heads suggested that given the conditions, moving it that day might not have been the best idea but the flight sergeant was having none of it. The Argosy was moving that day.

An hour later, the riggers were called together in the hangar kitted out in wet weather gear and boots. Armed with shovels, a Sherpa minibus took us across to the western side of the airfield where the Tug Master tow vehicle, that can tow anything the RAF operates, was 100 yards off the taxiway, down to its chassis in the quagmire. The Douglas tractor, an equally robust piece of kit, was fitted with a winch and a plough but was only succeeding in ploughing the ground. The bomb disposal guys were called out to hitch a strop to the Tug Master, attaching it to the FV432 troop carrier. Alas the armoured fighting vehicle, promptly sat up on its tracks at a 30-degree nose-up angle. The Tug Master was going nowhere, so out came the riggers, using shovels and boards to dig it out. Covered with mud from head to foot, finally the Tug Master was pulled out onto the boards and back to the perimeter track. Amazingly, the Argosy didn't move that day. Suffice to say that the senior NCO was rather sheepish at the beer call later.

With Charlie still engrossed with the raft-race scene, he arranged for us to take part in a charity event in Perth—not the big boys one, thank goodness. The rafts for this occasion were to be a standard shape and size so 'Crafty Crabs Two' was built. A team of six travelled down to Perth in a Sherpa with Charlie towing the raft on his car. The race was to be down the River Tay, with a runner picking up a flag from a stop point, then racing back upstream to the start/finish line. Our craft was not the fastest on the water, but our runner certainly was, so we set off upstream well in the lead, paddling like mad against the current, trying to find the unmarked finish line, calling to people on the bank. We finally found that we had finished and won £5 gift vouchers. All in all, it was a great day and a good evening out.

My time at Lossie was coming to an end, but the World Cup of 1986 and a heatwave that hit 'Ice Station Lossiemouth' at the same time, saw three weeks of glorious weather. The Scots were shouting "Portugal, Gol" when England lost. The English were hanging Danish flags from the dead Buccaneer in D Hangar. Lineker's hat-trick generated English cheers from both north and south blocks. The hot weekend brought the crowds out to sunbathe on East Beach along with the rest of northern Scotland. The 'Hand of God' goal caused uproar in the NAAFI.

But it was time to pack my 'tri-wall' box, clear from Lossiemouth and head for Germany. I would be charged for losing my identity card on East Beach during my last week only to find that it was handed in the day afterwards. That was my last day at Lossie. I took a taxi and a train back home on leave before attending another course before I was Germany bound. My next visit to Lossiemouth was to attend a Jaguar Q course over six years later. The Germany tour was, alas, not a patch on the Lossiemouth tour as life on a maintenance unit never could be.

CHAPTER 7

God's Little Aerodrome

Ray Deacon passed out as a boy entrant air wireless mechanic from RAF Cosford in December 1959 and was posted to the Central Flying School (CSF) at RAF Little Rissington. His first three months were spent in the Scheduled Servicing Flight but he did not like the dull routine of servicing aircraft by numbers and switched to No. 2 Handling Party operating Vampires. In early 1962, Ray departed the plush green pastures of the Cotswolds to begin a two-year tour in the hostile deserts of Aden with No. 8 Squadron at RAF Khormaksar. Spending two years in Aden and a number of desert outposts, a trip in Sydney Camm's most beautiful aircraft, the Hunter, was an experience he never forgot. Returning to the UK he attended his fitters course at RAF Cosford. Returning to Little Rissington, once more with No. 2 Handling Party, this time the unit was equipped with the Varsity. His final RAF tour was at Fairford working on the Red Arrows Gnats of the CFS Detachment. Having left the RAF in 1967, he held fond memories of his time at Little Rissington and Khormaksar, so he studied official records pertaining to both stations and the units operating from them. In the years 2002 to 2006, together with three former RAF colleagues, he co-authored the book RAF Little Rissington: The CFS years, 1946 to 1976. *His first missive on the Middle East entitled* Hunters over Arabia: Hawker Hunter operations in the Middle East *appeared in April 2019, followed by a companion volume called* Tales from the Front Line: Middle East Hunters.

Having passed out from boy entrant air wireless mechanic training at Cosford as a senior aircraftman, I was posted to RAF Little Rissington where I arrived in the late afternoon of 29 December 1959. With most people still on Christmas leave, the camp was deserted and felt rather isolated.

A comparatively small airfield, Little Rissington was perched on top of a Cotswold hill, some 730 feet above sea level, making it the highest airfield on mainland UK. The Gloucestershire countryside was a delight during the warm summer months and the camp offered spectacular views across the lush, green hills.

The airfield had been home to the Central Flying School since 1946. The school's purpose was to train pilots from the RAF, Royal Navy, Army Air Corps and countries around the world, to become qualified flying instructors (QFI). Having formed in 1912, CFS was the oldest flying training school in the world and it still is.

The airfield comprised three runways laid out in the conventional 'A' pattern and five main hangars on the north side of the airfield. These were numbered from one to four from west to east, with No. 5 to the north of No. 3 Hangar. A large maintenance unit occupied the area to the south of the runways but was rarely used during this period. In 1960 the squadrons were distributed around the airfield:

- Scheduled Servicing Flight (SSF) occupied No. 1 Hangar and was responsible for carrying out minor and major servicing on all of the unit's aircraft.
- No. 1 Squadron (Provost and Jet Provost) and the Handling Squadron (Anson and Varsity) were assigned to No. 2 Hangar.
- No. 3 Hangar was home to Rectification Flight. Among its responsibilities were aircraft primary servicing and the repair of more serious defects.

RAF LITTLE RISSINGTON FROM THE AIR. THE HANGARS ARE NUMBERED.
(SIR JOHN SEVERNE)

- Nos. 2 (Vampire) and 3 Squadrons (Meteor and Canberra) were located at opposite ends of No. 4 Hangar.
- No. 5 Hangar was equipped as a paint shop and contained the aircraft finishing section.

As a flying training station, a five-day week, from Monday to Friday with normal working hours from 09:00 to 17:30 was in force.

Soon after completing the arrival process, I was assigned to SSF but being an outdoor type, I hated the feeling of being enclosed. Life was made palatable by the airmen who worked there as they were always up for a laugh and a leg-pull. We were issued with individual tool kits and to ensure none were left in the aircraft, weekly tool checks were carried out under the watchful eye of a senior NCO. As we sat on the hangar floor, the SNCO called out a particular tool and we reciprocated by holding up the same tool from our own kit.

I had the misfortune to work for a dour senior technician of the air radar trade, a real creep, with no sense of humour and not liked by other airmen. He saw me as someone to boss around but you can only endure psychological bullying for so long. Having completed a primary inspection on the solitary CFS Valetta, my personality-deficient tormentor ordered me to rub down the roof-mounted aerials to the bare metal, wait for him to inspect them and paint them again. As I knew I had carried out the task as per the manual, I refused and he stormed off in a huff, muttering something under his breath. Some ten minutes later I was summoned to explain my actions to Sergeant Pat Trumper, my direct boss, in the Radio Servicing Flight who informed me in no uncertain terms, that a senior tech had the same authority as a sergeant. With the threat of a charge hanging over me so early in my career, I was let off with a warning and as punishment, transferred to No. 2 Handling Party (HP).

Flight line crews were known as HPs, each having a responsibility for first-line servicing and support; 1 HP to 1 Squadron, 2 HP to 2 Squadron, 3 HP to 3 Squadron and 4 HP to the Handling Squadron. My two years on 2 HP saw some of the most rewarding and entertaining days of my life. I worked with a great bunch of 20 or so airmen who consisted of a mix of national servicemen and regulars, many still in their late teens. Morale was high and when times were slack or bad weather prevented flying, we played volleyball against the aircrew and got up to all sorts of mischief.

Although we had 20 Vampires on the inventory there were seldom more than 14 available at any one time. To ensure sufficient aircraft were available for the 0900 take-offs, our working day began at 0830. After a hearty breakfast, a ten-minute walk to the hangar and a change into denim overalls, our primary task was to carry out pre-flight checks on aircraft allocated for the first sorties, a schedule having been drawn up by our line chief, Flight Sergeant Tucker.

It was then all hands to the hangar. Each of the huge doors was opened by two men winding on a large handle, with additional muscle from half-a-dozen bodies pushing on the trailing end. The six doors were mounted on tracks and all needed to be opened. For fun(!), the middle pair was propelled at as fast a rate as possible, so that they crashed into the buffer stops with an almighty bang. The aim; to see how far we could get them to bounce back. Each door weighed several tons and the consequences of one coming off the rails would have been catastrophic, but the safety aspect seemed to go over our heads.

In 1960 to 1962, the 2 HP groundcrew establishment comprised a mix of 'old' lags, with active service on front-line units, and keen young airmen, like me, on their first postings. Apart from a couple of oddballs, it was a great mix and everyone got along fine. Except for the occasional incident necessitating his attention, Chiefy Tucker kept himself to himself and Sergeant Jack Castle kept out of the way, leaving the daily routine in charge of Corporals 'Tom' Thomas and Des Mutton. Corporal Tom Thomas had just returned to the UK following a three-year tour in Australia during the H-bomb tests.

NO. 2 HANDLING PARTY IN THE 1960S. RAY DEACON IS FOURTH FROM THE RIGHT. (RAY DEACON)

Although conscription ended in 1960, four of the group were national servicemen and none of them liked being in the service. Senior Aircraftman 'Taff' Evans was the more philosophical of the bunch and the first to return to civvie street in the early autumn. On his last day he was seen off with a huge party in the Old New Inn in Bourton-on-the-Water and, being Welsh, he led a repertoire of bawdy songs that must have been audible along the high street. Bob Hambly came from Jersey and he departed a few weeks later, leaving just the Summers twins. Electricians by trade, one was outward-looking and friendly with a permanent grin while the other was the complete opposite. Being identical, we had to be careful when referring to one about the other as they were easily offended.

To support the flying effort, aircraft refuelling and tractor-driving services were provided by civilian staff of the Refuelling Flight, accommodated in a crewroom in No. 3 Hangar. They were a bunch of characters from villages in the surrounding area with strong Cotswold accents and were responsible for driving the fuel bowsers and towing the Vampires in and out of the hangar. The No. 2 Squadron apron was situated adjacent to the east end of No. 4 Hangar and could accommodate ten Vampires at a time. Once the aircraft were on the line, Chiefy would pass a message to the aircrew office to let them know flying could commence. At the other end of the hangar, Flight Sergeant 'Jock' Hutson would be chasing his No. 3 HP airmen as they checked their Meteors and Canberras.

As the first instructor/student pairs signed the Form 700s, Chiefy Tucker would slide back the wooden panel in the hatch linking his office to our crewroom with a loud clonk, the signal to end our darts and card games and for starter crews to head for the line. The starting procedure was standard practice; the instructor and pupil checked their aircraft for signs of damage, the flying control surfaces for full and free movement and checked the tread depth and pressure in the tyres before removing the pitot head cover. Having verified that the safety pins were correctly inserted in the ejection seat guns, they climbed into the cockpit. Meanwhile, the starter crew plugged a trolley-acc into the power socket and checked that the chain attached to the nosewheel chock was not trapped under the tyre.

Having assisted the pilots to strap themselves in, handed them their helmets and plugged in their radio transmitter leads, the ejection seat pins were removed, shown to the pilots and stowed in storage pockets on the side of the seats. The canopy was then closed and the steps moved away from the aircraft. Pre-flight checks complete, the captain gave a twirl of a forefinger, reciprocated by the airman, and pressed the engine start button. To the sound of the crackling igniters, the Goblin slowly spooled up until the fuel ignited with a loud whoosh and a sheet of flame from the short tailpipe; an illuminating sight at night. A final check of the instruments followed by the chocks-away signal by the captain and the starter took up a position ready to marshal the aircraft safely away. Finally, the ground equipment was repositioned, ready to receive the aircraft on its return.

Time to relax and return to the darts, cards and a mug of tea. On sunny days, high spirits led to high jinks, some of which would have got us into serious trouble if caught. Disappearing onto the roof to avoid Chiefy's monthly hangar clean-ups via an unguarded ladder on the side of the hangar, or racing the station warrant officer's flatbed trolleys across the pan and through the water splash at the bottom of a ramp by the

GROUNDCREW REFUEL A VAMPIRE AT RAF LITTLE RISSINGTON IN 1960. (RAY DEACON)

rifle range, were a couple of antics that spring to mind. Another risky pastime involved chasing the civilian drivers as they wound their tractors through the trees beside the hangar in an attempt to pull the engine cut-off. It was a miracle no one got hurt.

One of SAC Roy Bagshaw's favourite epithets was that 'Rissy' could endure four seasons in a day, and it often did. The term 'Harry Clampers' described a foggy day and these were worshipped by the groundcrew. The Vampires would be pushed to the sides of the hangar and the pilots challenged to a game of volleyball, which we inevitably lost.

The daily ritual of the mid-morning NAAFI van with its cups of chi (tea) and wads, was greeted by shouts of "NAAFI-UP" echoing round the hangar. One almost inedible delight, commonly known as 'the Sinker', consisted of a variety of crushed dried fruits lumped between two layers of 'granitised' pastry. It could take an hour to eat and gained the name 'Sinker' on account of the effects on the stomach after eating more than one. You only tried that once.

All too soon the high-pitched whine of Goblin engines could be heard as they approached over the threshold, the signal to present ourselves back on the line. Having marshalled the Vampires in and positioned the access steps against the fuselage side, the ejection seat pins were inserted in the guns as the aircrew ran through their post-flight checks. While the turnround teams began their checks, a pair of bowsers were moved into position alongside the first two aircraft, enabling those assigned to refuelling duties to begin the time-consuming chore of filling the five gravity-fed tanks. To remove air pockets that usually formed in the tanks, the airmen bounced up and down on the wings until the bubbles stopped. Each turnround took some 20 minutes to complete and the aircraft declared serviceable and ready for the next sortie, or unserviceable if a defect had been reported.

Problems reported by the aircrew were rectified by the responsible tradesman. Defects involving wheel, radio, radar and ejection seat changes, were carried out on the line but more serious defects were handled by Rectification Flight. The airmen would collect the defective aircraft and tow it up to No. 3 Hangar for attention.

Tom Thomas was a laid-back kind of guy who tended to encourage rather than cajole his men to carry out their tasks. He also liked to lend a hand during busy periods and, on one occasion, detailed himself as starter-crew for one of the flight commanders, Lieutenant 'Dickie' Wren, Royal Navy, who was keen to get airborne for a practice solo aerobatics sortie. Having strapped him in, removed the ejection seat pin and showed it to Dickie in the prescribed manor, Tom placed it in the stowage pocket on the side of the seat and closed the canopy. The aircraft started up and taxied out. "Easy," Tom thought to himself but while walking back to the office, the thought struck him that he hadn't taken the pin out. Overwhelmed with doubt, he dashed into the office, phoned the tower, gave the aircraft number and requested it be returned to the line for checking. By now the Vampire was accelerating down the runway and it seemed an age before the engine throttled back. Tom then had the embarrassing task of greeting the bearded instructor when he taxied in before checking the location of pin. Nothing was said, but I could see him glaring at me as I mouthed OK and gave the thumbs up.

In the pub that evening, Tom told us he need not have worried as he had removed the pin but the incident had probably upset Dickie Wren enough to spoil the enjoyment of his aerobatic session. On his return, Dickie had a quiet word with Chiefy Tucker who, being a wise old bird, said nothing. Next morning, however, he gathered the groundcrew around a T11 in the hangar and told Tom to give a presentation on the removal and stowage of ejection seat safety pins; a lesson he said he never forgot.

As flying was continuous throughout the day, groundcrew were split into two shifts over the lunch break, the first departing for the airmen's mess at noon and returning in time for the second shift to take its 60-minute break. On the occasions when we encountered students while on our way to the mess, we would spread ourselves along the road so as to make them salute each airman they passed. Occasionally, we reversed our tunics yet, amazingly, nothing was said as they raised their hands to the salute. SAC Dickie Baston had a kiddie's scooter which he rode to the mess without being challenged.

The afternoon routine was similar to that of the morning, each aircraft flying a further two or three sorties. At the end of the day, as the aircraft were refuelled and after-flight checks completed, the Vampires were towed into the hangar and the hangar doors closed in double-quick time; then off to the mess for a meal and an evening out in a local pub. We often wondered how the 'time and motion' boys recorded the blinding speed with which the aircraft disappeared into the hangar.

Night flying was undertaken over a couple of evenings towards the end of each course and to keep the groundcrew fortified, the mess delivered sandwiches in cardboard boxes. Among the delicacies was a culinary delight called 'Prairie Chicken Sandwich', bread interlaced with chicken and synthetic cheese. At the end of the night-flying session, which could last until 0200 during the summer, it was off to the mess for supper, a heaped plate of greasy chips, beans and rubberised eggs washed down with thick-stewed tea. Not the healthiest of diets.

In early 1961, several inches of snow fell across the camp, too deep for flying. We decided to build the biggest of snowmen out on the pan where it could easily be seen. After an hour of hard graft our masterpiece had grown so high to make it impossible to lift the heavy head onto the shoulders. Not to be defeated, the body was re-sculptured into a piece of modern art. The light-hearted rivalry that existed between the handling parties was demonstrated after airmen from No. 1 HP pulverised our work of art during our lunch break. On our return we knew who the culprits were and by way of revenge, we attacked their

GROUNDCREW PREPARE A VAMPIRE FOR A SORTIE AT RAF LITTLE RISSINGTON IN 1961. (RAY DEACON)

crewroom with a barrage of snowballs, severe enough to keep them pinned inside. Very soon, airmen from the other HPs joined in and before long, a massive snowball fight spread the distance from the top end of No. 2 Hangar to the bottom of No.4, much to the delight of staff in the control tower who sensibly kept their windows firmly shut. Words must have been passed down as Chiefy Tucker braved the barrage to order us back to the crewroom.

The temperature overnight dropped low enough to freeze the snow and to make matters worse, another six inches or so fell in the early morning. Although the snowploughs fitted to the front of the bowsers cleared the fresh snow, a thick sheet of ice remained. Chiefy instructed us to push a pair of Vampires out of the hangar and, manned by a couple of instructors, they were started up. The intention was to use the hot jet efflux from the Goblin engines to blast the ice away. As huge chunks flew across the pan, the jets began to slide on the compacted ice, so we lined up along the wing leading edges and pushed hard against them as power came on. It worked perfectly preventing the slippage and after a couple of hours, a large patch of apron had been cleared.

SAC Tony Algaze was a real character who hailed from Falmouth. On days when Rissy was clamped in, he could chatter away continuously about any subject in a strong, stuttering Cornish accent. Occasionally, he would utter sentences that were complete gobbledegook, much to the delight of a captive audience. A variation of this dreamt up by SAC Willy Guilmant, suggested we reversed the spelling of our names. We soon became accustomed to referring to our mates as Samoht, Wahsgab, Nocaed, Notsab, Llednulb, and so on. Chiefy Tucker and the pilots had no idea what or who we were talking about and visitors to the crewroom thought we were bonkers. It wasn't long before the name 'Crazy Gang' began to stick.

As our crewroom was rather dingy and draughty due to the door which didn't shut properly and opened at will, we attached a cord to the door and routed it over the wall above it, attaching the other end to the duty roster board, the weight of which pulled it shut. Every time the door was opened the board went up and down as intended. This didn't please Chiefy if he was writing as the door was opened.

Social life at Little Rissington was good. Being a long way from civilisation—the fleshpots of Cheltenham were 20 miles distant—much of our spare time was spent in the NAAFI where a pint of scrumpy cost ten old pence and a pint, one shilling—the 'billing shitter' as it was commonly known. Off camp, we were blessed with a number of excellent pubs and regular trips were taken to villages with exotic sounding names such as; Bourton-on-the-Water, Stow-on-the-Wold, Chipping Norton, Great Rissington, the Barringtons and Kingham. One of the closest was The Merrymouth Inn on the Burford road which could be reached by walking across the airfield and a couple of fields. Routine orders stated that airmen were not permitted to cross the runway when night flying was in progress but this did not deter us. The relaxed way of life on the camp contributed much to the camaraderie that existed at Little Rissington.

In an attempt to brighten up the crewroom, the walls were covered with beer mats and pin-ups and the area outside adorned with various trophies each acquired on evening raids to local hotspots. A bus stop graced the corner of the hangar and a much-admired hanging basket hung above the crewroom doorway. This was purloined from The Rampant Cat, a pub located halfway up Burford High Street. After an evening's binge in the bar, we carted it to Tom Thomas's Austin Somerset. As it was dripping water and too large to be squeezed inside with six inebriated airmen, it was perched on the open boot lid which was hinged at the bottom. Tom maintained a steady 35-40 mph all the way back to camp through narrow, winding lanes and try as he might to dislodge it, the basket was still in situ as we rode through the camp gates and dropped it off by the crewroom.

The next object added to our expanding trophy inventory was a large folding ice cream sign that was lifted from the green outside a Bourton-on-the-Water cafe by a couple of our intrepid chaps who walked it all the way up Rissington Hill. It was placed in a prominent position outside Chiefy's office. Instructors and students appreciated these enhancements and would quietly smile as they walked out to their aircraft, enquiring as to the flavours of our confectionary. Not to be outdone, they had decorated the officers' mess with Shell signs removed from the top of a petrol pump. Our newly found pastime, however, was short-lived.

A few days later the ice cream sign was spotted by Little Rissington's sole RAF policeman, Corporal Norman Ratcliffe, as he made his security tour of the camp on his bike. He had been informed of a complaint from a Bourton cafe owner about one of her signs being stolen and believed the culprits were airmen from the camp. When he discovered it standing outside our crewroom, he retrieved it using his Land Rover and took it back to the guardroom. When the station duty officer arrived, he ordered that those responsible be charged with theft. As soon as he left, Norman contacted the station adjutant, Flight Lieutenant 'Bunny' Austin, and put it to him that it was unfair for airmen to be charged for collecting souvenirs from their nights out when the discovery of a number of Shell tops in the officers' mess was considered high spirits. Nothing more was heard on the subject and as Norman liked the sign, he set it up in the guardroom.

After an evening's session in the NAAFI, where the bar closed at 2230, we often took trips to the Windrush transport cafe on the A40, some six miles away, for a fry-up. One night after a heavy session in the bar, Mickie Blundell and Willy Guilmant departed for the cafe on their Lambretta scooters with Dickie Baston and me on the rear pillion. The lane from camp to the Barringtons was narrow and fairly straight but the final mile was narrow with several sharp bends. Despite the intake of alcohol, getting there was no problem and we enjoyed a grease-laden snack before heading back. Willy's scooter was slow to start and as Mickie and Dickie disappeared out of sight, we tried to catch them up. The lane leading away from the A40 was narrow and steep with a sharp bend at the bottom. Approaching too fast, we instinctively leaned over, the scooter sliding sideways until its wheels hit the kerb. The bike stopped dead and the force of the impact catapulted us over a low stone wall into a cabbage patch. On realising we were not hurt, we burst out laughing in relief but when a light from a nearby house came on, we quickly staggered back to the bike. Although the fairings were buckled, it started and we departed in haste.

On another night when the camp was shrouded in thick fog, SAC Dave Lee invited Mickie Blundell and me for a run to the A40 transport cafe in his brand-new Ford Anglia; a present from an aunt, he said. We were well-oiled after an evening in the NAAFI and, although Dave managed to keep the verges on either side at bay, he drove too fast towards Great Rissington, boasting how fast he could go in dense fog. His tune quickly changed on reaching the first junction where the road kinked to the left as he couldn't see anything through the murk and alcoholic haze. We smashed into the banking at the start of the kink. With no seat belts, we were tossed about and apart from a few bumps and bruises, we escaped injury. Our spirits somewhat dampened, we clambered out, only to find the front wheels pointing in opposite directions. We had no choice but to trudge back to camp and leave the exposed vehicle where it stood. The following morning, in front of his sniggering mates, a red-faced Dave had to explain to Chiefy that he needed a couple of hours off to retrieve his car.

An evening out in a Bourton-on-the-Water pub usually ended with a prank and the occasional confrontation with the law, the village bobby, Sergeant 'Jock' Watts from Scotland. One evening, while walking from The Mousetrap Inn to catch the last bus back to camp, Roy Bagshaw decided to test his strength. As he walked past a pair of gateposts, he decided to remove one of the concrete balls mounted on top. Having lowered it to the ground, he proceeded to roll it down the high street, when who should come along but Jock Watts.

"I don't know where you think you're taking that, laddie but you can take it back from where you found it," he bawled. So Roy rolled it back to the gate and somehow lifted it onto the gatepost. Needless to say, Jock detained him long enough to miss the bus and as he would have to walk back to camp, he was let off with a warning.

A couple of weeks later, while waiting to catch the bus back to camp after an evening in The Old New Inn, we decided to lift a big, wooden sign from outside the Witchcraft Centre and carry it over to the river. Safely aboard and using our hands, we began to paddle towards the Birdland Wildlife Centre. On approaching the second bridge, who should be standing on it, arms folded, a scowl from ear to ear, but our friend Jock Watts. The immortal words: "And wherrr do we think we'rrre goin' wi' that?" bellowed across the village green. "Back to camp, constable," came the insolent reply—no respect for rank. "Oh no yerr not laddie, let's be having yerr." So once again we'd been foiled and forced to return our ill-gotten gain to its rightful place.

The groundcrew on Nos. 2 and 3 HPs got on well together and would help each other out when the need arose, in the hangar or at the bar. This did not stop the practical jokes, as on the occasion when Roy Bagshaw hid Jock Hutson's bike by hoisting it up a tree on a rope outside his office. The Chiefy didn't spot it dangling in the breeze and spent an hour searching for it in the hangar. Although we couldn't see him, the Gaelic expletives could be heard echoing round the hangar when he discovered it. He never did find the culprit.

Up until mid-1960 and despite the unit's training mission, it was rare for the groundcrew to experience trips in the Vampire. This changed, however, with the appointment of Squadron Leader Peter Hicks as OC No. 2 Squadron. On one occasion when I was strapping him in for a solo flight, I asked him if it would be possible for some of us to fill empty seats. Lo-and-behold, within a few weeks, most of the would-be jockeys were to experience a flight in the jet-propelled trainer.

My flight was in XD383/VW on 9 September 1960 with Flight Lieutenant Peter Broughton at the controls. During the pre-flight briefing, Peter stressed the point that should we experience a serious problem, he would order me to eject using the immortal words, "Eject, Eject, Go!" adding that if I made any reply, I would be talking to myself. That instruction has remained with me to this day. Having taken us up to 40,000 feet, Peter showed me how to perform loops and barrel rolls before letting me have a go. An unforgettable experience.

Two days before the 1960 Christmas break and in appreciation for their hard work over the year, eight airmen were invited to fly as passengers in an eight-ship formation. I sat beside the squadron leader in the lead aircraft, XK586/VO, which was not my preferred position as I wanted to take photographs. Being at the front made it impossible to turn my head far enough to the rear. We took off in box-fours and headed south-west in a steady climb into a gap between two layers of cloud and changed to arrow formation to execute a few turns. Dropping down to 1,000 ft, a customary festive flyby was carried out over Kemble and Brize Norton airfields. All too soon, we were back at Little Rissington and breaking in sequence, from echelon formation for a stream landing.

Vampire T.11, WZ416/VF was the third trainer off the production line back in 1953. After an instructor reported that it would flip onto its back during high-speed stalls, the station test pilot, Flight Lieutenant Peter Marsh, was summoned to carry out an air test. This took place on 30 October 1961 and I managed to talk him into allowing me to sit in the right-hand seat. Peter warned me that the test could be hairy but, nevertheless, I was determined to give it a go. Little did I know but I was about to experience one of the scariest episodes of my life.

Following a standard take-off, Peter trimmed the aircraft for a steady climb using a high-power setting while writing notes on a knee pad. During the climb he explained the fundamentals of a high-speed stall and how he proposed to test for it. If the aircraft behaved as reported, he would have to repeat the test and check it out in a spin. Only now did it dawn on me that I should have heeded his advice and remained on the ground.

Some 20 minutes into the flight and with 40,000 feet indicated on the altimeter, we levelled out, accelerated to something approaching maximum speed and began a slow bank to the right. As Peter pulled ever tighter on the stick, the G-force increased and the aircraft began to shudder violently until suddenly, it flipped over to the left and onto its back, exactly as reported. Having regained control, Peter made a few notes and repeated the exercise with the same outcome. A few more notes and then two high-speed stalls to the left. This time as the buffet came on the vibrations increased but the aircraft remained under pilot control. More notes.

Now for the spins. Having never experienced a spin and not knowing what to expect, we flipped over and descended vertically in a clockwise spiral at a disorientating rate of rotation. When Peter applied what I later learned to be anti-spin aileron and opposite rudder to correct the spin, the combined effect of severe vibration and heavy stick forces prevented him from holding the column to the left with his right hand while trying to reach the air brake handle with his left. Having tried unsuccessfully a couple of times, he ordered me to help him hold the column over which I did without hesitation. By now I was 'passing bricks' and fearing the dreaded words, "Eject, Eject, Go!", the brakes flipped open and the Vampire slowly recovered in a controlled vertical dive. Yet more notes! "Is that it, sir?" I politely enquired in a pleading voice. "No Deacon, it is not," came the sharp retort. "Each test is performed twice."

So up we climbed to start another spin to the right with the same nerve-racking result. The final pair of tests comprised spinning to the left and, as these were completed without incident or assistance from the shattered passenger, we headed back to Rissy.

WZ416 was parked in a corner of our hangar to await rigging checks which were carried out by my close friend and photographic buff, Tom Thomas. Using a set of jigs, he was able to determine that one tail boom was higher than the other and that this was the probable cause of the high-speed stall problem. In short, the airframe was twisted. A week later, 'Victor Foxtrot' was flown to RAF St Athan, ostensibly for scrap, but records show that it was refurbished and re-issued to No. 1 Flying Training School in 1963.

Over time, competition for flights amongst the groundcrew intensified, and Mickie Blundell gained credit for using his initiative. When he arrived at the hangar each morning, he would walk past the pilots' crewroom and check the flight detail board. If there was a slot with DP, or dummy pilot, against it, he would rub it out and insert his name. The aircrew got quite used to this and would often call him in to don a flying suit, electric hat and leg restrainers.

On one occasion, having been asked what he would like to do, he replied that he would like to fly as high as the Vampire would take him. At around 42,000 feet, ice began to form on the instrument panel as the needle on the RPM gauge started to drop. The tone in the pilot's voice suddenly changed as he belted out the instruction: "When I say prepare to eject, eject, go, you had better be gone by the time the word 'go' is out of my mouth or you will be on your own." After a couple of attempts the Goblin relit with a defining thump in the back as the aircraft surged forward.

Mickie also enjoyed the experience of being a passenger on an air test following a minor inspection, the best bit being the loose article check. This consisted of the pilot moving the stick in a circular motion as if stirring a cup of tea, and inverting the aircraft to collect any debris that fell into the canopy. Fortunately, there were no tools!

In January 1962, the CFS fast-jet squadrons, Vampire, Meteor and Canberra, moved on a six-month detachment to nearby RAF Kemble to allow heavy maintenance work to be carried out on the main runway at Little Rissington. A couple of weeks into the detachment and while watching a pair of CFS Hunters take off, I was called into Chiefy Tucker's office and informed that my overseas posting had come through. It was the dreaded Aden. My heart sank. Having entered Germany three times on the preferences form and listened to countless horror stories from airmen who had experience of the place, the prospect of two years in the desert filled me with dread. There was no point in dwelling on it I thought, I might as well make the most of my final few months at God's little aerodrome. Three years later I would be back at Little Rissington and working on the Gnats of the Red Arrows, but that is another story.

CHAPTER 8

Not Such a Nice Day in an MRCA— Sweeping the Wings the Hard Way

Bill Brown joined the RAF in 1977 as an airframe mechanic and served at RAF Lossiemouth servicing Jaguars. After a short time at the maintenance unit at RAF St Athan he transferred to the Tornado serving on a number of units in the UK and Germany. He finished his RAF service at Waddington in the tyre bay where his service had begun some 23 years earlier. Since retirement, Bill left to work on the Tucano upgrade programme before spending eight years in prison, happily as a maintenance engineer! He is an avid car enthusiast and built his own Robin Hood kit car with his son, racing with the RAF Motor Sports Association at home and overseas, and winning the RAF Championship in 2012. He was clerk of the course at the Barkston Heath Sprint for some years but now enjoys a slower pace of life.

By 1990 I was a war-weary corporal rigger with nearly 14 years' experience on Panavia's finest, the Tornado GR1 bomber. A gift for your wife after all these years we are told is supposed to be gold; a symbol of both wealth and optimism. Unfortunately for me, I had none of the former and a very low version of the latter given that I had recently returned from a three-year posting in glorious RAF Germany on No. 31 Squadron at RAF Brüggen, with three years living the dream, working first line, getting 'rates' and petrol coupons, eating 'bratties' and drinking Grolsch, working hard and playing harder. The aircraft was good to work on. My experience was mostly at third line so the line work on the squadron was new to me but very interesting. Life was good. Then like they say, all good things must come to an end. Mine didn't just end; it all fell apart. Marham? I had never put anywhere near Norfolk on my dream sheet for postings. I had wanted Scotland. Perhaps it was the administrators' punishment for my three years of fun?

Fast forward a couple of years, to find me settled in at the Tornado Aircraft Servicing Flight (TASF) at Marham working on Team 3. It wasn't that bad to be honest. Sure, some of the work was repetitive but, on the whole, it was acceptable and my fellow inmates made for some interesting and fun times. This TASF was a fairly standard set-up where each aircraft team was made up mostly of riggers who owned the aircraft and did the vast majority of the work and all the cleaning up at the end of the day. Occasionally, the sooties and fairies would show their faces as well. The trail of tie wraps around our aircraft alerted us to the presence of an electrician-type person.

Minor servicing started with us airframe types removing all the panels before the fairies removed a black box or two being extra careful not to touch anything dirty. The engine chaps were quite the opposite when winding out their engines while spilling fuel and oil all over the place. Finally, the lekkies added to the mess with their discarded cuttings. Once this exciting phase was over, the humdrum servicing commenced, usually lasting a few weeks but sometimes months passed and the poor aircraft was still dangling on its jacks, waiting for spares, gathering dust. During this period the fairies had nothing to do at all so were kept very busy at bridge school or playing 'Uckers'. For the uninitiated, this was a type of Ludo for men. The fairies were not very good at board games, so tended to stick to bridge or amuse themselves by trying to work out if the TV detector van really worked, or fabricating a

A TORNADO GR4 WITH THE TRAILING EDGE FLAPS FULLY EXTENDED. (CRAIG SLUMAN)

'Spot-the-Ball' predictor. It kept them happy though.

Towards the end of the servicing, the riggers would work night shift so we could do the important functional checks; waggling bits up and down, back and forward, without constant interruptions of the lesser trades. This was one such night shift but it certainly did not go as well as it should have. The night-shift rigger crew was made up of a newly promoted, very keen but not-so-knowledgeable sergeant, aided by myself, a junior technician and a senior aircraftman. We got to work that evening tasked with the simple job of fitting the leading-edge wing nibs and slats before doing a full high-lift wing-sweep (HLWS) functional test. After that it was anything else that took our fancy before supper time at 2230, then home to bed. Yes, I know, it's not exactly a night shift but that's what we called it, and that's why we all liked it.

On this occasion the port slats were being a right pain to fit, even though they were usually a doddle. In fact, once on a previous squadron, we had changed a slat that had been hit by a bird, without even removing the drop tanks. The pilots, who were desperate to get back to Brüggen, did the functional checks with the engines running. But I digress …

The slats were unusually stiff to move along the tracks so we spent a long time adjusting rollers, re-adjusting rollers, cursing the day shift, re-adjusting the rollers, cursing the day shift some more until eventually, we got them working correctly. Phew, a cup of tea and now for the HLWS functional.

Electrical power and hydraulics up and running, we started the test. Straight away we had a problem, we were getting an asymmetry indication as soon as we moved the flaps and slats. To explain, each wing has two asymmetry position transmitters which tell the high-lift wing-sweep control unit (HLWSCU) if there is a difference between the movement of each set of flaps and slats. We looked at the air publications (APTs), tried different things from said APTs but to no avail. We discounted the earlier slat problem as irrelevant and consulted the

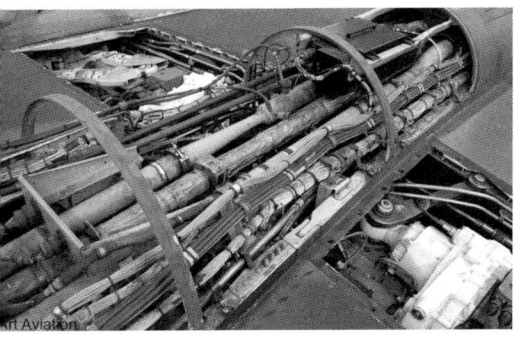

owner's manual. Everything pointed towards a problem with the rigging of the HLWSCU but due to our earlier problems, it was well past supper time and everyone else in the hangar had gone home. The prospect of starting a job we were very unlikely to finish did

THE TORNADO HIGH-LIFT WING-SWEEP CONTROL UNIT EXPOSED. (CHRIS WILSON)

not appeal to me so I suggested to the sergeant that we should not even start as it was not the type of job that can be handed over to the next day shift very easily. But the keen, but clueless, sergeant insisted we continue with the job. "OK," I said. "I will go and lock up the hangar."

We were the only people there so I left him to his plans. I was in no rush to lock up as I had already had enough of a certain person's 'push-on-itis'. When I returned to the aircraft, I found the sergeant, and the two juniors sitting on the spine.

They had got a short way into the printed-out maintenance procedure but had come to a halt because they could not find where the fescalised portion on the HLWSCU was—that's the shiny bit on the actuator. That's where you fitted the backlash tool to take up any slack in the inner realms of this magic box. The HLWSCU is that black thing you can see lurking underneath the spine pipe work between the two wing sweep actuators. Can you see the shiny bit? No neither could they.

I pointed out the shiny bit and told the sergeant that we did not have said backlash tool and a trip to the squadron would be necessary—but all sensible people would have gone home by now. The sergeant decided to search our stores for something, even though he didn't know what it looked like. Ho hum!

I sat with the lads and waited. Eventually, our intrepid explorer found nothing in stores and he returned empty handed. Finally time was called and he sauntered off to fill in the shift diary looking very dejected. He was defeated and he knew it because in his distraught mind his sergeant stripes were hanging in the balance.

Back to the real world and I asked the lads how far had they got. I seem to recall paragraph 4.1 but don't hold me to it. They had managed to disconnect the feedback shafts which are a mechanical linkage to the HLWSCU which allows all the fancy computer stuff to know where the high-lift and wing-sweep devices are positioned. They had gone no further so, in a big red pen, I put a line across the page where they stopped and at the top, I wrote 'Done' and below the line, I wrote 'Not Done'. This was exactly what had happened and there was no way anyone could think otherwise, and of course the sergeant was filling in the shift handover diary to confirm. I made sure we had a big sign: CAUTION, DO NOT APPLY HYDRAULICS. It was positioned on the rig and we disconnected the electrics, put the tools away, had a quick sweep up, cleared up the electrician's mess and we were gone.

Next day I was up early as I had a day-release college course in King's Lynn

THE TORNADO THROTTLE BOX.
(DAVID GLEDHILL)

learning to wire up houses so I was not scheduled to do a night shift. After my course I was at home enjoying my tea when I got a call from work suggesting I went in. Why? I asked but they would not tell me. Guess what? I didn't go in.

The following day the whole story became clear. The day shift—commonly known as 's**t shift'—had turned up and found the aircraft with its flaps and slats fully retracted, with the wings fully forward, just as we had left it. The shift leaders had decided to have the 'erks' wire lock the flap rollers and leave the rest of the HLWSCU rigging job to the night shift. Did I say it was not a good job to leave for the other shift? To wire lock the rollers, the flaps needed to be down and there are two ways to do this. The first is to use hydraulics and the other is manually to wind them down. You would think the large sign on the rig saying 'CAUTION, DO NOT APPLY HYDRAULICS' would be a clue but sadly no.

The day shift removed the sign, throwing it to the ground, connected power and hydraulics (at 270 Bar) and lowered the flaps and slats. Surprisingly, all went well to this point and power and the hydraulics were turned off. It had been a narrow escape and, thereafter, a leisurely day was spent wire locking the many rollers and, of course, playing Uckers.

Approaching the time for the night shift to arrive, the decision was made to raise the flaps and slats so that the team, without me of course, could carry on the complex rigging process. By this time, they had actually read the 'Done/Not Done' advice which I had left on the desk but it would appear the diary had not been filled in properly, although they knew that the feedback shafts had been disconnected. The 'Done' section had included disconnecting said feedback shafts but after much head scratching, they must have decided how to get the flaps and slats back up ready for the night shift's arrival. Obviously, now they could see that the feedback shafts were playing no part in the process, they would decide to manually wind the flaps and slats up. Surely, they would … wouldn't they?

When hand-winding you disconnect the port slat shaft, connect a socket and speed brace and get your SAC to wind furiously, until the port slats reach the bottom of their travel. Then you do the same for the port flaps before repeating the process on the other side. The procedure would not disturb anything on the HLWSCU because the feedback shafts were disconnected so it had no clue where all these bits were anyway. Of course, it was going to be rigged so that everything would line up again. The whole process would take 20 minutes at most and that includes waiting for the SAC to catch his breath and moan, "Why me?"

Common sense, sadly, failed this day because the decision came from the leaders-of-men, (sergeants and above), that speed was of the essence. In their view, because the flaps and slats had come down using 270 bar of hydraulic pressure without causing any problems, the wing-sweep lever had not been touched therefore, the flaps and slats should go up again using 270 bar of hydraulic pressure without any problem. The leaders-of-men were confident that it would be a lot easier to ram a load of hydraulic pressure into the system and select up! This would be a decision that came back to haunt a number of people.

Electric power was called for. Beep went the horn as the rush of electric fans drowned out the previous tranquillity. Hydraulics on, was the next command, and with a blur of the SAC's wrist, 270 Bar of hydraulic pressure flowed from the rig. Flaps down came the shout from an intrepid leader. My corporal mate in the cockpit selected flaps down and, with a rumble, they moved as predicted, followed closely by the slats which were just gliding perfectly on their tracks, thanks to the night shift's hard work. It was at this point things quickly started to look bleak for further promotion within the team.

Unfortunately, when the slats reached the bottom of their travel there was a large jolt and the wings decided to swing backwards rocking the aircraft on its jacks. This would have been fine had the flaps been up but instead of fitting neatly into the pressurised bags on each side of the fuselage, the flaps were forced at very high pressure into the fuselage skin. My mate in the cockpit described the sound as large bangs and lots of popping sounds as the rivets holding the skin in place gave way. Electrical power and hydraulics were speedily cut and all that was left was a deathly silence, broken only by the sound of fuselage rivet heads plopping to the ground, mercilessly shattered by the unexpected retraction of the wings and flaps. Very quickly, 'trolls' turned up. The sooties came running, the office staff put down their books to find out what was going on, and even the fairies stopped their game of Uckers to come and see. Everyone gathered round to gloat, laugh, cry and generally, to feast their eyes on this rather sorry-looking aeroplane. All you could hear from the chief's cabin, was sobbing. It was not long after that I got the telephone call.

Things were rather subdued in Aircraft Servicing Flight for quite a while afterwards. Team 3 suffered the mandatory humiliation, metered out by the other teams, albeit with good humour. The toilet wall artists quickly got bored and started on another victim. 'Crash and Smash' had sent over a team of experts to fix the damage, although it's a

VOLUNTEERS AT COVENTRY AVIATION MUSEUM CHANGE A TORNADO WING. (PHOTOGRAPH COURTESY OF COVENTRY AVIATION MUSEUM)

shame they didn't let us do it ourselves. After all, we had done our battle damage training but hey ho. The fuselage needed extensive repairs and the wings were both replaced. With the total cost in the millions of pounds, obviously, heads needed to roll.

Sadly, there are no pictures from the 'Crash and Smash' wing change but it was probably something similar to the efforts of the Coventry Aviation Museum above. Just squint your eyes a bit.

Step forward nearly a year later, to the Board of Inquiry, now known as a Service Investigation. It all looked very serious but, thank goodness, nobody was at fault—so said nobody on Team 3. Obviously, the MoD could not get the cash back but they wanted someone to blame for the alleged blunder.

Things were strange the day the inquiry started. The hangar seemed sort of quiet and even the banter had stopped; well maybe not all of it but there were certainly fewer grown-ups in the hangar. The board consisted of an officer or two and an RAF policeman which was a strange addition I suppose, but certainly the presence of a police-type added to the drama of the day.

The sergeant was the first to be called in. He was as white as a ghost and this man had a lot to lose yet this was his chance to save his career. Only a few hours later they were finished, and the sergeant, hanky in hand and tears in his eyes, left the room. Now it was my turn.

Remember, I was a seasoned corporal, nearing the end of my service, going nowhere, just biding my time until a return to 'civvie street' so this was not really much of a worry. I was also confident that I had not done anything wrong. When I went in, the policeman was the only one present as the officers had gone for tea and scones with the boss. We had to wait. Obviously, you can never trust a policeman but he seemed like a nice chap and we got talking. He was very interested in the hangar and the work we did and he asked me what job I was on at the time. As it happened, we were working another skewed wing/flap problem so I decided to hit 'Mr Plod' with some aeronautical jargon, thinking I would baffle him: "Oh we have an asymmetry problem with the high lift system." "Have you tried the APTs," came the immediate reply.

I was shocked to say the least. No wonder the sergeant had red eyes when he came out because this copper knew the Tornado HLWS system inside-out. I asked him if he had some strange type of rigger fixation and where on earth he had gleaned his information, given that his normal job consisted of looking at faces on ID cards and arresting drunks in the NAAFI. Apparently, as part of the inquiry he was sent on the HLWSCU course so that he could understand what us techie types were babbling on about. It also helped him detect any bullshit that may be spouted by the accused.

When the officers returned, they were nice and friendly and tried to make me feel at ease, making it clear this was not a criminal investigation which made me wonder why the clued-up policeman was there. It was not at all what I expected. Even so, I was still pretty relaxed. The serious stuff began and they asked about me, my welfare, how long had I worked there, where I worked before, if clothing stores had my size of socks, and numerous other seemingly, random questions. They wanted to know that there were no underlying reasons that could have caused this minor disaster (check out that for a pun). Then they started on the build-up to the event, my part in the team, the people involved and whether we were trained and competent for the job. They asked who was in charge that night but I was surprised at the question and explained that the sergeant was in charge. They revealed that during his interview, the sergeant had said that I, the corporal, was in charge and that he was only there for independent checks. I pointed out to the board that, had I been in charge, we would have all gone off after supper, like normal.

More and more questions came my way and it was becoming like a game of table tennis. The balls kept coming over and I calmly returned them, time and again. This went on, and each time my response was met with a slight nod of the head. I imagined this was an acknowledgement of my being correct but I suspect that if they did this with the sergeant, he may have thought that the nod was a sign of his impending doom.

They asked about the slat fitting. They asked about the HLWSCU backlash tool and why we didn't have one in Aircraft Servicing Flight (ASF). They suggested it would be easier if there was one in our stores and I agreed. They then asked whether the wing-sweep lever lock was fitted. I confirmed it had not been fitted but countered with that it was not mentioned in the maintenance procedure and also the fact I had never seen one in my 14 years on this aircraft. I even questioned its existence as this tool was the Tornado equivalent of the dinosaur.

In the image on page 93, the wing-sweep lever is in the top right in the fully forward position and the flap lever on the left alongside the throttles. You can see that there is no lock fitted to the wing-sweep lever. None of us had ever seen such an item.

They asked a lot more about the shift including who wrote the 'Done/Not Done' annotation on the maintenance procedure which made me chuckle. They also agreed it was straight to the point and obvious as to how far the lads had got in the job.

When the board made its findings, the wing-sweep lever lock was mentioned and they criticised the fact that it was not mentioned on the maintenance procedure for the HLWSCU, suggesting that it may have held the lever rigid enough to stop the tiny movement that caused the wings to sweep so far back. This criticism was not levelled at us, of course, because we were only following the procedure at the time. The board cleared the junior ranks of negligence, as the airman who removed the 'No Hydraulics' sign was not expected to think for himself—perish the thought. The leaders of course earned 'full buffoon status' losing any hope that their future dreams might include the role of station commander.

So, what did we learn from all this? Well, I would think the biggest problem was that an accurate night-shift diary was vital. A push to finish the job, even though it was never going to happen that night, might not be the safest course of action. Equally disturbing, was the removal of the warning sign that was left on the hydraulic console. The team tasked with lowering the flaps on that fateful day should have noticed a huge obstruction, covering all the dials and wiggly switches. The warning of peril should hydraulic pressure be pumped into this poor aircraft was a clue. Even worse than the first application of 270 Bar pressure was that, by the time they raised the flaps, they had already had a near-miss and the warning sign should have broken the chain. So the version of 'Tornado Russian Roulette' was ill advised.

The final conundrum was the HLWSCU rigging tool which would include the elusive lever lock. Well they are dead right that ASF should have owned one but the 'RAF bean counters' held the answer to that question. Counting the cost might have occupied their time.

One of the more memorable events of that posting, I think it safe to say that none of us who were involved will ever forget it. The aircraft was eventually fixed by 'Crash and Smash' and, after a bit of paint, you would never have known the difference. As far as I know it served out its time until the iconic Tornado fleet was retired in 2019, some 20 years after me.

CHAPTER 9

The Dead Cat in Gibraltar or Death on the Rock II

Terence 'Paddy' Doyle joined the RAF in 1975 as an aircraft apprentice air-frames/propulsion and after training, his first posting was to RAF Lyneham on C-130 Hercules. Moving to RAF Kinloss Paddy found himself on Nimrod Line Squadron for a seven-year stint, latterly as the SNCO in charge of Visiting Aircraft Servicing Flight (VASF). He completed his time in Scotland as an instructor on the Nimrod Maintenance School. In 1987 he served in Hong Kong on Wessex Servicing Flight before a further tour at Kinloss as a Nimrod crew chief and latterly the crew chief instructor on the Nimrod Maintenance School. In 1998 he left the RAF and joined BAe Systems at Warton, initially on the training course design team for Nimrod MRA4 but then in Flight Test, supporting the first flight of the MRA4 from Woodford and then Warton. The demise of MRA4 saw him casting around for anoth-er position and an opportunity arose as the flight test control engineer on the Lockheed F-35 at Naval Air Station Patuxent River in Maryland where he has been since June 2011. In his spare time Paddy has been exploring the USA, playing golf and riding a Harley Davidson.

In February 1985, Spain fully re-opened its border with Gibraltar and shortly afterwards, I found myself on detachment from RAF Kinloss aboard a Nimrod crewed by No. 120 Squadron. The aircraft could carry up to 25 people. The usual crew complement was around 13 comprising a mix of officers and NCO

NIMROD MR2, XV239, AT GIBRALTAR IN MAY 1991. (TERENCE DOYLE)

aircrew. The groundcrew, led by an aircraft crew chief, usually made a further six or seven.

A pre-detachment briefing had warned us to be on our best behaviour if we crossed the border and strangely enough, we were. Back then, there was a wide boulevard from the border leading towards the town of La Linea. For many years, every time I walked up that boulevard there was a dead dog lying somewhere alongside the road. At a guess, I would say the local council wanted to send some sort of message to the Gibraltarians and would regularly deposit one on the road at night. We did hear of some arrests for dancing naked in a fountain in La Linea town square and our immediate thoughts turned to some of the characters in the crew. It turned out however, that the culprits were from the Royal Navy. Our crew was keeping its powder dry for a more outrageous stunt.

We tried a few bars in the town and found them too quiet for our liking so headed back into Gibraltar to more regular haunts. Our usual, well-worn route would start in the Piccolo in Catalan Bay and then move on to the happy hour in the Caleta Palace hotel which, for our crew chief, was more of a parade than an option. We would then walk back past the camp and head to Bianca's in the marina to continue drinking, followed by the now defunct Paddingtons, the Horseshoe, Gibraltar Arms, Angry Friar and various pubs in Irish Town including Buccaneers. The evening would often end up at the infamous Lotte's Bierkeller on Engineers Lane, one of only two bars in Gib. that stayed open until 0400. The other, the Hole in the Wall, was more of a matelot/gay bar, which the RAF rarely visited.

The night wore on and we staggered our way at some point late in the night, back to RAF 'North Front'. We had after all, to launch the jet on a Gib-Gib trip the next morning. With the Nimrod, these trips were usually six or seven hours long, which gave us ample time to rest and recuperate, either back in our beds or in the crewroom back at the Visiting Aircraft Servicing Flight. Meanwhile, the aircrew had to work.

Early next morning my alarm went off and I made my way to the room opposite in the upstairs corridor of the sergeants' mess to wake up the crew chief, as we had arranged. The light was still on in his room and he was mostly on the bed, still fully clothed after a night of refreshment. He was surprisingly, easily roused but I had to find his Anadin and then left him to it. I went back to my own room, got my shower kit and padded towards the showers. Halfway down the corridor, I was somewhat surprised to see what appeared to be a dead cat, laying against one of the room doors and there appeared to be a bit of a bloodstain. Shaking my head, I hurried on to the showers.

Drying off, I could hear a few more bodies up and about; doubtless our NCO aircrew up for their flight. There were a few catcalls, guffaws and some loud man-induced mewing noises echoing around the corridors. I made my way back to my room noticing the cat had now disappeared. Having changed and feeling barely human, I decided it was time to see how the crew chief was faring. Much to my chagrin, he was, after a mere couple of Anadin, way more bright-eyed and bushy-tailed than I considered he deserved to be.

Needs must, so we called transport and made our way over the runway to the aircraft and enjoyed an uneventful launch. I was feeling slightly better after a cigarette and looking forward to breakfast in the mess. The crew chief had plans for a liquid lunch later in the day at the Piccolo which was an old Nimrod habit, acquired before the days of mobile phones when you could sit in bars like the Hacienda, close enough to the runway to enable you to see the aircraft, doing the almost compulsory rollers, before a full stop landing. This ploy would give enough time to get back to the flight line before the Nimrod taxied to a halt. The Piccolo seemed to be a fair distance away at the top of Catalan Bay and I thought it a bit of a stretch to make it back in time, but he knew the owners and he was, after all, the crew chief.

Taking the transport back to the sergeants' mess, me and the crew chief, being the only senior NCO groundcrew, tucked into a fried breakfast. I think it was a Saturday but by this time, most of the rest of the sergeants' mess residents had eaten breakfast so we had the dining room to ourselves. As we ate, further laughter and meowing sounds were coming from the staff in the kitchen. We chuckled, speculating, or should I say confirming each other's theory, about the culprit. Coffee and cigarettes followed in the ante room before we decided to go upstairs to our rooms for a quick nap and change into civvies. As we climbed the stairs, I noticed a couple of chalk circles on the steps. They were around an inch in diameter but I was certain I had not noticed them earlier. Entering the corridor, we were greeted with a full crime scene investigation and part of the corridor was taped off with police crime scene tape. I noticed further circles leading to a larger cat shape chalked outside one of the doors. A gaggle of RAF policemen had arrived and cameras were flashing.

A couple of Special Investigation Branch (SIB) RAF policemen, instantly recognisable by their ill-fitting blazers and poor taste in ties, spotted us and called out: "Are you two with the Nimrod?" An answer in the positive saw them, purposefully, striding down the corridor towards us.

To the crew chief: "What time did you get in last night?"

"Not sure, I'd had quite a few."

Turning to me: "What about you?"

The crew chief responded quickly: "Ah, he was with me."

Now the truth was, I had not been with him by the end of the night, having been unable to keep up with his, almost legendary, drinking prowess. I had sloped off back to the camp on my own. As I passed the hexagonal-shaped school on Winston Churchill Avenue, I recall having to step around our friend the dead cat on the pavement. I presumed it had met its end after being hit by car.

Meanwhile, back to the interrogation. I decided it was better to keep quiet and agree with the crew chief rather than contradict him and invite further questioning. I certainly wasn't going to mention that I'd seen the cat the night before.

The first 'blazer and tie' asked me what I had been wearing the previous night. I described my jeans, top and trainers. The second 'blazer and tie' then asked the crew chief: "What about you?" He couldn't remember whether he had been wearing a white or a blue top but the first 'blazer and tie' replied: "It was a blue top." The crew chief seemed nonplussed for a half second before replying: "How the f***ing hell do you know that?" "I saw you in the Horseshoe around midnight," was the response.

The crew chief did a passable impression of a goldfish whilst searching for a response before the second policeman interjected, his attention on me: "Can I see the clothes you were wearing?" I agreed and we went into my room where he examined my outfit, in particular the jeans and shoes, clearly looking for bloodstains. Dejected, he returned to the corridor to find the other two re-enacting a similar scenario. The 'blazer and ties' conferred in a huddle before announcing: "OK you can carry on; we've finished with you two."

I had dearly hoped they would warn us not to leave the Rock but they were a cut above the average RAF 'plod' and, after all, they surely hadn't made it into the SIB without showing a modicum of more common than fashion sense.

Now should anyone be upset about disparaging remarks about RAF policemen, I give you this vignette. We had collected, as tradition dictates, trophies from a visit to a US Naval air station, including the large, rubber, welcome mat from outside the chief petty officers' mess. It showed the base crest and read 'Welcome to the CPOs' Mess'. Unbeknownst to us, as we rolled it up and prepared to hide it behind a hedge for later collection, it was strengthened with metal, probably lead, to stop it being blown around in a hurricane. It was seriously heavy. It returned to the UK strapped to a nitrogen bottle trolley, in an RAF Hercules. Ripping up the threadbare carpet in our crewroom, we laid out our latest acquisition and gave it a clean. It lasted only a day before the RAF police confiscated it. The owner had reported it as a theft and wanted the people responsible brought to book.

It soon transpired that three suspicious-looking characters had been seen in the CPOs' mess foyer trying to lift more trophies. Two were easily identified by the descriptions as a propulsion sergeant and a flight-line mechanic. A third man, some potato-faced nonentity, (yours truly), could not be easily identified. To their credit, whilst being interviewed by the RAF police, the perpetrators did not grass me up, claiming I was some American they didn't even know. The propulsion sergeant, faced with a constant barrage of you did it, eventually became fed up of this tack and blurted out that he couldn't have done it as he had a bad back. As soon as the words left his mouth, he realized he had just implicated himself and waited for the inevitable question, how did you know how heavy it was? The question never came but the one that did was: "Can you prove it?" Of course, he could and did.

They were left with a villain and the propulsion sergeant sweated for a while afterwards, thinking that some investigative supervisor somewhere in the chain of command, would uncover his inadvertent admission. It never came.

Meanwhile back in Gibraltar, having been dismissed by the 'plods', the crew chief and I changed into civvies and re-convened in the ante room to discuss developments. We managed to collar one of the mess staff and it seemed that the cat had been thrown out of the window into the back garden of the sergeants' mess. The body had been collected and bagged by the RAF police who were taking it to the only vet in Gibraltar for a post-mortem. They were investigating the possibility that the cat had been brought into the mess and killed in some sort of satanic black mass ritual. Now I can't confirm any of that as true, although the cat going out of the window certainly fitted the theory as it had disappeared whilst I was showering. The satanic black mass ritual theory would fit, presumably only if the plods had spent many boring nights on duty reading Dennis Wheatley novels. Perhaps there was some kind of Holy Grail in the minds of law enforcement officers when investigating such activities?

I don't recall whether we made it to the Piccolo for lunch but I do recall the team seeing in the jet. The junior ranks groundcrew who had listened avidly to our accounts of the morning's activities as we waited for the jet's return, did not hold back. We indulged in some good-natured banter, including catcalls and jibes. I was surprised that there was no police presence to greet the returning aircrew who climbed onto their bus carrying their gear. Just as the last guy disappeared inside, a plethora of blue lights headed across the ramp towards us and several RAF police vehicles surrounded the crew bus in a dramatic scene, somewhat reminiscent of an episode of *The Sweeney*.

Perhaps they thought the poor driver would be 'car-jacked' by the crew and make a break for the Spanish border a few hundred yards away. I would like to say they had a police dog with them but that would be wishful thinking on my part. Perhaps they feared for its safety and left it in the kennels? At the bus, the disproportionate number of policemen, including the two 'blazer and ties', jumped out of the vehicles, first sending a couple of uniforms onboard in case there was any trouble. After a while, the bus set off with its 'blue-light escort' as we finished our flight servicing and put the aircraft to bed.

The crew chief arranged the customary parade for the groundcrew to attend happy hour at the Caleta Palace Hotel later that evening before he and I retired to the sergeants' mess for a stiff drink. Usually, our NCO aircrew would have arrived after their flight debrief but, as we entered the bar, it was strangely empty. Mehidi, the Moroccan barman, looked at us quizzically and asked where everyone was. He too was used to hearing the Nimrod land, giving him time before the bar got busy. We asked him if he had heard about the cat. As the penny dropped, he nodded his head and uttered an 'ahh' sound. Eventually, the aircrew arrived to the bar and more of the story emerged. Two of our intrepid crew, whilst returning to camp in an advanced 'state of refreshment', had spotted the cat and decided, as people in that state often do, that it would be a good idea and a jolly jape, to take it back to the mess. Presumably, just before they got to the main gate—I seem to recall that it was manned in those days by locally employed, MoD Police—they realised it might not go down too well to be seen carrying the cat.

The low, white, stucco wall of the adjacent North Front Cemetery provided the solution. Bordering Halifax Road, it lay adjacent to the sergeants' mess outside the camp. It is not clear how delicately the cat was delivered into the cemetery, but having passed through the main gate and by now out of sight, they jumped the wall and retrieved their prize. Of course, it would be great fun to put it in someone's bed and, even better, if they could somehow tuck the poor creature in for the night. Satisfied with their work, they had retired.

It would not have been too long before our poor victim returned to the Goldilocks scenario. He suspected that he knew the culprit and arrived at the crew chief's door, dead cat in hand. Aiming to return the poor thing to its 'un-rightful owner', he could not break into the room so he left the cat outside the door in the corridor which is where I had spotted it sometime later.

Eventually, the culprits confessed to their antics under RAF police questioning and likely under pressure from the aircraft captain. Sometime later they were released, the incident having gone all the way up to Air Commander Gibraltar. We were ordered to leave in shame the next morning.

That night a big storm blew in and an easterly gale howled across the rock. By morning, it had not abated but we turned up and started preparing the aircraft for departure, somewhat surprised to see the Gibraltar Airways Vickers Viscount parked and blanked. The aircraft hopped over to Tangiers a couple of times every day and we had never seen it grounded. Checking with VASF, they told us the that the winds were too bad for it to fly which was not a good sign.

Pulling the blanks from our engines, the wind spun up the low-pressure compressors to an impressive speed never before seen. That was all the engines except number four which was not turning. I was not there as the engines man, rather as a 'spilt brain' technician (dual airframes/engines), the official engine man and the crew chief got together in a huddle but things did not look good. A fault being carried showed a high debris count on the magnetic chip detector (MCD) on the number four engine which meant that the detector had to be removed, inspected and replaced with a fresh one after each flight. We dug out the detectors from the previous flights and looked at them and, yes, there was black sludge evident but no apparent increase in the amount. No one was experienced in specialised early failure detection skills to be able to make a call on the amount of sludge, so when the captain was brought into the conversation, he asked for advice on how the problem would normally be tackled. Being the more experienced and senior engine bloke, I told him that we should wait for the wind to abate, do an engine ground run, shut down and time how long the engine took to get to a stationary condition. From memory, it was a minimum of 45 seconds, otherwise the engine should be rejected. The captain told us that, given the events of the previous day this was not an option and as the engine had worked fine on the last flight, we were leaving. Instructed to refuel to 76,000 lbs the decision drew gasps. With only 6,000 feet of runway, in the summer heat, the aircraft would normally take off with around 65,000 lbs. At least it was February and the wind was blowing hard so we completed the aircraft preparations as instructed. Taxiing to Runway 09 at the marina end of the peninsular, I listened intently on intercom as we increased power against the brakes prior to take-off. The throttles advanced and the engines seemed to be giving good power before the brakes released and the aircraft jumped forward like a scalded cat, quickly gathering speed. The take-off was surprisingly smooth and, looking out of the window, I realised we were already over 500 feet high by the time we crossed the main road to Spain which intersects the runway halfway along its length. It was good to be airborne! After an uneventful sortie, we arrived back at Kinloss. The next day I followed up on the fault to find out that the MCD had been inspected post-flight and an engine change was underway.

As an epilogue and more than six years later, I was by then a Nimrod crew chief myself and once more on detachment with No. 120 Squadron. We are in Andøya in the Norwegian Arctic Circle, staying in a hotel in the town of Andenes called the Andrikken. There was a fine stuffed arctic fox in the foyer but, having hosted crews of maritime patrol aircraft for many years, it was attached to the reception desk by a heavy chain, preventing anyone from taking it for a walk. In the dining room, one of the older sweats on the crew was regaling those who had not been on the squadron for long, with the 'Dead Cat in Gibraltar' legend. By then, the story had morphed and the crew were, supposedly, playing 'mess rugby' in the bar with the dead cat. After an errant pass, the dead cat landed in the lap of the mess manager's wife and …

It all went downhill from there!

A great story; a great legend.

CHAPTER 10

HMS *Ark Royal*—the Last Farewell

Robin Trewinnard-Boyle started his Royal Navy engineering career on the Sea Harrier FA2 before moving onto the Harrier GR7, and had a varied career on both fixed-wing and rotary-wing aircraft with embarked experience. In 2010 he was the senior air engineer on HMS Ark Royal, *responsible for the Air Engineering Department, its workshops and personnel. After the defence cuts of 2010 he was selected to become the military maintenance officer for the F-35 Integrated Test Force, NAS Patuxent River, Maryland in 2011. This first-hand knowledge was later used in the Carrier Strike Capability Development Team in preparation for UK F-35B sea trials and entry to service of the Queen Elizabeth-class aircraft carriers. Leaving the Royal Navy in 2018, he now works for Nova Systems Europe, specialising in flight trials planning, whilst working for the Lightning Delivery Team as a Royal Navy reservist.*

The announcement of the axing of HMS *Ark Royal* and Joint Force Harrier (JFH) in the 2010 Strategic Defence and Security Review (SDSR) came as a complete shock to those of us who made up the ship's company. I was on the bus down to the dockyard from my married quarter when my wife called. She asked whether I knew anything about it as she had received a text from a friend in London asking where we were moving to next. When I got to the ship the whole

DAVID CAMERON ON THE FLIGHT DECK
OF HMS *ARK ROYAL* IN HALIFAX, NOVA SCOTIA.
(ROBIN TREWINNARD-BOYLE)

place was in uproar. Some of the ship's company had seen it leaked on the ten o'clock news the previous evening, it was all over the front pages of the newspapers, and everyone expected that the officers knew it was going to happen and blamed us for not telling them first. Of course, we were all completely in the dark too, including the commanding officer, Captain Jerry Kyd, RN. At about 1100 he called everyone together in the hangar, known as a 'clear lower deck', where he gave an impassioned speech to say that he had now spoken to the First Sea Lord and he would do all that he could to find out what would happen next and let us all know as soon as possible. After we were dismissed everyone returned to their mess decks and the bars opened, almost like a wake for the ship, as there didn't seem a lot of point in doing any work. The main excuse was that we needed to use up the bar stock before we decommissioned and we were helping the 'pussers', the supply officers. We felt particularly betrayed as only a couple of months earlier, the prime minister, David Cameron, had visited the ship whilst we were alongside in Halifax, Nova Scotia. We had bent over backwards to welcome him onboard, along with a demanding media contingent, and he had stood in front of us all, praising our efforts and promising a great future for carrier aviation. We also felt betrayed by our own First Sea Lord, an ex-submariner who appeared to have protected HMS *Astute* and its successor, now the Dreadnought class, submarine programmes at the expense of the Fleet Air Arm and our aircraft carriers.

It was our 25th anniversary year, we were the youngest of the three Invincible-class ships, there was a royal visit in November to mark the occasion and special china plates had been commissioned. How could this be happening? Her Majesty the Queen visited the ship on 5 November, just days before we sailed for the final time, walking up the brow and commenting on 'The Queen Mother's Step', a specially cut-out piece of deck under a water tight door, that could be removed so that the Queen Mother could come onboard 'her ship' more easily. The Queen Mother had always considered the *Ark Royal* as her ship, having apparently insisted on the name change of the third ship of the Invincible class from the planned HMS *Indomitable*, and that passion had passed to her daughter. She kept her opinion on the decommissioning to herself, or maybe just spoke to the captain, but she looked disappointed and angry about the whole thing to those of us on parade to greet her.

Roll on a month or so and the ship was already clearing itself of all non-essential items even though we would be sailing for one last time. Some personnel had already moved onto their next assignments and a lot of effort was being made with 'Drafty', Royal Navy manning, to try and ensure our personnel went to roles that would suit them rather than just filling up slots in random places around the Fleet Air Arm. Naval Manning had also been kept in the dark so the sudden requirement to find roles for an entire aircraft carrier's worth of people, alongside all the air engineers, suppliers, meteorological officers and aircrew of Joint Force Harrier was a real task. Groundcrew who had been working on Sea Harriers at Yeovilton until 2006, had moved their families to Rutland under the expectation that the Harrier Force would keep them in that part of the country for some considerable time, but now found themselves faced with a move to the Royal Naval Air Station Culdrose a mere four years later. Likewise, some of the RAF engineers on JFH had spent their entire careers moving between RAF Wittering and RAF Cottesmore and now faced retraining to a different aircraft type and a move to RAF Lossiemouth. Through unsympathetic eyes this could be seen as 'life in a blue suit' but the personal implications for the careers of spouses and partners and schooling of children caused considerable grief. Under these uncertainties we expected the personnel to continue at the pace and level of professionalism they had before their lives had been thrown into turmoil.

A POINT CLEARLY MADE, ALTHOUGH THE PILOT WAS NOT WING COMMANDER LINK TAYLOR, WHO UNWITTINGLY FOUND HIS NAME IN THE PAPERS. IT DOES NOT APPEAR TO HAVE AFFECTED HIS CAREER TOO BADLY AS HE IS NOW AN AIR VICE-MARSHAL. (ROBIN TREWINNARD-BOYLE)

Careful and considerate management was required.

The plan was to conduct Exercise Joint Warrior with Army Air Corps Apache attack helicopters before heading to Glen Mallan in Scotland to de-ammunition the ship of its no longer needed air weapons, then to return to our 'birthplace' on the Tyne to say goodbye before a final foreign run ashore in Hamburg. It promised to be a busy time for the air engineering department that I was heading up, getting the army up to speed with operating in the maritime environment and supporting Apache, whilst planning the major evolution of getting thousands of pounds of high explosive (HE) safely out of the magazines and ashore. After that we would be receiving four Harrier GR9s from RAF Cottesmore, two from No. 1(F) Squadron and two from No. 800 Naval Air Squadron, for a symbolic, final embarkation and departure.

As it turned out, the work up with Apaches became critically important to the UK, as just weeks after HMS *Ark Royal* was decommissioned, the Libyan conflict flared up. The Apache teams had practised loading Hellfire missiles and 30-mm shells onto the helicopter in particularly challenging weather off the coast of Scotland. It was exactly what they subsequently needed, albeit in the somewhat better weather but more pressured operational mission, in the Mediterranean. As news reached the UK about the fighting in Libya, a rumour spread around the ship that the prime minister himself had questioned how long it would take us to reverse the decommissioning and set sail. However, by this point we had had engines, diesel generators and other essential pieces of machinery and equipment removed to assist in the overhaul of HMS *Illustrious* in Rosyth dockyard. As much as those of us onboard wanted to assist, we knew that the call had come too late in the day for us to be capable. The Apaches were deployed onboard HMS *Ocean* and did sterling work, although how much more effective would air support to the campaign have been if HMS *Ark Royal* with a full deck of Harriers had still been available?

NO. 1 (F) SQUADRON HARRIER GR9S AFTER THEIR FINAL LANDING ONBOARD HMS *Ark Royal*, NOVEMBER 2010. (ROBIN TREWINNARD-BOYLE)

De-ammunitioning the ship became significantly harder than expected due to exceptionally cold weather after a lot of rainfall. The entire flight deck became covered in sheet ice which needed to be chipped away by hand before it was safe to start moving pallets of bombs and bullets around. Although a routine procedure, it had to be done carefully and safely with a particular eye on the accounting. No one wanted to be responsible for a missing 500-lb Paveway bomb. This was purely an air engineering department task, so whilst we were busy, the rest of the ship took a few days to enjoy the beautiful Scottish scenery.

Our stop at Glen Mallan also coincided with Taranto Night, the annual commemoration of the Fleet Air Arm's Second World War attack on the Italian port of Taranto. This attack, using outdated Swordfish biplanes on 11 November 1940, was extremely effective and caused significant damage to the Italian fleet, allowing

HMS *Ark Royal*, R07, SEEN OVER THE WINGS OF THE FINAL HARRIERS EVER TO GRACE HER FLIGHT DECK. (ROBIN TREWINNARD-BOYLE)

freedom of movement for the RN around the Mediterranean. It also showed how effective carrier aviation could be against an enemy fleet in harbour, a lesson not lost on the Japanese who subsequently started planning the attack on Pearl Harbor. Our guest of honour for the last-ever Taranto night was the legendary Jock Moffett, one of the few surviving Swordfish pilots and the pilot who put his torpedo into the stern of the German battle cruiser *Bismarck*, crippling it and allowing the RN to avenge the loss of HMS *Hood* and to sink her. He was

RN AND RAF GROUNDCREW PROUDLY STANDING NEXT
TO THEIR AIRCRAFT PRIOR TO THE FINAL-EVER LAUNCH
OF HARRIERS FROM THE RN AIRCRAFT CARRIER.
(ROBIN TREWINNARD-BOYLE)

on top form and, as expected, had some wonderful stories of his time on the third HMS *Ark Royal*. He also had some interesting opinions of fellow legendary naval aviator Winkle Brown, which can be best described as 'not complimentary'.

The arrival of the last Harriers caused quite a stir. The 'goofers' deck was full of as many spare hands as were available as everyone wanted to see the last-ever landing of a Harrier onboard a Royal Navy aircraft carrier. The jets arrived as planned flown by two RN pilots and two RAF pilots. Despite the bitter inter-service fighting that had preceded the SDSR, the Joint Force Harrier was exactly that and everyone was hurting, wondering what the future held. Despite strict instructions not to do anything controversial, as there was a significant media contingent onboard, one of the RN pilots placed a poignant sign in his windshield—FOR SALE (*see page 110*). Whilst causing amusement to us all, it did of course end up all over the newspapers. The pilot was flown off by helicopter back to RAF Cottesmore where he was severely reprimanded. In the end the jets were sold off to the US Marine Corps for spares, in my mind a fate better than the Nimrod MRA4 suffered after being cut in the same review. Unsurprisingly, everything went smoothly, with the deck crew and maintainers as professional as ever. After all, just a couple of months ago we had been operating with 12 Harriers at pace, training for operations; having only four jets was easy.

Having embarked the jets we headed to Newcastle, sailing up the Tyne for one last time, with the ship's company in 'Procedure A', lined up along the side of the deck. The No. 1(F) Squadron flagship, Harrier ZG477, was deliberately chosen to take pride of place on the ski-jump ramp as we sailed in, showing that the pain of SDSR was shared across both the RN and RAF. The welcome we received in Newcastle was fantastic. We opened up the ship to visitors and it seemed the whole city queued up to see her and say goodbye. Some of the men who had worked in the dockyard to build her only 25 years earlier, brought their whole families down to point out bits they'd done and areas that they'd worked on. The whole city of Newcastle seemed to share our pain and took it personally that we were being chopped.

After an amazing few days, we sailed away with the tune of Rod Stewart's *Sailing* blasting out over the ship's speakers. The entire riverbank was lined with spectators, waving and cheering and from Newcastle down to Tynemouth, ships tooted their horns and flags were waved. It was an incredibly emotional send-off as we headed into the cold, stormy weather and a grey, lumpy North Sea. Maybe people's eyes were watering because of the biting cold wind?

As we sailed towards Hamburg the moment came for the Harriers to leave us for the final time, never to return. In torrential rain and a bitter wind, they were towed into position at the stern of the ship and prepped carefully by their ground-crew. A mix of RN and RAF engineers from RAF Cottesmore, they knew they were taking part in a historic moment. No-one wanted 'their' jet to go unserviceable on start-up and be left behind.

The aircrew had been carefully selected, two RAF and two RN, with the honour of being the last pilot to launch being given to Lieutenant Commander James Blackmore, RN of No. 1(F) Squadron flying ZG477, the squadron flagship. Squalls of rain continued to lash the deck as a Sea King Mk 7 of No. 849 NAS lifted from the deck with a camera crew ready to record the event. 'Goofers' was full again, with ship's crew, squadron staff and embarked journalists. Brian Hanrahan's famous phrase from the Falklands conflict: "I'm not allowed to say how many planes joined the raid, but I counted them all out and I counted them all back" was echoing in their minds, knowing that this time, none of them would be coming back.

RUNNING IN FOR A 'LOW SLOT PORT' FLYPAST. (ROBIN TREWINNARD-BOYLE)

After interviews with the camera team, recording it all for the Discovery Channel series, the pilots crewed in and the mighty roar of the Pegasus engines echoed out over the choppy waters. The well-oiled procedures of working a flight deck, one of the most dangerous operating environments in the world, kicked in and the four jets sat waiting for the command from 'FlyCo' to launch. The green light hanging above the flight deck came on.

With RAF pilots and engineers serving on No. 800 NAS and RN pilots and engineers serving on No. 1(F) Squadron, this event was very much about showing the public and our own senior officers—who we felt utterly betrayed by—that carrier aviation in the 21st century truly was a joint endeavour and would remain so into the future. The first two jets taxied out, conducted their final checks and the engine noise grew to the familiar whining crescendo, the jets straining at the leash to let them fly off the ski jump one last time. We carefully watched for any signs of tyres slipping on the drenched deck. When the flight deck officer (FDO) raised his green flag, the first jet hurtled down the deck and leapt into the air, blasting spray and warm jet exhaust over those of us on the flight deck, rapidly followed by the second and third jets. A slight pause followed as Lieutenant Commander Blackmore took up his position, lined up along the runway, keeping his thoughts to himself on what this launch meant. Releasing his brakes, he tore down the deck and was gone, joining up with the others in a circuit overhead. The flight deck, that had been so loud just moments before felt very empty and quiet, the miserable weather reflecting the mood, especially those of us who had previously worked on JFH.

We had been told that there would be a flypast. It was the traditional thing to do when a squadron leaves the carrier, saying goodbye to the many people who they had worked with whilst embarked. Everyone stayed on deck or headed to the top of the ramp to watch. The first pair of jets, one from each squadron, appeared out of the gloom in tight formation. Edging lower to the water and at full power, they blasted past and headed straight on into the clouds, the Pegasus engines screaming and streams of contrails being left behind. Finally, the last pair came into sight astern of the ship, maybe a little lower than the first pair, maybe a little faster, shattering the gloom with one last, magnificent blast of jet-engine noise and power. Slicing down the port side of the ship they broke across her bows and vanished into the sunlight that was just breaking through the thick cloud, returning to RAF Cottesmore.

Once again, the eery silence was deafening before a chatter broke out amongst the deck crews of well, that's that then, and in a way, I think most were happy that they'd done their job safely and efficiently for one last time but now they were cold and wet and fancied a cuppa. As the Harrier groundcrews disappeared from the deck we quickly reset and readied ourselves to recover the Sea King Mk 7; although the day was all about jets the rotary guys were just as important to carrier strike and were themselves facing an uncertain future with the much-delayed Merlin Crowsnest.

By the time we got to Hamburg, the Sea King and its team had also returned to RNAS Culdrose, marking the last RN helicopter to take off from the deck of HMS *Ark Royal*. The final helicopter was from No. 32 Squadron when we were alongside in Portsmouth, but that's another story. The pent-up emotion of events needed to be blown away before we returned to Portsmouth for the final time, for which Hamburg was an ideal location. Sir Donald Gosling, long-time supporter of the Royal Navy and its sailors, joined us and personally handed out cash from his own pocket to every sailor onboard. Having been a sailor himself he knew that morale was pretty low and that a trip round some of the more interesting parts of Hamburg would help. He treated the wardroom to an exceptionally upmarket dinner and also seemed to take the decommissioning personally. By all accounts he had spoken to everyone in authority that he knew, to try and use his influence to reverse the decision. It wasn't going to make a difference in the face of the severe financial crisis in MoD.

Having started my career on the Sea Harrier FA2 shortly before they were retired, then moving to RAF Wittering onto the Harrier GR7 and T10, I feel a real sense of privilege to have been part of the ship's company of HMS *Ark Royal* during this turbulent time in the UK's history of carrier aviation and hope that political short-sightedness, inter-service battles and lack of defence funding do not ever impact our armed forces so much again.

CHAPTER 11

Tornado Aircraft Servicing Flight on Operations

As a 'scaley brat'—a service dependant—Jordan Harkins grew up with a deep interest in aircraft watching Tornado F3s at Leuchars from his primary school playground. It seemed inevitable that he would join the RAF and did so in 2013 as an aircraft mechanic. After basic and initial trade training, he joined No. 8 Squadron as an aircraft maintenance mechanic. After trade training, he joined the Tornado Aircraft Servicing Flight at Marham in 2016 and, within two years, was posted during the Tornado drawdown to work on Typhoons, with No. 29 Squadron, where he now serves.

My second hour passed in the departure lounge at RAF Brize Norton. Having arrived just before midnight, I knew well what to expect from my fourth deployment on operations in a year. In preparation, I had explored all possible avenues in order to entertain myself for the usual hop to a 'distant Mediterranean island'. I would be away for a month and was a little apprehensive about venturing down route as my wife was pregnant with our first child. I decided that Netflix films were the order of the day. As I looked around, I recognised faces from the past, either from training or places I had been posted; catching up helped pass the time.

I am a bit of a self-confessed geek; I will often watch from the window of my married quarter at the jets coming and going. To that end, I was looking forward to getting on the Voyager, the RAF's transport aircraft. Take-off was normal, right up until we felt the engines wind back earlier than usual followed by a sharp change of direction. After a short time circling Brize, I was settling back into the departure lounge once again. It was a bird strike. A tired-looking departure lounge employee rolled in a trolley of hot drinks but a further two hours passed before I heard the calls to board. For a second time, those lucky enough to have found an adaptor plug, removed their phones for the journey ahead. I soon found myself on the phone to 'the missus' who had been watching my progress on an aircraft-tracking application and had seen the odd flight path. She was alarmed that the pilot had 'squawked' emergency before landing.

Walking down the large white steps was a relief after a busy flight south. The local city glistened through the night sky in the distance and the thick heat was a warm welcome. The transit accommodation awaited. Arriving at the block, we figured out who was going where, arranging ourselves so that our four-man rooms were made up of two from each shift, allowing us a little more breathing space. Our accommodation, fashioned from what may as well have been ISO containers, was no bigger than a decent-size bathroom. Rank was irrelevant here; the snorers were put together, for the rest it was first come first served. We arranged the contents of our black ops bags into double lockers, some of which were a little shoddier than others. Some lost out and were given bunk beds but would, instead, move the top mattress onto the floor. One guy always draped an extra sheet over the side of his bunk for a bit of privacy—I never asked what he wanted privacy for …

'Team Takeaway' offered our small deployment of 14 airman the opportunity to, once again, settle into our somewhat familiar surroundings. The occasional sound of RB199 or EJ200 jet engines reminded us that this was far from a holiday. Time passed quickly as we reacquainted ourselves with the dartboard and pool table. I made a quick Skype call to the wife before crawling under the well-used dark blue duvet courtesy of Her Majesty, resigned to an 0600 start.

The detachment members were well accustomed to short deployments to the island, their reputations as experienced Tornado crew proceeding them. This particular team was short of a sergeant, which meant that my shift would be run by our most experienced corporal. The rest of the night shift would be made up of myself and three others. We knew it would be tough being a man down, but this seemed only to motivate us more.

The first day on the airfield underlined that this would be no holiday. Aircraft neatly parked across the pan under shelter hung low with live stores, rarely seen back home. While this deployment would have its fair share of laughs, the sight was a stark reminder of why these aircraft were here. These were no longer just good-looking fast jets; they were killing machines. Fortunately, we were able to set up a speaker and blast out music while we worked. It amazes me still how some good music can motivate a team to work as we did.

The aircraft we had been deployed to work on had a reputation as 'a bit of a dog', and the Form 700, the aircraft's logbook, confirmed this. Endless pages of acceptable deferred faults (ADFs) were added to our usual Primary Star workload and we would need to fix those too. We began to remove the skin and look deeper. As technicians, we like to solve problems—it awards us a sense of achievement—but here, in the sticky heat of our shared hangar, each problem we uncovered would potentially mean a delayed trip home. In the UK we would be allowed plenty of time to complete a Primary Star servicing, but out here we would have very little flexibility. Realistically, the job could be finished within ten days for a good jet but this one was a challenge. We kept our hopes up and planned for some heavy shifts but, unlike deployments gone by, we knew by the end of day two, that we would be lucky to return this GR4 on time. Often I found myself in discussion with someone from the squadron which went something along the lines of:

"So how long are you out here for?"

"Just two weeks, you?"

"Really? Part-timer! I'm out here for three months!"

Of course, short deployments are beneficial, however, while the squadron would often have a portion of free time, we would be hard at it throughout the day. Not that I complained of course, as time flies when you're having fun. The digs from the squadron guys were soon to be silenced when they learned how often we went out there. In just over a year, I flew on the Voyager 15 times. It was an odd number because of the bird strike on this trip. This amounted to more time away than those on the squadron. It was so bad that we were on first-name terms with most of the mess staff.

I'm rarely a person for wearing sunglasses but after the first couple of days, I couldn't go without them. It was a rookie mistake for not bringing my own with me. I got up early after a nightshift and opted to walk down to the shop on base but I had forgotten quite how hot it was during the day and was sweating buckets by the time I finished my 15-minute walk. A quick scan through the fakes and I was wearing some 15-Euro Ray Bans. Sorted! With my earphones reinserted for the walk back, and sipping my lukewarm water, I caught a glimpse of something dart across my path. It took a moment for my brain to process what I'd seen—just a small newt. Embarrassment crept in, shadowed by a sarcastic comment about soiling myself as I realised there were people behind me who had watched me jump out my skin.

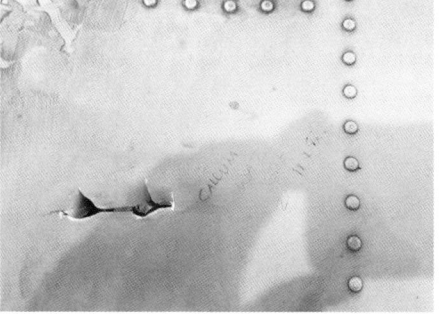

A STRAY CAT TYPICAL OF THOSE OFTEN ATTRACTED TO RAF DETACHMENT DISPERSALS AROUND THE WORLD. (JORDAN HARKINS)

THE HOLE PUNCHED INTO A GR4 AIRFRAME AFTER A DOOR WAS INADVERTENTLY CLOSED. (JORDAN HARKINS)

A hungry stray cat waited patiently in our office. Four of us were preparing for the start of our shift, discussing the plan for the evening. One of the dayshift lads had managed to close a door while a component was in the wrong position, punching a nice clean slit on the inside skin of the aircraft. Rather predictably, stores didn't have a spare available, so it was put on D-state. That means the spare will have to be flown out from Leeming, on priority demand. It's strange how a common problem will bring a shift together, as is often the case with shift rivalry, but on that note, B shift was always the better shift …

The end of our shift arrived and we got changed ready to return to the accommodation. I had left my beret on top of my bag in the locker room which turned out to be a big mistake. What I can only describe as the 'King Kong' of moths had decided to nest in my beret and it looked a tad threatening. Into a plastic bag it went but I was already planning a trip to clothing stores to organise an exchange. Later in the afternoon, assuming the stores people would be back from lunch, I took a walk down past station headquarters, towards air traffic control, between which I found clothing stores.

As I got closer, I heard two Tornado GR4s at the end of the runway, heat-soaking the engines before going 'through the gate' into reheat. I hung back a little, knowing that they would be passing low as they got airborne. The deep rumble filled the air; a sound that we had become accustomed to. I pondered the thought of putting my fingers in my ears, seeing the first GR4, at less than 100 feet and climbing past me, two perfectly formed reheat cones out the back end, gear still travelling. As the pilot disengaged the reheat, a dark plume of unburned fuel poured out from beneath the rear fuselage, although it was perfectly normal when reheat was disengaged. The shimmering heat haze had barely dissipated before the second GR4 passed, a blur of grey, the iconic image captured in my mind's eye. The pilot rolled left immediately, trying to catch up with his leader before disappearing into the sky, leaving only a distant rumble and the smell of burnt fuel in their wake. I arrived at clothing stores, only to find out that, on this station, they are open for only three hours in the morning. Life could be relaxing serving on a Mediterranean island! Beret-less I would be for now.

A few shifts into our detachment, we decided that we needed to socialise a little more. The long days meant that most of our free time was spent in bed or eating, so a little relaxation in a social environment would be beneficial. I'm not one who spends every night in the bar and, obviously on working nights, this was out of the question, so we opted to spend a bit of time outside the block after our shift. The morning was fresh, and yet to be thickened by the heat. As the sun rose, we soaked up the morning heat as if we had just arrived on the island for a lad's holiday. Still dressed in our personal combat system (PCS), our combat gear, the song *Wonderwall* by Oasis, played from someone's phone as one of the boys broke out a set of cards. We were worn out after a night shift, still dirty and nursing the usual cuts and scrapes that are to be found on a techie's arms but this was a highlight for me. Nobody spent the morning staring at their phones or playing pool or darts. We just had a good, old laugh between mates. By the time we headed off to bed, full of abuse and banter from the morning's antics, it was 24 hours since I had woken up.

After a second, but this time successful, attempt to get a new beret, I grabbed my washing from the laundry. Walking back to my room, one of the boys asked me what washing tablets I was using. "Fairy," I replied. My colleague laughed and asked for a second time. As he took the bag from me, he turned it around, pointing to the picture and writing on the front, I realised my mistake. For the last few days, and for the whole of the previous deployment, I had been using dishwasher tablets to wash my clothes. There are words to express my thoughts, however, I'm sure you've already thought of your own by now. As it turned out, I wasn't the only one to have made this mistake, given that the packaging for the offending items were almost identical to the liquid tablets I had intended to buy. You live and learn.

After the first three days, we found ourselves in good spirits, despite numerous problems with the aircraft. The weather was warm enough to enjoy, even at 0400 when we ended our shifts. A couple of us may have acquired an extra set of combat trousers to cut down, converting them into shorts. We all regretted the decision of the powers that be who have decided that shorts are no longer an acceptable item of working dress.

Detachments could cause many pressures amongst the team. I often found myself losing interest at this point when members of the team started to get at each other's throats for no real reason; this time was different. While there was plenty of banter and abuse being thrown around, nobody had fallen out, despite spending 90 per cent of our time together. This was astounding. We were even on good terms with the squadron management for a change, which did not always apply. Sometimes, station augmentees could be excluded from the squadron 'family'. The squadron even offered extra manpower if needed. I will always remember the SEngO, who would often pop by the jet, just to have a bit of a chat with the lads and see how we were getting on. He was very good at relaxing the team when we felt under pressure, and the biscuits he brought along were always welcome.

We were at the turning point of the scheduled servicing of the Tornado and just four days in. This was surprising but reassuring, as it was rare to be at this stage so quickly even on a good jet, never mind one that had an ADF log as big as the Yellow Pages. The next stage was to rebuild the aircraft, having inspected what was required, swap out the life-expired components and repair the odd bit of damage. One of the components I had to replace was the auxiliary air doors. I had done this job many times before and knew I could complete the task quickly, opting to do the job myself, freeing up some manpower to crack on with the more time-consuming tasks.

Where the rear of each door met the fuselage was a panel, held on by a number of captive fasteners. As some of these were inside the intake, I had always been extra vigilant to ensure that they were securely attached. A few weeks later, I learned that one of the fasteners had worked loose, somehow overcoming its captivity, causing damage to an engine in mid-flight. There were 75 points of contact that were evident as it had made its way through the engine, if my memory serves me correctly. Fortunately, I was confident that I had done no wrong and that, on completion of the job it was securely fitted. It is just one of those things that can happen and was viewed as a learning point. Every Tornado should be inspected regularly to ensure that all the captive fasteners were secure.

As we rebuilt the Tornado, a couple of small, unexpected snags were found but were quickly overcome. As anyone who has worked on fast jets will know, rebuilding after deep servicing can be a bit of 'trial and error'. The nibs on the wing gloves which house the Krueger flaps, were re-attached. A new radome was fitted because the pitot probe was bent on the old radome. As we closed it for the first time, a gentle push upwards helped the new shoot-bolts slide into position. The panels which could be re-attached went back on and the jet began to take shape once again. We started testing each system down to component level, including hydraulic power checks, a high-lift check, wing-sweep movement, valve checks, checking for environmental control system leaks and brake functional tests to name a few. Each new component was tested individually, of course. While carrying these out, I noticed someone had added a smiley face to the little red button on the pilot's stick. We aimed to please! Providing everything was successful, the day shift would be able to start functional checks of the engines. With the end of the shift approaching, I saw the blackness over the sea start to lighten, giving way to the deep royal blue of morning, quickly fading into brilliant reds, oranges and blues. A storm cloud was the only thing spoiling the vivid sky.

By day seven, the jet was at crunch point. That day we were scheduled to tow the jet to the running pan and carry out tests under power. This was often when progress could reverse and, unfortunately, that's exactly what happened. I had spent the afternoon staring at a computer, looking at married quarters that had been offered for my next posting. It was an unwelcome reminder that my time on the Tornado was coming to an end. After hours of comparison, I had sent off my choices to my wife so she could have a look. She was able to pop across to our new base for a closer look, and that let us come to a decision. With the strains of detachment, it was one less stress factor to worry about. It also demonstrates the strains of being a 'service wife' and the burdens that they have to shoulder in our absence.

Back to the jet which had been left on the running pan. The day shift had run into a few issues, meaning that they were unable to start the tests but being outside at night had its benefits. At least we would not be sweating and sunburned by the time we finished our shift. The downside was the insects. I cannot tell you how many little, green bottles of mosquito repellent we went through during the detachment but it wasn't enough. It was too hot to cover up but there were too many insects not to. It was a 'lose-lose' situation.

Our 'engine runner' jumped in, did his checks and sparked up one of the engines. It was a tense moment for us as all our hard work had led to this moment. The engine spooled up with a deep thud as the ignition kicked in and smoke cascaded from the engine doors while the residual fuel escaped from the gaps. I remembered my first engine run when this was all very new, not knowing if this was normal. Now, I stood and watched as the expected happened, but 'the why and how' in my head, explained the phenomenon. As the engine settled back to idle, our man in the cockpit checked the instruments before running up to 'max dry' for heat soak checks. I got comfortable for the ten-minute soak, adjusting my ear defenders but, in the process, accidentally allowed some of the pure, RB199 noise to hammer my eardrums. I was quick to secure my ear defenders back in place! The ground runner alerted us that ten minutes was up triggering a series of checks. My supervisor signalled each person to complete the assigned task that had been briefed before engine start. One of these was to climb up onto the wing, walk across to the starboard side with a heat gun, and to check an exhaust pipe. This provided pre-cooled air to the front of the jet, ensuring it did not exceed a given temperature. All OK. Another was to complete a leak check on the 'alien' which I had removed in order to fit a new water extractor. I had to adjust the main fuel control unit, which, although electronically controlled, had a mechanical back-up. It controlled the acceleration and deceleration time of the engine, from idle to max dry and required careful adjustment which was, again, very much 'trial and error'. Being attached directly to the engine, it meant opening the engine door, sticking my hand, wrapped in a high-visibility jacket for heat protection—very professional—past hot pipes. Rotating an awkwardly placed square key, I altered the fuel flow. I was relieved that I finished the task quickly. It was then on to the fun bit, the reheat runs. Reheat calibration was part of the check and was quite a spectacular sight when it's dark but I'm sure a few choice words were spoken about us on station that night. Thank goodness that, with operations underway, we had permission to carry out the test throughout the night if needed.

With the test almost finished and, mostly successful, there was one final run-up to maximum power. We were almost there when a fuel pump caption illuminated on the central warning panel in the cockpit. Shutting down abruptly, we began to ponder the impact on our departure date. We dragged the jet back into the hangar but with the clock showing 0600, we left a handover briefing for the day shift and set off back to the mess.

We arrived the next day for what we hoped would be our final night shift but the hope quickly faded with the sunset. Listening to the handover brief, the pump caption had been caused by—you guessed it—a faulty pump in the belly of the aircraft. The day shift had already swapped it for a new pump so we were back to the running pan for a final check. There was an immediate failure. Inside the pump is a non-return valve which had been fitted facing the wrong way. This sounds like a stupid mistake but the diagram in the technical manual was very easy to misinterpret. The replacement was pretty much a full night's work, so after defuelling, the aircraft was dismantled once more. Now, we had thought we were being clever by only defuelling the fuselage fuel tanks and not the wing tanks. Being anhedral in design with the wingtips lower than the wing root, we had not expected problems. Unfortunately, as one pipe was disconnected, a river of fuel dumped on the guys working below. Thinking it would soon stop, a waste bin was emptied and quickly placed back under the pipe. The bin was soon full so a second bin appeared. The second bin was also soon full. And so on. ... Eventually, the flow stopped and with the non-return valve correctly orientated, off we went once more to the running pan. The day shift promised to take on the final tests, leaving us to a nervous day's sleep. Would we get home on time?

I woke up, the odour of fuel still smelling strongly in the corridor from the discarded, heavily doused coveralls. My phone was flashing, telling me I had a notification, so I opened it expectantly. The jet was done and had been handed back to the squadron. I breathed a sigh of relief, knowing I would now, most likely, be returning home on time. Everyone got together and our next couple of days was quickly planned. We were lucky to be where we were, with a beach within the station bounds, a go-kart track and a bustling city just 20 minutes' drive away. We opted to head to the mall in town and while we were there, I bought clothes for my son for the very first time. It was something new and I felt strangely uncomfortable yet emotional. It was a great feeling.

The weather had taken a turn for the worse but for over five years, I had always enjoyed watching the biblical thunderstorms. It never disappointed. Luckily, the weather was due to clear up for the following day, so we planned to go to the beach. It was a beach like no other. There were palm trees, loungers, fish in the sea, a bar and even wi-fi. With the occasional transport helicopter and fully armed fast jet passing overhead, this was the perfect way to end our deployment.

Sitting here now, finishing this off in a gap at work at my new station, I cannot express how much I would do it all again. The world is changing and technology is improving. The Tornado changed over its service life, adapting to the tasks, thanks to all those who worked on the modification programmes. The jet served on operations continuously throughout its life, operating well beyond its original capability. The ladies and gents who worked on the Tornado are, and will be, the final fast-jet breed. It, for me, was the last of the great aircraft our Royal Air Force operated; a pure-bred fighter-bomber and reconnaissance fast jet. The legacy it leaves behind is ever present on the active airfields that remain.

CHAPTER 12

Gas, Gas, Gas

David Roy joined the Territorial Army in 1983 and the regular army in 1986 as a full-time member of the Ulster Defence Regiment. He then joined the Army Air Corps in 1988, leaving in 1991 to go to university. He deployed with No. 4 Regiment AAC, equipped with Lynx and Gazelle helicopters, and was sent to the Gulf from Detmold in Germany. He humbly explained that, with the war quickly over, the groundcrew followed along and tried to keep sand out of their rifles. After university he trained as a teacher but is also a prolific author with over 40 books on Amazon Kindle.

It was January 1991 and we were about to go to war. It had taken some time to decide that the Army Air Corps was going to be needed and exactly how they would be used but here we were; asleep. "Gas, Gas, Gas, NBC State Black." The words came over a radio that I hadn't even noticed before. We were at war.

The lights snapped on to reveal a scene of utter bedlam. Ben had jumped down from the top bunk and was partly into his uniform. Soldiers hopped about with two legs down one leg hole, or trying to get their head through a sleeve of their jumper. Let's not trivialise this event. The troops were terrified and, apart from anything else, the warning we had just been given was the one we should have got when they were *fully* clothed and *fully* suited. 'Gas, Gas, Gas' was supposed to mean that you put your respirator on. Only that. Some were trying to get their NBC suits out of their webbing when their uniform was only partly on. The webbing, over 30 years old and useless to the last, had not been designed to take an NBC suit in the first place. The straps were too tight, knuckles were grazed, there was swearing and fighting for breath.

Chaos:

Noddy suit on.

Inner and then outer gloves.

Mask on.

Blow out hard to get rid of the old air inside the mask.

Our drills were in disarray. Someone had omitted to tell us that the war was starting. A minor detail, except that it was us who would have to fight the war and to do that, we would have to survive an NBC attack. When we were completely kitted up, we checked each other, examining the fit of every part of the NBC kit, just as we had done in training so many times and then wondered what to do next. Every sense was smothered by the suits. Muffled voices broke the silence and we looked at each other in that special, sincere, NBC way to make sure that the person with whom we thought we were conversing was aware of this fact. Some men stood in huddled groups, others sat, alone with their stifling fears.

So, this was war, eh? Rather like piles! You never think that it will happen to you. I sat on the edge of my bed; my webbing belt tight around my waist. I held my rifle by the stock, the butt supported on the floor and weighed up the pros and cons of the situation. The pros were … sorry, *the* pro was, clearly, I wasn't dead. The cons? Well, they were a book in themselves.

After a while nothing had happened so, presumably, our leaders supposed that we were now aware, in some primitive way, that the war had begun. Thus far, none of them had come to confirm or deny this fact. I stood, removing my webbing and informing Ben that I was going back to sleep. Ben nodded silently. Our corporal further down the hut, was also silent and, most likely, afraid. But there seemed little point in staying up. Some of the others were following suit and despite their fears and the masks which seemed to threaten suffocation, they did indeed sleep. Never had their night-time breathing been so laboured. And that was that. That was how war began and, for me at least, it was a welcome anti-climax. This, I supposed, was the phoney war.

In the morning we were still in full NBC kit. People tried to get on with something, anything, but above all we needed information. We wanted to be told about the precise nature of the situation in which we found ourselves and yet no one had even been to check on us. We were sheep without a shepherd. It was safe to assume that the coalition had initiated the war in some way and that the

TOP: A TORNADO GR4 BEING TURNED ROUND. THE REFUELLING PROBE IS EXTENDED
FOR INSPECTION. (CRAIG SLUMAN)

BOTTOM: A SQUADRON OPERATIONS COMPLEX AT MASIRAH IN THE 1980S.
THE COMPLEX WEARS THE BADGES OF SOME OF THE RAF UNITS THAT
OPERATED THERE OVER THE YEARS.
(DAVID GLEDHILL)

CLOCKWISE FROM TOP LEFT: THE TEAM PREPARE BLACK MIKE FOR THE FIRST ENGINE DROP. (JOHN KENDAL)

THE SUPPORT RIG IN PLACE BENEATH THE ENGINE. (JOHN KENDAL)

'BLACK MIKE', PHANTOM FG1 XT582, AT COSFORD AIR SHOW IMMEDIATELY FOLLOWING ITS REMOVAL FROM RAF LEUCHARS. (DAVID GLEDHILL)

'BLACK MIKE', PHANTOM FG1 XT582, AT RAF LEUCHARS AWAITING STRIP DOWN. (JOHN KENDAL)

THE BUCCANEER FLIGHT LINE AT RAF LOSSIMOUTH WITH BOTH CAMOUFLAGED AND GREY COLOUR SCHEMES PRESENT. (JIM SIMPSON— 3ADIMAGES.CO.UK)

TOP: A HUNTER OF NO. 20 SQUADRON. THE SQUADRON OPERATED THE TYPE AT RAF TENGAH, SINGAPORE IN THE 1960S. (JIM MASON)

BOTTOM LEFT: GROUNDCREW PREPARE A HUNTER FOR FLIGHT. (JIM MASON)

BOTTOM RIGHT: MIST ALONG THE LOCH SIDE AT GLEN MALLAN. (ROBIN TREWINNARD-BOYLE)

NEXT SPREAD: A PENCIL ILLUSTRATION OF A JAGUAR GR3A IN MAINTENANCE BY THOMAS CLIVE WATKINS. THE 54(F) SQUADRON JAGUAR WAS UNDERGOING MINOR MAINTENANCE IN AUGUST 2000 IN ENGINEERING WING. THE DRAWING SHOWS A GROUP OF AMF AVIONICS TEAM TECHNICIANS DISCUSSING A WIRING FAULT IN THE LASER RANGING AND TARGET-MARKING SYSTEM.

Aircraft Maintenance Flight

Royal Air Force Coltishall

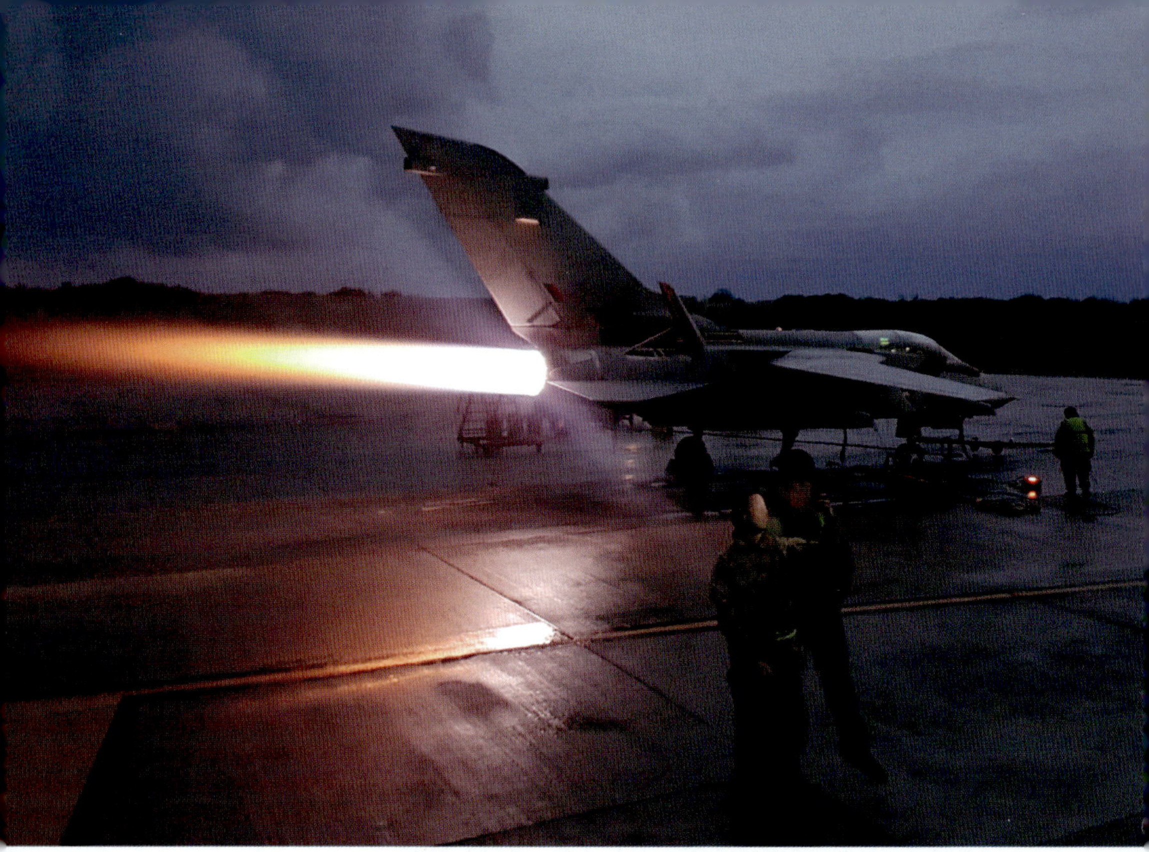

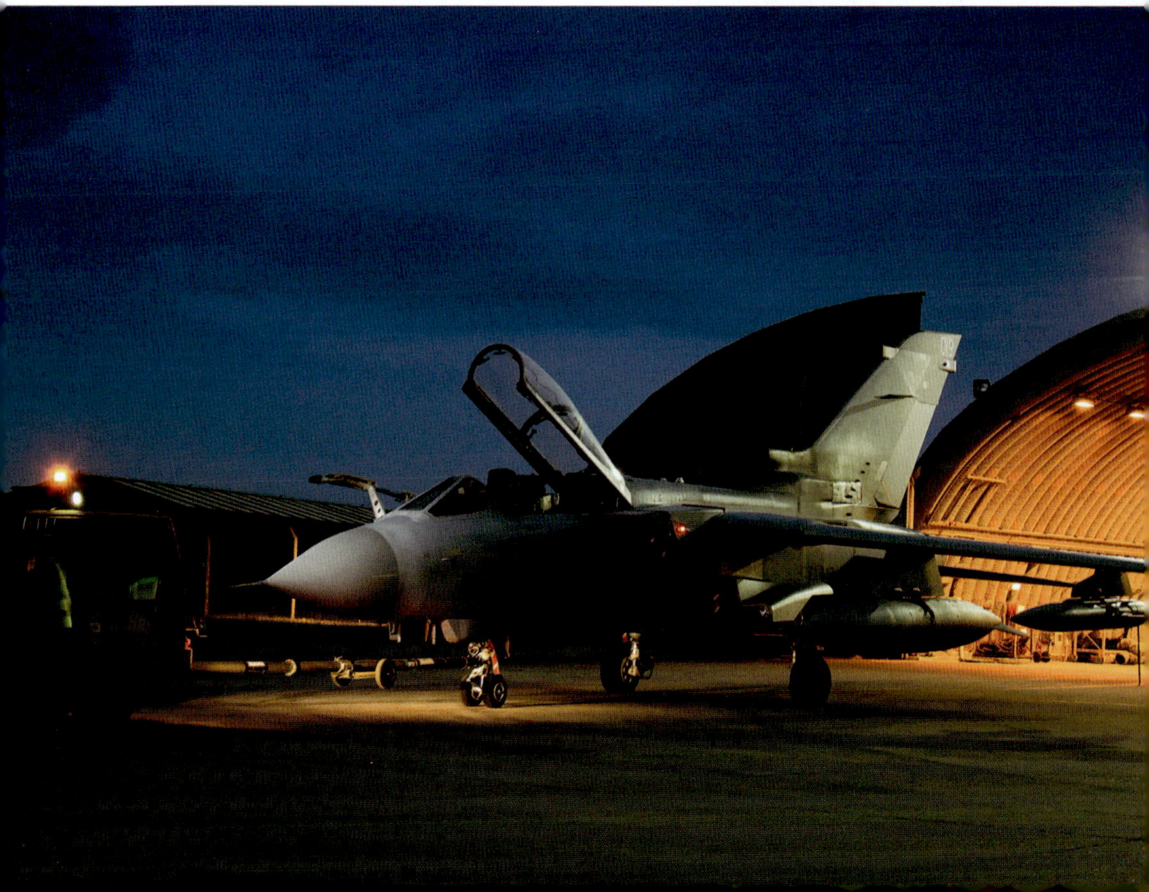

TOP LEFT: A TORNADO GR4 ENGINE RUN. (JORDAN HARKINS)

BOTTOM LEFT: A TORNADO GR4 IS TUCKED AWAY FOR THE NIGHT. (CRAIG SLUMAN)

ABOVE: FLT LT EM RICKARDS LAUNCHES FROM THE FLIGHT DECK FOR THE LAST TIME. (ROBIN TREWINNARD-BOYLE)

MIDDLE: THE FINAL FLIGHT DECK, HMS *Ark Royal*, 24 NOVEMBER 2010. (ROBIN TREWINNARD-BOYLE)

BOTTOM: A STUNNING SUNSET IN THE MEDITERRANEAN. TORNADO 2250-LITRE EXTERNAL FUEL TANKS RING THE DISPERSAL. (JORDAN HARKINS)

TOP: CHRIS WILSON SEEING OFF RED 1, SIMON MEADS, FROM THE LINE IN CYPRUS 1999. (CHRIS WILSON)

MIDDLE LEFT: CHRIS WILSON JOINS THE DYE TEAM ON THE RED ARROWS 1999 FAR EAST TOUR. (CHRIS WILSON)

MIDDLE RIGHT: CHRIS WILSON'S FIRST FLIGHT IN A RED ARROWS HAWK, XX306, WITH WING COMMANDER JOHNSTONE. (CHRIS WILSON)

BOTTOM RIGHT: SEEING OFF A SECTION OF VAMPIRES. (RAY DEACON)

TOP: THE LAST FAREWELL.
(ROBIN TREWINNARD-BOYLE)

ABOVE: SUNRISE IN THE MEDITERRANEAN.
(JORDAN HARKINS)

RIGHT: AN APACHE AH1 OPERATING FROM
THE FLIGHT DECK OF HMS *Ark Royal*
IN 2010. (ROBIN TREWINNARD-BOYLE)

TOP LEFT: A BEDFORD
FOUR-TON TRUCK IN IRAQ.
(DAVID ROY)

TOP RIGHT: A NIMROD R1
ON THE APRON IN OMAN.
(JIM PHILLIPS)

LEFT: E-3D SENTRIES
DEPLOYED IN OMAN.
(JIM PHILLIPS)

RIGHT: VULCAN MB2 XH558.
(CRAIG SLUMAN)

BOTTOM: NIMROD
MR2 XV229, OF NO. 206
SQUADRON, AT GIBRALTAR
IN APRIL 1993. (TERENCE
DOYLE)

TOP: CUTTING A STRIKING POSE, BUCCANEER S2, XV353 OF NO. 208 SQUADRON, IN ITS NATURAL HABITAT. (LINDSAY PEACOCK)

BOTTOM: BUCCANEER S2 XV353 OF NO. 208 SQUADRON OVER THE MORAY FIRTH. (LINDSAY PEACOCK)

ABOVE: A SHACKLETON AEW2 CAPTURED IN FLIGHT BY A PASSING PHANTOM CREW.
(TONY DIXON)

TOP: BUCCANEER S2 XX900 OF NO. 12 SQUADRON AT RAF LOSSIEMOUTH. THE LANDMARK LIGHTHOUSE IS IN THE BACKGROUND. (LINDSAY PEACOCK)

BOTTOM: LIGHTNINGS OF NO. 74 SQUADRON. (RAY DEACON)

CLOCKWISE FROM TOP: A VICTOR
TANKER OF NO. 57 SQUADRON DESCRIBED
BY VIC WINWRIGHT IN CHAPTER 4.
(DAVID GLEDHILL)

THE CREW ENTRY TO A VALIANT BOMBER.
(DAVID GLEDHILL)

A SHACKLETON MR3. THE MR1 DESCRIBED BY
ERIC DUNN IN CHAPTER 5 HAD A TAIL WHEEL
CONFIGURATION AND NOSE RADOME SIMILAR
TO THE AEW2. (DAVID GLEDHILL)

A VULCAN BOMBER ON WHICH VIC
WINWRIGHT WORKED. XH558 THE LAST
AIRWORTHY VULCAN FLIES ABOVE XM594
AT NEWARK AIR MUSEUM. (DAVID GLEDHILL)

CLOCKWISE FROM TOP: A VIEW FROM THE RUB. (JORDAN HARKINS)

AND RELAX. (JORDAN HARKINS)

THE ADOUR ENGINE FITTED TO THE JAGUAR. (CHRIS BODEN)

A BIRD STRIKE REPAIR TO XZ109. (ALLEN VERNON)

THE RAF COLTISHALL AMF TEAM WORKING ON THE JAGUAR DISPLAY TEAM PRIMARY AIRCRAFT, XZ103, IN 2005. (GRAHAM HAYNES)

FROM TOP LEFT: ZG477 IN HER STRIKING
DECOMMISSIONING PAINT SCHEME.
(ROBIN TREWINNARD-BOYLE)

VAMPIRE XD550 TAXIES OUT
FOR A SORTIE. (RAY DEACON)

HUNTER T7, XL565, SIMILAR TO THOSE
OPERATED AT RAF LOSSIEMOUTH AS
BUCCANEER TRAINERS. (CRAIG SLUMAN)

FROM TOP RIGHT: SAILING UP THE
TYNE, PROUDLY DISPLAYING THE NO. 1(F)
SQUADRON FLAGSHIP, ZG477. (ROBIN
TREWINNARD-BOYLE)

A VAMPIRE AT LITTLE RISSINGTON.
(RAY DEACON)

HUNTER T7, XL565. (CRAIG SLUMAN)

CLOCKWISE FROM TOP:
THE PATROL VEHICLES.
(DAVID ROY)

A BIRD'S EYE VIEW OF A
TORNADO SERVICING.
(JORDAN HARKINS)

JIM PHILLIPS WITH FREDDIE
FLINTOFF. (JIM PHILLIPS)

A TORNADO GR4 UNDERGOES
A PRIMARY STAR SERVICING.
(JORDAN HARKINS)

TOP: A JAGUAR T2 SIMILAR TO THE ONE FLOWN BY CHRIS BODEN FROM GIBRALTAR. (CRAIG SLUMAN)

MIDDLE: A LIGHTNING PRINT PERSONALISED FOR MARTIN GOODWIN BY HIS FORMER BOSS ON NO. 5 SQUADRON. (MARTIN GOODWIN)

BOTTOM LEFT: RN AND RAF GROUNDCREW PROUDLY STANDING NEXT TO THEIR AIRCRAFT PRIOR TO THE FINAL-EVER LAUNCH OF HARRIERS FROM AN RN AIRCRAFT CARRIER. (ROBIN TREWINNARD-BOYLE)

BOTTOM RIGHT: A NO. 41 SQUADRON JAGUAR SINGLE-SEATER RETURNING FROM A SORTIE. THIS IS SIMILAR TO THE ONE DESCRIBED IN CHRIS BODEN'S TALE. (GRAHAM HAYNES)

ABOVE: SCUD ATTACK? (DAVID ROY)

BELOW: AN RAF CHINOOK LIFTS FROM A FORWARD-LANDING ZONE. (DAVID ROY)

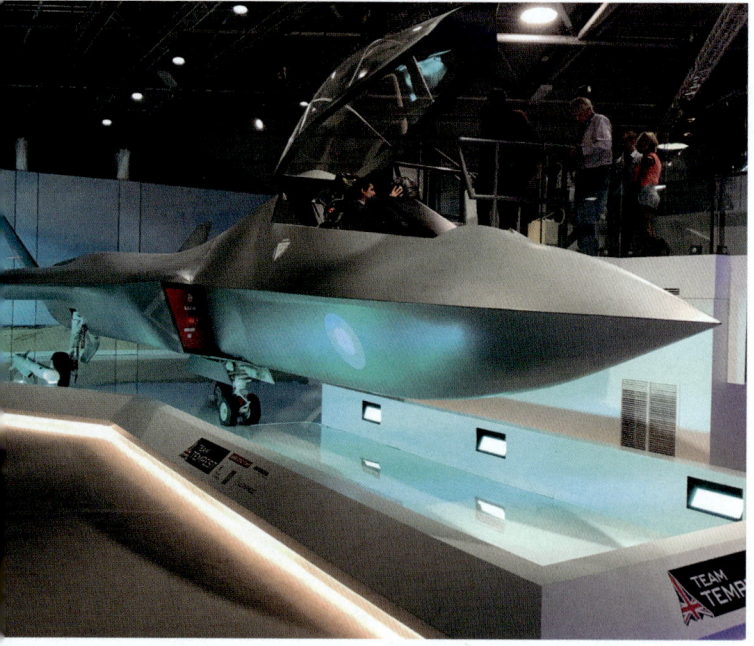

CLOCKWISE FROM TOP LEFT: RIER XV741—THE LONDON TO NEW YORK AIR RACE WINNER—INSTALLED AT BROOKLANDS MUSEUM. (CHRIS WILSON)

HARRIER, XW269, AFTER RESTORATION. (CHRIS WILSON)

A BATCH OF JET PROVOSTS AT JET ART AVIATION. (CHRIS WILSON)

TEMPEST CONCEPT MOCK-UP AT FARNBOROUGH IN 2018. (CHRIS WILSON)

TORNADO GR1, ZA399, TORNADO F3, ZE256, AND A JET PROVOST AT JET ART AVIATION. (CHRIS WILSON) panic-driven measures were aimed at countering a possible response from the Iraqis. It didn't look as if such a response was forthcoming, but this was neither confirmed nor denied.

Only one civilian camp worker turned in that morning and was alarmed to find everyone covered from head to foot in protective clothing. A warrant officer, not renowned for his compassion, gave the man a piece of almost-useless, chemically resistant fabric to put over his face. The recipient of this magnificent western beneficence, smiled and bowed to show his thanks shortly before dying. No, he didn't really die, but if there had been poisonous chemicals in the air, then he would have. The cloth was a placebo. His benefactor strode off noncha-

DAVID ROY ON DEPLOYMENT DURING THE FIRST GULF WAR. (DAVID ROY)

lantly, sealed off completely from the outside world. The man who ran the camp laundry felt no such loyalty to the soldiers and did a runner. The linen limbo only ended when he was tracked down and brought back to camp at banana point. Only then did people get their underpants back and, let me tell you, if there was one thing some of them needed, it was fresh underpants. Outside the camp gates, the world still turned.

Before the wakeful part of the morning was too old, we were told to unmask and we did so with relief, ending our pulmonary constipation. We took our first NAPS tablets—another belated measure. Nerve agent pre-treatment set (NAPS) tablets were supposed to build up our immunity to, as the name suggests, nerve agent. Why hadn't we been taking them before now? Well, we had to from now on. Some people suffered from side effects and stopped taking them before too long. I did not approve of such a measure.

The squadron sergeant major (SSM) sought out his driver—me—that morning but he looked tired. Why? He was certainly much more flustered than usual. "Paddy, get the wagon ready. We're going to recce. a new location for the squadron," he said with great weariness. The war, just a few hours old, was taking its toll on him. I had to remind him of further bad news too.

"It's got no alternator, sir," I told him. "What?" he said. There was more than a trace of annoyed panic in his voice. "No alternator, sir," I repeated. "It won't start." I had not kept this information secret from him. "Well, why hasn't it got one?" "It's bust. They ordered a new one, but they sent the wrong type. We're waiting for the right one."

He shrugged helplessly. I could tell that by some strange, unexplained act of the universe, it had become my fault that Solihull's finest product did not work. Admittedly the timing was poor but only in a normal world could I have avoided the blame for this and I did not, presently, live in a normal world. There was pent-up fury in the SSM's face, which even a huge moustache could not disguise. He seemed to mentally take a deep breath before speaking again. "We'll have to go without it," he said at last, his face red with anger and anguish. "I'll try, sir," I said doubtfully. My words were directed at the SSM's back. He was walking off by this time.

Necessity being the mother of invention, my first task was to get (steal) a functioning battery and to swap it for 44KF88's rather non-functioning one; having no alternator meant that the existing battery was flat. It was 'as flat as a dodo' or, to put it another way, 'as dead as a pancake'. Stealthily, in broad daylight and in plain view, I loosened the bonnet on one Land Rover, detached its battery and carried it over to '44'. I did all this whilst crushingly depressed but I was tough back then. Sometimes.

Shortly after this, the SSM appeared and I started the wagon. Every click of the indicators, every time the wagon was started or the wipers were used, drained the battery a little bit more; irreplaceably so. Having no alternator meant that the battery would just get flatter and flatter, deader and deader, more dodo-ish and more … well, you get the idea. As for using the headlights, I didn't even want to contemplate that. Hopefully we would be back before it was dark. The only thing in our favour was that the wagon had a diesel engine which drained the battery less quickly than a petrol type would have done.

Of course, we found our patch of desert and the sergeant major decided that it was large enough to accommodate the squadron should it need to bug out. To be honest though, the desert was a huge empty space which probably would have had room for the entire army of every nation had they needed to move. With our recce complete we returned to camp and the Land Rover got its new alternator the following day.

Life, if that's what you called it, went on. This was, for us anyway, a continuation of the phoney war stage of the conflict and we went about our business,

THE ARMY AIR CORPS VEHICLE COMPOUND. (DAVID ROY)

perhaps with a wary eye on the sky above, perhaps not. No Scud missiles had yet been fired at us, but our early warning system was up and running, although it was spectacularly unsophisticated. It was the lot of the signaller in the operations room to alert the camp to possible missile attack and to do this he had to run around shouting, "Gas, Gas, Gas". Yes, it was that good. Added to this, was the fact that the signaller would be wearing his respirator, which would muffle his voice terribly. All in all, it would be a less than operatic performance. There would also be a considerable delay between the signaller getting masked up and actually getting to the accommodation to deliver his warning because there was no point in him running outside unprotected and then dying before he had warned the others of the danger. Still, it was only life or death. The modern British Army, eh? Unbeatable.

Our hut contained mostly Command Troop personnel, with one or two store-men and clerks thrown into the human soup for good measure. One of the clerks, a hard case from Leeds, was acting as driver to the ops officer. In this capacity he, presumably by default, attended the same briefings as his boss and was therefore privy to plenty of high-grade information. The soul of discretion and acting on a strictly need-to-know basis, he would tell his hut mates everything that he found out. He thought that they needed to know. We were getting ready for bed when he came back one particular night, and we gathered round as he shared with us the latest intelligence. It was like prisoner of war camp gossip and he was our only contact with the news that really mattered. We took him seriously, never more so than tonight.

"Don't get too comfy, lads," he warned. He had no neck and his head swiv-elled like a budgie as he spoke: "This place is targeted for a Scud attack tonight." He had our attention and we waited eagerly for him to continue. How could anyone know this, I wondered? Was the cleaning lady at the Iraqi's Kuwait headquarters a mole, or did they publish their intentions in the Iraqi edition of *The Sun*? "That's what they said at the briefing," he continued, warming to his theme, his eyes gleaming with excitement. "There was this major there who says which town is going to get a Scud attack. He's been right every night so far and tonight it's our turn." His eyes were wide as he spoke, as if telling a ghost story. He certainly believed that what he was saying was true.

For the last few nights, getting ready for bed had meant putting on our NBC suits and so it was tonight. Nobody was prepared to disbelieve what they had just heard, but if this missile really was coming our way, why couldn't we have been told about it officially? It felt like the old tradition of soldiers as mushrooms was being maintained—kept in the dark and fed on s***.

"Why has no one apart from you," I said, pointing to our mole, "told us about this? Officially, that is? It's soldiers like us who have to fight this bloody war, so why don't our leaders tell us this sort of thing?" He had no answer. No one did. I shrugged and let it go. We didn't have a union and he wasn't the shop steward.

The old Scud missile, a superseded Russian design, was reputedly very inaccurate. This led to the joke, don't take it personally if one hits you—it was probably meant for someone else. I took no solace from this fact, if indeed it was a fact. If our Scud did hit somewhere else, then surely someone else's might hit us. Besides which, this part of Saudi Arabia was so full of troops that it would be difficult to fire a missile and not hit a military target of some sort. The enemy could certainly assume that, once fired, inaccurate or not, it would land somewhere.

We all reacted privately in different ways to the news but I had a certain amount of faith in our training and in our NBC kit, which we had always been told was the best available. I didn't assume that I would necessarily die in a gas attack. I wasn't an enthusiastic soldier but I was a good one. Barring a direct hit, I stood as good a chance as anyone of seeing this through. In contrast, our corporal lay corpse-like on his bed, as if accepting the fact that tonight he would die. His nerve was already gone. We were all nervous, jumpy even, but he was just plain scared and unable to hide it. It was uninspiring, worrying and bewildering. Bloody hell, I thought, as we drifted off to sleep.

"What the f**k was that?!" shouted one of my roommates. An explosion in the distance jolted us into frozen wakefulness like an electric shock. There was an open-mouthed silence so intense that I could hear Ben swallow. At the far end of the room, our corporal was scurrying about like a frenzied hamster and then there was a second explosion. Someone helpfully shouted, "Gas, Gas, Gas" but we were already masking up and breathing out heavily as taught, expelling pockets of polluted air from our masks. The lights came on, making me feel strangely vulnerable, but we acted in unison and with purpose. This time we had been prepared, if only by accident. This time we had been warned and that made all the difference. Suit fabric rustled and rubber gloves snapped on. We were once again sealed off from the outside world, with its smells and, to some extent, its sounds, but I could hear Ben saying, "F***in' 'ell, f***in' 'ell," over and over again, like an urgent, terror-filled prayer. Suddenly he appeared in front of me like a green phantom. He was profoundly agitated.

"Check my eyes, check my eyes," he pleaded, the words muffled. I led him to the centre of the room and stood him below the light, tilting his head back until his eyes were clearly illuminated by the harsh fluorescent tube overhead. His pupils were okay, his eyes tearful. He'd had a shock, thinking that he was contaminated by nerve agent, but that was all he was suffering from—a shock.

"You're okay, Ben," I said reassuringly keeping my voice calm and nodding until Ben started nodding as well, believing his friend's words. "Your eyes are watering, that's all, but you're okay." Ben gave one last affirmative nod as I clapped him, sturdily, on the shoulder. The attack had begun only seconds before and I'd had no time to ponder the veracity of the earlier claims but the second-hand prophesies certainly seemed to be coming true. If those two bangs weren't an indication of an attack, then what were they? It really didn't take a genius to connect one thing with the other. I thought about the times when I had checked the skies for incoming missiles. When it had finally happened, I was sound asleep and dreaming my civilian dreams. There was a ruckus. Shouting. Frantic and discordant, interspersed with another noise like pathetic whimpering. A man afraid to die, pleading for his life. Human and yet inhuman. The separate elements came together quickly, but still in distinct stages.

"Shut the f***ing door!", shouted a trooper. He was young. Only in the army for months. My gaze followed the urgent path of his words and, sure enough, they led his eyes to the bottom of the hut. Others joined the trooper, the originator of the plea, shouting the exact same thing: "Shut the f***ing door!"

It was not polite but it was heartfelt and unambiguous. The object of their pleading was no surprise. Our terrified corporal was standing in the open doorway with his back to us all. His head was raised, presumably to scan the skies but he could have been baying to the moon for all we knew. These reasonable entreaties to shut the door went on until, shockingly, he turned to speak to us. His voice was wavering, desperate but crystal clear, "I can't find my respirator," he wailed and indeed his face was uncovered! It was a moment of horror for the other soldiers. For some time—it seemed an age—no one could speak. We were under attack. We were masked up. It was obvious what he needed to do. Put on his respirator. He had already outlined the problems he faced and was in no fit state to find his own solution. So panicked was he, that he couldn't sort himself out, but as far as the rest of us were concerned this was it. This was our promised Scud attack and 'our Scud' had been laden with deadly chemicals.

No one had ever faced these dangers for real before, at least not since the First World War. No one knew exactly what to expect. I closed my mind to any other interpretation of events. We had been attacked by chemicals but to know what dangers we faced was a big part of the battle. Know your enemy. Saddam had fired a missile full of toxins at us. Fact.

"Shut the f***ing door and find it!" The corporal turned again; his face contorted in terror but then began rummaging through his kit which was a start. Someone shut the door. It was an extra layer of protection against the unseen gases which poisoned the air outside, albeit a flimsy one. Our corporal was almost in tears, frustration and fear combined, like a man on the gallows being given some unattainable means of escaping the noose.

"Where the f**k is it? I can't find my respirator," he repeated. I watched and shook my head bleakly. I was reminded of Wilfred Owen's poem, *Dulce et Decorum Est*– with the line, 'flound'ring like a man in fire or lime'—who dies horribly when exposed to poison gas. Another corporal walked calmly over to his bed post and unhitched the respirator that had been carefully, and forgetfully, placed there for instant access. He handed it to its owner, with a disdainful shake of his head. The NCO pulled the ugly rubber mask on and breathed out gratefully. Of course, had there really been any gas in the room then he was already dead. "Daft sod." The words were said with contempt.

We were all silently staring at the NCO now. No one spoke. None of us could quite believe it. We had just watched a man's self-respect crumble, like a pillar of sand. More to the point, we had been unwilling witnesses to that same man exposing his true nature. I doubted if any of us wanted to see that unedifying spectacle repeated. I knew we weren't heroes but I also now knew that our corporal had failed the test.

We remained in our full NBC suits until we heard the strained but earnest "All Clear" from the duty signaller. I loosened my hood and tore the mask from my face with exaggerated relief. It fitted neatly onto my knee as I sat and pondered the night's alarming events. Ben sat next to me. "Bloody hell, I thought that was it," he said seriously. "You thought you were a goner, son," I said beginning to wipe the sweat from the inside of my mask, "but at least you knew what to do."

To my astonishment no mention was ever made of our Scud attack. It was years later that it came to light that Saddam had launched a missile at us that night but that the powers that be didn't want to worry us.

Bless 'em.

CHAPTER 13

Life at Binbrook

Martin Goodwin joined the RAF at a tender age in October 1975, purely out of a love for aviation. Before that he has been a persistent visitor to the careers information office in Reading from the age of 13; "Gizza job, mister," he was heard to say. During a long career of over 30 years, Martin served on a variety of units in the UK, Germany and Kuwait. He worked on Canberra, Devon, Jet Provost, Andover, Jaguar, Lightning, AEW Nimrod, Hawk, Skyhawk, Tornado GR4 and Tornado F3 as well as being an instructor at Halton and running the Sentry AEW Maintenance School. Since retiring from the RAF he has worked for BAe Systems and Northrop Grumman in a number of roles, in support of the Boeing E3D Sentry programme at Waddington. He recently took up a more central role in the Intelligence, Surveillance, Target Acquisition and Reconnaissance (ISTAR) Force headquarters at Waddington. He became a gliding instructor in 1984 and amassed over 650 hours before taking up powered-flying and taking a share in a Cessna 172. Although he has now hung up his flying boots, he enjoys photographing aircraft when the opportunity presents itself and retains his lifelong passion for aviation.

Life on a Lightning line was challenging, hectic, manic, rewarding and occasionally downright bizarre. I was a line corporal for the first 18 months on 11(F) Squadron from 1982 to 1985. My squadron boss was Wing Commander John Spencer. He was known as a stickler by both his pilots and groundcrew alike.

He didn't suffer fools gladly and could cut steel with his glare. Communications weren't the best in those days and I found myself, I know not how, facing two Lightnings taxiing back to the pan but there was no see-in crew. OK, no issues. I marshalled the first in, gave him the 'brakes on' sign and moved on to the next jet. "Crap, it's the boss."

John Spencer was 'old school'. He wore a distinctive, two-piece, silver helmet. None of the new modern stuff for him. The silver helmet, attached to several tons of noisy machinery came towards me. I knew the minimum was a bollocking for being unprepared so I marshalled him in properly, checked his tyres, 'chocked' him and he shut down. I grabbed the aircraft ladders so he could get out, not wanting him to wait a second more than necessary.

Firstly some background knowledge. The aircraft ladders have four steel 'balls' that slot into four slits in the fuselage of the jet. This was on the port (left) side, which is also the side where the in-flight refuelling probe was mounted. It was a permanent fixture and very strong. On fitting the steps you jumped on the bottom rung to ensure the balls were correctly slotted but that day something went wrong. He was already cross and glared at me from the cockpit, put his own seat pins in and descended the steps.

As he got level with the refuelling probe the two top balls sprung out of their slits as they had not engaged fully. I could say that everything got a bit hazy, however, things did not go hazy at all. I remembered every nanosecond in excruciating, glorious technicolour. The ladder pivoted outwards on the bottom two balls, at which stage he let go with his hands and the probe hit the back of his knees before both his feet came, smartly, off the rung of the ladder. Toppling backwards over the top of the refuel probe, Newton's third law came into force and his legs shot skywards. The next rung of the ladder caught both of his shins and painfully arrested any movement in that direction. With his legs stuck in the ladder and his knees wrapped over the probe, the only thing the rest of his body could possibly do was to fall upside-down over the probe. Wing Commander Spencer and Corporal Goodwin ended up eyeball-to-eyeball, with him upside down.

Now, as a steely-eyed fighter pilot, he had been inverted many thousands of times in his illustrious career, however, never at zero miles per hour. 'I'm so dead' was my predominant thought. 'My career is over, officially'. The only possible recovery action was to punch him between the shoulder blades with enough force to swing him back over the probe, whilst then holding the bottom of the ladder to stop a repeat performance. It worked. He descended onto terra firma, glared me into a six-foot grave and marched off. I wanted to cry and I think I may have passed a little pee …

Maybe 40 minutes later the call came through: "Corporal Goodwin, Boss's office. Blues and hat!" I quickly changed into a smart(er) uniform, grabbed my beret and hot-footed to the hangar. On entering the outer office, his adjutant gave me a stage performance look of horror and pulled a finger across his throat. 'I'm dead,' I thought. On the call I marched in and threw up the best of best salutes and stood rigidly to attention, focusing my gaze just above his eye line. It failed. I could feel his eyes boring into me and I was forced to lower my eyes to meet the glare.

It went on too long for comfort. Eventually he spoke: "Hat off and sit, Goodwin." My bum hit the seat so quickly. He spoke again: "My shins hurt a lot, my back hurts but your face was an absolute picture!" I stared back aghast. "Yours was as well, sir," was all I could muster. He smiled and the atmosphere changed in a heartbeat.

We laughed that day and we laughed again, decades later, on a sunny day on the grass at Bruntingthorpe when we related the tale to several people who just wouldn't believe it. It was true, trust me. He passed away some months later. RIP. He was a true fighter pilot.

✳

"Emergency state 2, emergency state 2, emergency state 2, 11 Squadron aircraft, one POB. Recovering with a hydraulic failure."

It was a cold Binbrook winter evening; gin-clear skies for a change. I was the 'ramp tramp' corporal, an experienced aircraft tug driver and I had been waiting in the line hut for the next job. In case of emergency and regardless of the outcome, we always deployed a tractor and towing arm to the end of the runway, in case the aircraft shutdown and needed towing back to the pan. I grabbed the undercarriage locks and shouted through the hatch for a liney to assist.

The line controller had already shouted, calling me to use the western perimeter road—the peri-track. I thought this was strange, so I requested clarification. He called air traffic control, and yup, they wanted me to use the western. We jumped onto the open-top David Brown tractor, grabbed the towing arm and set off. Heading down to the QRA sheds, onto the dark side of the airfield, past the reheat de-tuners and up the western peri-track, it just didn't feel right and we didn't have a Storno radio.

As we made our way around the road, I could see the blue lights of the emergency vehicles on the other side of the runway. I could also see several Lightnings in the visual circuit, their white anti-collision lights flashing away. Pulling up facing the emergency vehicles, with maybe 4,000 feet of runway remaining to the north, we watched the aircraft in the circuit. Some landed but others overshot back into the circuit. It was all a bit lonely without communication so I shouted at Al the liney who had come with me, that when the fire trucks headed off, so would we.

More jets landed but then as one touched down, the fire trucks moved and followed it down the runway. I crashed through the gears and charged after them as they disappeared into the distance, leaving us in the middle of a very big, very dark, very foreboding runway. More white 'anti-cols' overhead announced more Lightnings arriving back in the circuit, all the pilots anxious to recover. My throat tightened. The Lightning was never flush for fuel.

The tractor could go no faster so I just kept looking around in case a stray aeroplane landed. Subliminally, I saw a steel rope in front of me. No issues, I thought. It's the Rotary Hydraulic Arrestor Gear (RHAG), which is an emergency arrestor device so the pilot can lower a hook and catch the cable if all else has failed. To allow for a clean engagement these cables are held off the ground, at about three inches high, by hard rubber rollers.

Within a second the night took a really bad turn. The tractor decelerated to a dead stop, I was thrust against the steering wheel and Al just disappeared off the front of the tractor onto the runway. What has just happened? It took about another second to realise that the rear of the towing arm had engaged the RHAG and it had functioned exactly as designed. The flashing lights from the waiting Lightnings were still in the circuit but the fire trucks had reached the, now stationary, Lightning on the operational readiness platform (the ORP). They looked miles away so I reversed the tractor so that Al could unhook the arm from the cable. Disentangled, we sped off as fast as the tractor would go, heading for the ORP.

Pulling up, I went straight to the sergeant fireman who was the vehicle crew commander and incident commander. When I explained that we had just de-tensioned the RHAG after our unexpected encounter, he went into a spectacular rant. He called the local controller in the tower and the waiting jets were diverted as a precaution. Not good! We quickly completed the safety checks and prepared the stranded aircraft, before towing it back to the line. I was summoned.

Before my arrival, the senior air traffic control officer (SATCO) had phoned the squadron duty authoriser and informed him that he wanted my spleen on a plate. I was to be charged; I was to be hung, drawn and quartered and the whole of the book would be thrown at me; chapter by bloody chapter.

My only ally in all of this was the line sergeant, a huge, jovial rugby-playing legend called Mo Puddick. When I briefed him about the phone call from SATCO, Mo took control. He called the tower and, quietly but forcefully, reminded them of the directive that had created the circumstances that led to the unfortunate incident. A silence ensued but I was still issued with the obligatory bollocking for being a 'biff'. Even so, with a quiet word, a positive outcome emerged from a potentially disastrous incident; the only casualty being my underpants.

✳

Sometime later, very early on a Monday morning on No. 11 (F) Squadron, I was with a liney, Reg, whose job it was to fill the aircraft with liquid oxygen. With me supervising, I decided we'd do it a bit differently as no one would be around for some hours yet. I was one of the few who was cleared to tow aircraft, so with Reg on the brakes in the cockpit, we towed two jets out onto the line—the concrete hardstanding in front of the squadron. We had opened both the inner hangar doors so, as long as I was on the centre yellow line, I knew the wingtips would miss the doors. It was, after all, the 1980s. I left Reg filling the liquid oxygen pot and went back to the hangar. Having had lots of practice, I could reverse the towing arm pretty accurately, so I hooked up to another jet. I walked around to ensure nothing was in the way and slowly, towed it out to the line. As I said it was the 1980s.

Having done this maybe seven or eight more times, things were going well and we had saved the shift a load of time. It would be 'smartie points' all round. Reg had finished replenishing the aircraft with oxygen and helped me with one final tow-out. At the end of the hangar was a servicing slot called 'Check 2'. Prior to a Check 2 servicing, the aircraft was washed by the civilian wash team, on the wash pan around the back of the hangar. With Reg in the aircraft and once more on the brakes I set off, moving carefully within the confines of the hangar. Maybe I should point out that the minimum number of personnel to tow a Lightning was five; the tower, the brakeman, one man on each wingtip and a controller, normally a corporal. Off Reg and I went towards the wash pan.

It was a clear morning but it had rained overnight and the ground was wet. The wash pan was circular, sloped downhill slightly and was surrounded, bar the entrance, by a small concrete curb. The entrance dropped slightly into the wash pan itself. My plan was to tow the jet in a circle and out of the entrance, stop, then reverse into position for the wash team. The plan went spectacularly wrong about three seconds after entering the wash pan. As I initiated a right turn, the aircraft went straight on. This had the effect of spinning the tractor and me, violently to the right. The back of the tractor—a big steel sheet—snapped the towing arm like a brittle twig. Undeterred, the tractor kept spinning to the right until it was facing the still-moving, monster I gulped.

It was a Mk 6 Lightning and the ventral tank, with its integral Aden gun pack, mounted the front right of the tractor. The missile slipper—the bit of metal the missile is mounted on—came quickly towards me. I gulped again.

I threw myself into the gear lever area, the slipper punching me a glancing blow to my right rib cage before ripping off the back of the seat and severing the flashing light mounted on a pole behind the seat. The aircraft main wheel hit the front of the tractor and we all changed direction. I was now going backwards. The nosewheel of the jet jumped the curb and sunk into the grass surrounding the wash pan before the tractor and me, tucked under the starboard wing. The tractor suddenly became a very large chock. I was too shocked to gulp!

THE 'TRACTOR INCIDENT'. A LIGHTNING VERSUS RAF TRACTOR.
(© UK MOD CROWN COPYRIGHT 1983 VIA MARTIN GOODWIN)

THE TRACTOR
TUCKED UNDER
THE STARBOARD
WING. (© UK
MOD CROWN
COPYRIGHT
1983 VIA MARTIN
GOODWIN)

As events had unfolded, Reg had dropped his gloves and was busy picking them up from the cockpit floor. He felt a couple of heavy bumps so looked up but I wasn't there, nor was the tractor. He flew down the ladders, yelling loudly but I couldn't answer as I had been badly winded by the blow to the ribcage. We exchanged pleasantries and I decided to summon help by radioing air traffic control on my Storno radio. All hell broke loose within a very short space of time as fire, police, ambulance, every man and his dog from ATC and every man and his officer from No. 11(F) Squadron arrived in our vicinity. Less welcome was the station photographer who arrived to record the heinous crime for evidential purposes. It was still fairly early and I was mightily impressed that they were all at work at that time of day.

For those aware of the military disciplinary procedures, I was charged. I saw the JEngO and was remanded.

I saw the SEngO and was remanded.

I saw the squadron commanding officer, a certain Wing Commander John Spencer, and was remanded to the station commander. I really gulped; this was getting serious.

It was October 1982 and the previous station commander had been gone about three months, so my testicles and spleen were to be saved. The new group captain presided over a brief one-sided affair, but he was a very nice man. I received two years informal reprimand, and was charged for ten per cent of the cost of the damage to the towing arm; £83 was quite a lot in 1982. Luckily, there was no mention of the damage to the tractor or indeed the ventral tank of the aircraft. Hat on, salute, march out. Left, right, left, right, left, right …

There in the waiting area was John Spencer. "Sit there," he growled. I sat.

He went into the station commander's office, the door shut and ten minutes later I was marched back in. I saluted and was told to remove my head dress and to sit. I sat. He spoke. I listened. My previous conduct, and the fact I was only two years away from promotion were taken into account. It was a double 'slap on the wrist'. Phew! Hat on, salute and get the hell out of 'Harry Staish's' office as quickly as possible.

A somewhat dejected Corporal Goodwin was glumly making his way back to the squadron when up pulls a service Mini. The door opens. "Get in, Goodwin."

John Spencer twice in one day. Dear God.

"Wasn't too bad was it?" he said, with a glint in his eye. "By the way, you are now promoted to be the squadron towing examiner."

It's a strange, old world.

✱

It was March 1985 and I knew my time at Binbrook was coming to an end as I had been selected for promotion which would also mean a posting away from RAF Binbrook. I actually ended up on the Airborne Early Warning Nimrod Development Unit at RAF Waddington. My analogy was that this move was the difference between speeding down the motorway in the outside lane at 100 miles per hour versus changing all four tyres on the hard shoulder. It was a different pace of life but that's another, sad story.

A German F-4 Phantom squadron was at Binbrook on an exchange visit to the squadron. They arrived and all was going well. I had done my stint as a line corporal and was now working in 'the shed' fixing any propulsion faults that occurred and believe me, there were plenty. The Lightning was a wonderful aircraft to watch flying but an absolute nightmare to keep serviceable. It was without doubt the hardest aircraft I worked on during my 30-year career.

Preparing for the exchange visit, one aircraft 'tower' from each of the line shifts was checked out on how to tow the visiting F-4s. The Form 600A, the service driving licence, was annotated to reflect the qualification. I was still nominated as the squadron towing examiner even though I now worked in the main hangar. The German F-4s were squeezed into our already crowded hangar when being worked on, so space was at a premium. It was teatime and the lineys had been sent for food in the mess. An F-4 had been in the shed for a propulsion snag that required a quick, non-reheat, engine ground run. The liney tower was not available so, as time was of the essence, the duty flight sergeant sought me out. Now many people working on No. 11(F) Squadron at the time will remember this man. He stood six foot six inches tall, had bright red hair and a temper to match. He took no prisoners and I vividly remember him informing an airframe chief technician what he was going to do to him after he had ripped his head off. The chief backed down and conceded the argument. The flight sergeant found me in the crewroom, supping a well-earned brew.

"Goodwin, tow the German 'Toom' out for a ground run."

"Can't Flight," was my glib response. "Not on my 600A."

I knew my rights, I knew the law, I was watertight. There was a brew to finish.

"Get your ******* backside out off that ******* chair and get into that ******* hangar and tow the ******* aircraft! **** the ******* 600A, you are the ******* squadron towing examiner you little ******* ****!"

In full flow this man would have given Alex Ferguson a good run for his money. Well, in the hairdryer mode of diplomacy. I thought that, as he had asked so politely, I would accept his gracious request and was soon inside the tractor with towing arm attached.

There are two background points for the story. Firstly, the open-top tractors—which I had the misfortune to both crash on the wash pan and to engage the RHAG with—had been replaced with a new design which had a metal and glass cabin, as well as many other creature comforts. Secondly, the Phantom towing arm was different to the Lightning and, therefore, OC Eng, the officer commanding Engineering Wing, had decreed that one would be sent from RAF Coningsby which operated Phantoms. This happened without further questioning as he was god as far as the groundcrew were concerned.

I arrived at the hangar to be met by the Germans who knew what they were doing, so we were soon connected and ready to roll. In true Germanic fashion they were correct and ship-shape in all departments: man on brakes in the cockpit, wingtip walkers to ensure the aircraft couldn't accidently hit anything and an 'UppenGruppenFuhrer' in charge of the whole thing. Off we went.

Getting out of the hangar was easy, and as it was a no-reheat engine run, we went onto the disused runway quite close to our own line; remember time was of the essence. We stuck the F-4 'arse to grass' so it would not damage the tarmac surface and they readied it for the run. As I was a propulsion man by trade, they let me sit in the back seat to see it in action. Billy bonus I thought. The engine ground run went to plan and lasted about 20 minutes, proving the fault was now cleared. We, (they), refuelled the F-4 and we set off to put her back in the same slot in the hangar to complete the maintenance. No issues at all.

Now, to an experienced aircraft tower, it was a matter of pride and street credibility to follow a set sequence. You got the wingtip as close to the hangar door as possible. You turned the aircraft as late and as tight as possible, to allow the whole combination to line up correctly on the white centre lines, before pushing it back into the slot. You reversed the tractor and aircraft into the hangar, as only weak and pathetic people stopped and turned the tractor around to push the aircraft in, (in line with station standing orders).

I slowed down on the approach and the German wingtip men jumped out of the tractor to see that I was safe … Nice and close … Easy does it … Past the white centre line … Easy does it … Turn now … Coming round nicely … GRRRRREEEEEEETWANGGGGGG!

What the f**k was that? I stopped pretty sharpish with the F-4 at about 45 degrees to the hangar doors. Please God tell me that I hadn't hit the hangar doors. But no, the UppenGruppenFuhrer was already at the front of his beloved aircraft, staring at the nose area with his hands on his hips. I joined him and we stared at the nose and then at each other.

The pitot tube, a hollow, metal tube which tells the pilot how fast he is going, is mounted on the front of the nose cone on a Phantom. It was bent. It was bent quite badly, actually. A quick look at the tractor showed a corresponding scrape on the rear left edge of the metal cabin. It wasn't a big scrape but that wasn't the

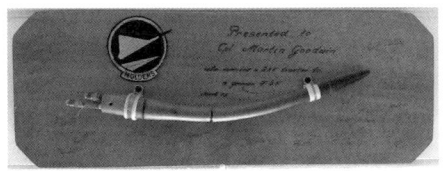

THE BENT PROBE FROM A LUFTWAFFE F-4F
PRESENTED TO MARTIN FROM THE VISITING
GERMAN SQUADRON. (MARTIN GOODWIN)

MARTIN GOODWIN IN THE COCKPIT OF
A LIGHTNING SOME YEARS LATER.
(MARTIN GOODWIN)

big issue. The big issue was the fact that the pitot tube was bent on the visiting Phantom and they were flying home in four days. There was also the small fact that this was my third 'towing incident' during my three-year tour. I felt a hard knot tighten in my stomach.

Yet again I was impressed at how many senior people arrived in such a short space of time. After a lot of head-scratching and pointing and measuring and photographing, the 'brass' decided it was safe to carry on and to put the aircraft into the hangar for further investigation. Therefore, they all stood there watching with more than a little interest as we reassembled the towing team and I, carefully, and I mean really carefully, pushed her back in.

My head was potentially on the chopping board again and I was wondering if my imminent promotion would be delayed, or indeed cancelled, if I was found to be responsible for this most heinous of crimes. The investigation went on into the night. The pitot tube was so bent it had to be sawed into two pieces to remove it. The Germans didn't carry a spare, nor did they have support equipment for such a job, therefore, everything had to be found and flown over from home base. Not looking good.

Two things happened to save Goodwin's bacon. Firstly, the investigation found that, as I was an ace tower, I had turned sharper than normal but this was acceptable. Pythagoras' theorem came into play and the pitot tube had struck the left rear of the tractor's cabin but why? Aircraft buffs amongst you, will be well aware that the German Phantom has its cannon mounted in the nose. This has the effect of making the nose cone some two metres longer than its British cousin. Therefore OC Eng's decision to bring an RAF item from Coningsby was the suspect and, indeed, the Germans should have been instructed to bring their own towing arms with them. As soon as this came to light the official 'let's crucify the guilty b*****d' line of investigation fizzled out somewhat. I have to say that, at that stage, I really didn't give a damn as my head had been removed from the chopping block. Secondly, they managed to get hold of the spares and to fix the probe to allow them to leave on time. All's well that ends well.

There was an obligatory beer call at the end of the exchange visit and everyone from the squadron was there including 'Harry Staish'. The visitors had brought over a number of steel kegs of the German 'golden nectar' and the party was in full swing. The official pleasantries were underway as squadron plaques and pictures were exchanged and the 'two-winged master race' (pilots), told each other how brilliant they were. A couple of the German groundcrew came forward with an empty beer keg and placed it at the front.

"Corporal Goodwin. Please come and stand on the barrel. Please come." I was assisted to the front of the assembled mass and climbed onto the upended barrel. The UppenGruppenFuhrer, actually a really, nice man called Franz, or Fritz, or something, came forward, gave a short speech and handed me a wooden plaque, on which was mounted the offending pitot tube, still in two pieces. The German groundcrew had signed it and it had been beautifully varnished. The applause was massive and I went red. I gracefully accepted the gift but was mindful of my exposed position. The risk of being caught for a 'Zulu warrior' prompted me to jump off the keg sharpish. "Speech, speech!" came the call from the Brit groundcrew. Should I? Why not.

"Gentlemen, I should like to make a few thanks. Firstly, I would like to thank the UppenGruppenFuhrer and his team for helping me in this matter and for being good eggs. Secondly, I would like to thank the flight sergeant for authorising an unauthorised tow—his ginger head disappeared into the crowd as he quickly, ducked down. Thirdly, I would like to thank the boss of 11 (Fighter) Squadron for being our boss (huge cheer). Lastly, I would like to thank the station commander as he is new to RAF Binbrook and doesn't remember me from the last time." This ended with huge cheers and much throwing of beer, mainly at me.

Both the boss and 'Harry the Staish' came forward to shake my hand. The night turned into a riotous affair with much singing of loud, boisterous and raucous songs and much drinking. I don't remember the end of the night but I vaguely remember the hangover from hell that lasted days.

There is a footnote. The plaque, which was presented to me that evening, has hung proudly in eight of my married quarters and houses since. It has, by tradition, always been the last item to be removed when we packed up and was the first item to be put up in the new abode. It has been in its current location since 1997 and I fully intend to have it in my coffin for my final journey.

CHAPTER 14

It Shouldn't Happen to an Engineering Officer

Jim Phillips joined the RAF as a flight systems apprentice in 1982 having previously failed to join as a pilot, navigator and engineering officer. He also failed to make the grade as a technician, instead being offered a cadetship and commission after a year. A four-year engineering degree with regular periods discovering RAF engineering resulted in not actually doing anything useful until the summer of 1989 when he was posted to RAF Brize Norton. Tours at Waddington and Wyton followed before some serious academics achieving an MSc in electronic warfare. Then something new; a tour at the Air Warfare Centre at RAF Waddington where he met Dave Gledhill. Over a decade of stations starting only with a 'W' spawned a yearning for something different, satisfied by an exchange tour in the USA. Inevitably the 'W' thing persisted at Wright-Patterson AFB. Returning to the UK, avoiding Waddington and Wyton but not the 'W', meant a posting to RAF Wittering. He broke the trend with, finally, a tour in Oman. Retirement followed back-to-back tours at Abbey Wood in military procurement which he continues to support.

A career in the RAF offers enormous opportunity to explore challenging, stressful and risky endeavours; sometimes these situations also stray into the ironic and comical. Every career is unique but built on a common framework

JIM PHILLIPS TAKES A BACK-SEAT HAWK TRIP. (JIM PHILLIPS)

that allows those who have experienced one to recognise the similarity of experience of others. My pathway into the RAF was un-uniquely unique, joining as an apprentice technician until a distinct lack of potential resulted in selection to be an engineering officer. Hence, while I spent most of the time as a 'boss', I understood, appreciated and sometimes even enjoyed, the pranks of my troops.

I was fortunate to enjoy an extended training course which was conducted periodically at university, with stints experiencing a wide range of RAF engineering. One high point was spent as a 'flem'—a flight-line mechanic—on the much-missed No. 233 OCU, or the 'Wildcats' as they were known. No. 233 OCU taught pilots to fly the Harrier GR3 at RAF Wittering, the home of the Harrier. This was just a few short years after the Falklands War where the Harrier had made its unique reputation. By 1986 the GR3s were worn out and about to be replaced by the new 'plastic' GR5 and it is fair to describe the Harrier Force as lively and brave. As a very green acting pilot officer (APO), a rank that no longer exists, I was dropped into this mix and it was heaven. Having previously sat through mechanics courses in airframes, and propulsion, and electrics—that was a long summer at RAF Halton—I did the flem course and arrived on the squadron as, probably, the oddest flem they'd ever seen. Nevertheless, despite being from the 'other side' as a commissioned engineering officer, the engineers took me in as one of their own and proceeded to teach me what books couldn't. I was also privileged to have two great examples of engineering officers in the SEngO, Neil Gammon and the JEngO, Dirk Bacon, who themselves were probably the subject of a joke by the posters. On a later tour Neil Gammon would become my long-suffering OC Engineering Wing.

I did watch another APO attempt to follow the air publications to the letter to conduct a before-flight (BF) servicing as part of the flem final test. As he wheeled a trolley loaded with all types of spares, including wheels, several types of oil and all the necessary APs, a small, muttering audience gathered and the guffawing grew as the minutes turned to hours. The BF took over two hours and was the engineering equivalent of a work of art; however, the extended debrief majored on time and the expectation of a BF taking no more than 30 minutes. Somewhat embarrassingly, my colleague became part of the small and select band who have ever had to re-sit a flem test.

Probably the best advantage of being on a squadron is the opportunity to fly. Have I mentioned lively and risk yet? Anyway, the day came and I met my pilot and off we went. There is nothing more exciting. Instead of me doing the strap-in, I was being strapped in by another flem and feeling on top of the world. As he finished, he smacked me firmly on the helmet which distracted me to the fact that he had flicked off the air supply to my g trousers. The Harrier with its high power-to-weight ratio was one of the fastest accelerating vehicles on the planet, if I recall 0 to 60 in 2.6 seconds. Before I knew it, we were airborne at low level with the English countryside flying by at seven miles a minute. The first event on this training sortie was to attack a petrol station, on the A43 I think. I'm not convinced that banking into a six-g turn was entirely necessary but, had my well-informed pilot not done that, I wouldn't have blacked out. It was maybe at that moment—meaning the moment I woke up of course—that I truly understood the vicious humour that exists 'on the line'.

We continued the flight, me feeling not quite as bright as when we'd taken off, and headed to a village called Broadway, known as the gateway to the Cotswolds. Why do I know this? Because at Broadway is a three-storey tower that rises on a hill above the village. As we tore across the countryside and the hill with its distinctive tower began to loom large, my pilot said, "Don't forget to wave". Seconds later we were on our side, grazing the tower about halfway up. On the top of the tower were some tourists staring down at us, open-mouthed at the unexpected sight of an RAF Harrier flashing by; and no, I didn't forget to wave. From there we followed the M6 north, taking a moment to go inverted and wave to surprised drivers through sun roofs.

The reason for going north was that the pilot had asked where I might like to go and, as this might be the only time flying a Harrier, I thought a flypast of my parent's house in Stoke would be good. Luckily, in the minutes before taking off I managed to call my mum and warn her. So, not so long later, there we were at low level over the house, wings waving so that we could take pictures from the 95-mm nose-mounted camera. I don't recall seeing my mum, but she recounted in fine detail the surprise from her perspective when I telephoned later that day. We finished the sortie by rising to 20,000 feet over Sheffield and doing some aerobatics. What a trip. I had two more trips in Harriers. On the second trip we took a bird-strike over Dartmoor and had to divert into RAF Chivenor where we happened to be going for a land-away anyway. I think every emergency vehicle on the base came out to meet us, blue lights flashing. My third trip was to return the same aircraft to RAF Wittering after having checked the engine and then signed for it myself. It always helps to concentrate the mind knowing you're going to fly in that aircraft.

The RAF routinely deploys forces to conduct operations overseas and these are known as deployments or detachments. The stress and pace of deployments can bring out the very best, and worst, in people. Tempers are easily frayed, but this gives opportunity for deeper friendships to develop. During the First Gulf War I was deployed to RAF Akrotiri in Cyprus where air defence was provided by six Phantoms from Nos. 19 and 92 Squadrons in the twilight of their RAF careers. It soon reduced to five after one was lost into the Mediterranean. Several good friends of mine were the JEngOs of this detachment and I was sharing the time of day with one when he took a call from OC Operations who was concerned to minimise the damage that possible missile strikes could do, and insisted that " … no two Phantoms should be on the same straight line". My friend's gentle correction that he meant no three Phantoms, resulted in a lengthy tirade about doing as one was told and not asking questions. Needless to say, that order could not and was not complied with.

My own time as a JEngO was on the Boeing E-3D Sentry aircraft, sometimes known as AWACS. Deployment with the Sentry to support the conflict in the Balkans in the first year of its service offered a significant challenge. Everyone was new to the aircraft; maintenance procedures were largely untested and spares were short. An initial deployment managed by my fellow JEngO, Paul Pearce, to Trapani in Sicily had gone well but now it was my turn to relocate the deployment for the longer term to an American base in northern Italy. I arrived with other deployment execs on a Friday afternoon. My groundcrew were expected the next day, and two aircraft on the following Monday, ready to fly continuous operations three days later. A meeting with our USAF hosts was going really badly with all requests for support being met with difficulty. The Sentry has low slung engines and is susceptible to foreign object damage (FOD) and I recall my requests for very early taxiway sweeping being met with unconstrained laughter, which I thought a bit rude. After a couple of very draining hours the base commander stepped in unexpectedly, declared us as the vanguards of Europe and that we were to be given everything we needed. The meeting improved considerably to the point that a dusty operations order for deployment of USAF AWACS was found. In addition to being offered my own hardened aircraft shelter as a base, I was driven to a field of neatly parked vehicles to, I thought, select a few for our needs; however, my hosts meant the whole field worth in accordance with the plan. There were 43 vehicles and I was only expecting 30 troops. With some disappointment I had to reject the ambulances, the staff cars and a couple of what looked like armoured-personnel carriers. I did ponder for a second over keeping a police car for myself but, sadly, common sense prevailed. Nevertheless, I kept a fleet of 'six packs'—trucks with a six-seater cab—and that proved very popular with the team.

Smug at our success, we embarked on an evening exploring Italy and, in particular, a previously unencountered liquid called grappa. That resulted in the inevitable hangover, but more seriously, I lost my voice at a time when it might have come in quite handy. The briefing to the incoming troops was a non-event. I was not able to warn them sufficiently about grappa and by the following day we had more casualties. Nevertheless, we threw ourselves into setting up our base and by arrival time, we lined up by the side of the pan ready to receive our chicks.

The first aircraft, ZH105, made an elegant arrival and a suitable entry of the RAF Sentry into operations at a USAF base. If only the second aircraft, ZH101, otherwise known as the Hindenburg, could have done the same. As we watched, many of us still in a fragile state, the aircraft dropped onto the runway with the heaviest of heavy landings, causing the whole team to wince simultaneously. In those early days of the Sentry there were many procedures that were still untested, including heavy-landing checks, so it was just my luck to have the opportunity to work through them for the first time away from our main operating base, when we were under pressure to perform. A debrief with the aircrew suggested elevator lock-up, making the situation even more concerning. While the checks were completed successfully, they did not uncover the cause and, with a sinking heart, I called OC Eng back at his home, where his uncharacteristic response of "Waddington nut house, Napoleon speaking," suggested a party in full swing. After several attempts the full severity of the situation was imparted, but sympathy was not forthcoming and the phone put down with the final words "you'll think of something" still echoing.

Now the way was clear for me to exercise my full engineering expertise, which of course meant debating with my SNCOs. The symptoms suggested that we needed to look inside the elevators, and as we dropped the first panel, a thick honey-like liquid dripped out. Another call to Waddington revealed that this might be corrosive protective compound (CPC) sprayed onto hidden surfaces to reduce corrosion. We then discovered that if we could see it, it was on too thick. See it? You could have cooked in it! It was this sticky gloop that was gumming up the works and we had to clean it up. This meant marshalling the whole team to remove panels and clean out the gloop with rags and alcohol, and the size of the task meant even using non-technical staff to help. After 60 hours of unbroken activity from when the aircraft had arrived, it was ready to air test. I sent the groundcrew and other helpers back to the hotel armed with a lot of my money and an order to have 'just one' and go to bed. Then as the brave leader I thought that I was, I demanded to go on the air test and was pleasantly surprised how obliging the aircrew were.

The Boeing 707 airframe is not as sluggish as it looks. When it was flown for dignitaries over Boeing Field in Seattle, the rebellious test pilot didn't do as he was told and rolled the aircraft, attracting instant wrath but cementing its credibility within the aeronautical community. Hence, taking off in a lightly fuelled Sentry was, I now know, like being in a fighter. With me in the fifth seat behind the pilots we spent a pleasurable time weaving in and out of a spectacular cloud scene, the manoeuvres becoming progressively more aggressive to test the full range of the elevators. Once completely confident, the pilots decided to add one unscheduled manoeuvre to the list, and stalled the aircraft. One moment I'm looking at fluffy clouds like the credits for *Toy Story*, the next I'm watching the parked aircraft on the airfield getting bigger. I recall hearing the flight engineer say with barely constrained contempt, "Captain, the JEngO has fainted". Clearly, he was mistaken but to be fair, I had been taken a little by surprise and I may have been mentally bracing for impact. Safe on the ground, I made my way unsteadily to our ops centre, interrupting a televised interview with the deployment commander who, unadvisedly, introduced what was possibly the least attractive advertisement for an engineering officer, speaking with a squeaky voice, unshaven and unwashed for many days, and white as a sheet from a recent near-death experience. I returned alone to the hotel hoping to slide in unnoticed to bed, but naturally the 'only one' party was in full swing and away we went.

After such an eventful start nothing else could possibly go wrong, but as the legions of survivors of RAF deployments will testify, it's only the depth that differs. So, buoyed with overcoming the early crisis start, confidence grew and

JIM PHILLIPS TAKES A BREAK DURING OPERATIONS IN OMAN. (JIM PHILLIPS)

a sense of invincibility set in; survivors also know that this is always the smug feeling that you get immediately before a disaster. A run of good luck and passable judgement meant that the aircraft were playing ball and presenting fewer and fewer problems, until one evening when the stars aligned and we had two serviceable aircraft ready for the next two launches. Knowing that I had a fresh groundcrew team arriving early the next morning for the second see-off, I allowed a very tired shift to go home to rest—meaning of course to drink the hotel dry first. This left just me and a stalwart chief who had been instrumental in taking a green JEngO through six weeks of a familiarity course on the aircraft. What could possibly befall this premier division team from glorious success?

As it happens, a rotor-dome failure on crew-in and the need to move a 14-man crew to the second aircraft to meet the see-off time, including the unfeasibly large amount of food that such a crew seems to need to survive on such trips. We made the see-off time—just—and as the navigation lights faded into the night, alarm set in as to how to repair the original aircraft ready for the next see-off with no groundcrew. How much of a challenge would it be for a slightly rotund chief, and a still green JEngO to replace a rotor-dome motor? We studied the job and prepared tools and spares before loading the cherry picker and heading skyward. The hatch at the bottom of a Sentry rotor dome is 90 feet from the ground, at which point we discovered we had a cherry picker with about an 82-foot reach. Now, I don't like heights but options were few, so the rotund chief and I climbed onto the railings of the cherry-picker basket to open the hatch and somehow scramble on board, despite the basket rocking like an old roller coaster. The job, however, went like a dream with the chief doing most of the work and me acting like a nurse in an operating theatre; teamwork is important at these moments. Once we had changed the motor, we had to get down which is when we learnt that exiting was much more difficult than entering, requiring an 'entirely safe'—health and safety aside—drop into the basket, and not forgetting the broken motor and tools either. We made it back to the safety of the ground and the rotor-dome tested satisfactorily; it even went round the right way. We also just made the second see-off time, but could not convince the arriving groundcrew that the JEngO had actually wielded a spanner, nor that the chunky chief had been able to squeeze himself in and then back out of the rotor-dome hatch.

On 4 July, I was honoured to be invited to the base Independence Day BBQ and to be asked for an interview on the base radio station. The Americans take independence very seriously as it underpins the whole ethos of the country and so I had practised in order to roll off some casually articulate answers on the day. The groundcrew were, I thought, busy maintaining the aircraft and I was looking forward to a rare period of relaxation on a warm afternoon with a cold beer. The moment of my performance arrived and a microphone was thrust in my direction. However, my heart stopped as a trumpeter started to play the British national anthem and from behind a nearby hedge the basket of the RAF cherry picker started to rise majestically. On board was the slightly rotund chief and another fellow chief both resplendent in homemade red coat uniforms typical of the British Army at the time of independence, complete with tricorn hats fashioned expertly from black tape. The second chief was famed for his ability with the fugal horn and he was playing the national anthem. The rotund chief was fixed, stiffly at attention, with a homemade rifle. The BBQ fell silent and everyone turned to watch. When the basket was at about half-height, the rotund chief executed a perfect present arms for the ascent to full height. As the trumpet fell silent, there was a moment's pause in which time I reflected on a career that was about to be cut short due to this diplomatic incident. The crowd erupted into laughter and applause as they were genuinely impressed at the impertinence of the chiefs and, as it happens, the rest of the groundcrew sniggering at the base of the cherry picker. The groundcrew got an unexpected invitation to the BBQ, but the chiefs spent most of the afternoon recreating the unexpected British intervention to never-ending applause.

The deployment drinking was mainly under control with just with one or two notable incidents. On occasion we were joined by the SEngO who, to be fair, while he meant well, was not the most joyful kind. His presence had a Transylvanian chilling effect on moral and so it was not uncommon to feign that the deployment was under control to allow him to go off and indulge in a bit of solo cultural tourism. To support this endeavour, a car would be left, exclusively, for him but this was to be the spectacular downfall of one chief technician. This chief had been throwing himself into work and play with equal vigour but had missed the transport to work on more than one occasion. Much more severe than the stern advice I was forced to give him was his own pride and so, late one evening and realising that he was again 17 sheets to the wind and would most likely sleep in, he showered, dressed in uniform and went out to sleep in one of the cars—you may already be one step ahead at this point. It was never established who was the more surprised, or how the SEngO didn't crash the car after the chief sat bolt upright behind him. We didn't see much of the SEngO on deployment after that, or indeed the chief.

Much later, I had the utmost honour of being the officer commanding Engineering and Supply Wing and deputy base commander of an expeditionary air wing (EAW), 902 EAW in Oman. Arriving was shocking, stepping out of an air-conditioned aircraft into 55° C heat I felt that I could never survive, but after a few weeks of focused acclimatisation—essentially walking frequently in the desert—the heat became less of a topic. With a population of about 250, made up of EAW personnel plus groundcrew and aircrew of a range of supported aircraft types, including RAF and RN plus a smattering of army, made for an exciting mix. Plus, having the air component commander (ACC) more than

1,000 miles away, forced certain freedoms and allowed both aspects of the typical 'work hard-play hard' to be played to the hilt. The aircraft at the base were of two types: ageing transports and complex electronic mission aircraft that some like to call 'spy planes', and each threw up unique challenges.

The routing of the supply chain meant that we were the last base in the region to receive spares, and this was a constant source of frustration as 'awaiting spares' became a miserable mantra. In addition, the RAF stores systems had recently been changed with some teething problems. We had waited many days for a specific relay which was holding back an aircraft from being able to perform a unique task, which itself was holding up a mission involving aircraft and ground troops. Hence, the calls from the ACC and his engineering staff became more frequent and less about the weather. Eventually the package arrived and my supply staff gave me the honour of opening it so that I could rush it round to the installation team. I ripped open the packaging to reveal 250 gleaming rivets that turned out to be for a helicopter elsewhere in the region. I wondered who would be the most irritated, us or the helicopter crew who had had a similarly disappointing discovery of our relay; but I needn't have worried as the ACC made it most clear where his greatest irritation lay.

On another occasion we needed seven separate items to make up a kit for a specific task. One box arrived with information on the outside showing it to be one of the items and we set it aside in anticipation of the other six. We waited, and waited and eventually contacted the source to chase the remaining six items. Without acknowledging any irony, the source confirmed that they had put all seven items in the box of the largest item but hadn't thought to identify this on the outside, meaning that we had the spares all along.

The play-hard ethic kicked in particularly strongly whenever anyone went home on R&R. Inevitably, their return would be marked by some prank or other. For example, I cannot confirm or deny my involvement in turning my warrant officer's (WO) office entirely pink, but for the full effect it was important to do a complete job including chair cover—our survival equipment section were mean seamstresses—and fluffy pink picture frames and my sanction was needed. However, this only raised the bar for my own R&R and I dreaded that return.

The base commander and I had the best cars on the detachment, not because of our status but because we occasionally had to entertain VIPs such as government ministers and senior officers. These cars were kept immaculate not only because of their main purpose, but because it was also the local law that cars had to be kept clean. I was in the habit of giving the car to the troops for the runs between domestic and technical sites and continued to walk to and from work across the desert with my WO after he had forgiven me. When it was my turn to go home for a week's R&R I played safe, or so I thought, and gave my pristine Toyota Prado to the loyal sergeant who ran Mechanical Transport Flight and who also shared my surname. I couldn't have made a worst choice as Sergeant Phillips was a seasoned prankster who had developed a very trusted relationship with the local car hire company. Hence, on my return a different car awaited. It was something about 20 years old, on its last legs and in a dire condition, covered in authentic poo and foliage. Reacting would have been futile, so I kept the car with gritted teeth for a week—which is about how long it took me to clean it unaided—before the troops were forced to return my real car as the prime minister was coming to visit.

JIM'S NOT SO PRISTINE HIRE CAR. (JIM PHILLIPS)

One evening a Tristar was returning from Afghanistan and we learnt that a couple of celebrities were on board, having visited for the Pride of Britain Awards. When we learned who they were, I called the physical training instructor and had him assemble all of the sports kit that he could possibly spare. As the aircraft stopped, we raced onboard to, respectfully, ask Gary Lineker and Freddie Flintoff to sign appropriate bits of sports kit. The two could not have been more accommodating of our hurried intervention, and many of the base personnel were rewarded in the following days by signed kit. The aircraft would be resuming its journey as soon as it had refuelled but it was at this point that Freddie made a request. At that time he lived in Abu Dhabi, which was only about 300 miles away, and wondered if we could help him to fly there directly rather than to return to the UK by military aircraft and then return on a civil flight. Of course I volunteered, not knowing the unspoken complication that would be caused by Freddie having never officially arrived in Oman. Moreover, he was injured and was on crutches. Nevertheless, sometime after midnight I drove Freddie to Muscat International Airport in my recently returned Prado. As he attempted to buy a ticket, the lack of arrival documentation became apparent. Not to worry, the airport had an office that can resolve such issues, but it was at the other end of the airport. With me carrying Freddie's heavy bag, and him swinging on crutches, we began a series of dashes up and down the airport attempting to resolve the arrival issue, and then buy a ticket. These dashes became more frantic as the flight time approached and, while I suspected Freddie had never trained so hard, I was certain that I hadn't. A ticket was produced with just a few minutes to go and Freddie made the flight. Despite intense provocation, he never lost his cool and I thank him for that. Naturally, with little sleep, the next day proved long and taxing. That is just part of the endless fun that deployments offer.

CHAPTER 15

My First Backseat Trip: Being in the Right Place at the Right Time

Chris Boden, wanting to follow in his father's footsteps, set his mind on a career in the RAF from the age of 14. He joined in 1976 in the aircraft mechanical electrical trade. After a first tour at RAF St Athan servicing equipment for the Vulcan, he served at Coltishall. Initially, he worked on Sea Kings and then moved into the electrical bay before finishing on No. 54(F) Squadron, servicing Jaguars. Tours at Coningsby and Leeming with the Tornado F3 followed before he left the RAF in 2000 having served for nearly 24 years. He returned to the Jaguar at BAe Systems Warton before moving to Marconi Communications involved in military projects. After a switch of role, he began working for Bombardier on the Voyager trains project and remains associated with the railways as the service delivery manager at Arriva Train Care. He maintains contact with the RAF community acting as the secretary for the XI(F) Squadron Association.

It was sometime in late April 1982, after the invasion of South Georgia by the Argentinians. I was deployed with a small Jaguar detachment to Royal Air Force Gibraltar (Gib). Something political had kicked off, possibly connected with the Falklands invasion. There was a hint that the Spanish were threatening 'the Rock' by carrying out simulated air attacks and Margaret Thatcher

160

expressed strong concerns over the vulnerability of the airport and garrison. As it turned out the Spanish were actually conducting some sort of amphibious exercise but with the Spanish air force as back-up. The UK response was to deploy two Jaguar GR.1s and a T2 to Gib.

I was a junior technician serving as an aircraft electrician in the 'lekkie bay' on the Electrical Engineering Squadron (EES) at RAF Coltishall, maintaining Jaguar and Sea King electrical components. By 1982 I had been in the RAF for over five years and had been in post at Coltishall for around 18 months. I'd been on a few detachments, here and there, and this was my second trip to Gib. I'd also been deployed, mainly for exercises, with all three Jaguar squadrons based at Coltishall. I'd been to Decimomannu in Sardinia with No. 41 Squadron and Tirstrup in Denmark with Nos. 6 and 54 Squadrons. With the permission of my chief technician and the EES flight commander, I maintained contact with the squadrons with the sole intention of continuing my flight-line training competency that I'd gained with No. 41 Squadron, as I wasn't particularly happy working in the bay. After all, I'd joined the RAF to work on aircraft and, although the bay was a learning curve, the lifestyle wasn't for me. With short trips away I had a taste of squadron life and was hoping for a posting out of EES as soon as possible. Volunteering for any, and all, of the squadron detachments, advertising myself as 'EES bay support', I was eventually allowed to join the 'sharp end', albeit for short stints at a time. This, along with a lot of general applications, known as gen apps, led to my permanent posting onto 54(F) Squadron.

The Spanish air force had been testing the RAF response to potential intrusions by operating their American-built Northrop F-5 trainers into Gibraltar airspace; a show of strength, I suppose. Spain was not part of NATO at that time so the UK politicians decided to deploy Coltishall-based Jaguars to Gib for several weeks. I was lucky enough to be selected to go on that deployment. I cannot remember which squadron was tasked but I'd like to think it was No. 54 Squadron which was to be my future posting. I also can't remember whether or not we deployed with aircraft that had received the over-wing Sidewinder missile modification. This allowed Jaguars to carry self-defence missiles without losing under-wing carrying capacity that was needed for bombs and electronic warfare equipment. I knew that the modification was in the pipeline and, as the Jaguars were expected to hold QRA, it made sense that the pilots would be able to defend themselves with something other than their 30-mm Aden cannons.

Once we arrived in Gib and by then working on the flight line, I was expected to carry out normal day-to-day aircraft servicing—the usual before-flight, after-flight, turnround and see-off/see-in duties. We were launching jets daily, some as active QRA responses but also a few routine sorties. We were playing the Spanish at their own game. I was working with a good crowd who let me do my fair share but also allowed me to gain more experience, clearing defects and undertaking fault finding. This experience was useful as I knew I would soon be attending a Jaguar 'Q' Course at RAF Lossiemouth.

We had one particular jet which the aircrew, known to us as 'jockeys', had managed to break quite early during the deployment. The fault seemed to happen only in flight, but soon it became apparent that it was only occurring when the jet touched down for either a roller landing or its final landing. The problem seemed to be with the fuel-transfer system, with the jockey reporting anomalies in transfer indications. Once the jet had landed, the refuelling process just would not work until a fuse in the roof of the nosewheel undercarriage bay was replaced. Replacing fuses in the nosewheel bay was never a straightforward process as it involved winching the main 28-volt battery out and then back in. The battery pack was installed in the bay with its own, built-in, hand-operated winch that made installation a little bit easier. However, the design of the battery box and winch installation was such that it was only intended to be used for removal and replacement. The issue was that every 28 days it was inspected as part of the maintenance schedule that was deep rooted in the rules and regulations for the servicing and maintenance of RAF aircraft. This occurred regardless of whether it needed changing or not. So, this battery was going to be raised and lowered more times in a week than was envisaged would be needed in a year … OK, I'm probably exaggerating.

The offending fuse was replaced and a full calibration of the fuel-transfer system was carried out involving a refuel, a defuel and a further refuel, before the jet was declared serviceable. The jet launched again and flew a full mission without a problem until it arrived back in the circuit for a 'touch and go', or roller landing. On overshoot, the jockey, once again, reported the same issues with the system. At this point us lekkies, the airframe and propulsion chaps, (riggers and sooties), all came to the same conclusion that the transfer fault was something to do with the fact that when the main landing gear touched down, the fuse was probably blowing.

After extensive fault diagnosis, including replacing numerous components both in the fuel-transfer system, just in case, and the undercarriage system, we thought we'd fixed it. The jet had been jacked up and powered up and the undercarriage had been raised and lowered numerous times, operating the weight-on-ground switches. We were at the point where we were absolutely sure everything was now working correctly. We had even checked out the wiring on either side of the fuse so that we didn't have to keep winching the battery pack in and out. That was it, job done; everything worked. The aircraft was lowered off the jacks, and another fuel calibration was carried out using the internal transfer system to pump the fuel to the bowser.

The next check was an air test. The same jockey took the jet for a spin as he was by now, intimately familiar with the problem. He had absolutely no issues during the air test until he undertook a roller landing. Hey presto, the original fault returned. The jet landed, taxied in and was marshalled to a stop and the engines shut down. It was my exasperating task to winch out that damned battery, only to find the fuse had blown again. In went another fuse, back went the battery. It's a good job we had a few in stock in the detachment kit.

A serious amount of head scratching ensued, including many more conversations and discussions with the engineering experts back at Coltishall but no one could come up with anything that we hadn't already attempted. Somewhere in all of the debate, a decision was made that it would be safe to fly back to Coltishall as there was no point attempting more repairs in Gib. Someone (me), however, would have to teach two of the aircrew how to replace the fuse in the nosewheel bay, including how to winch the battery out and in. The route back to Coltishall would, definitely, involve at least one transit stop at Nice in France for two jets. The sick jet would be escorted home, for part of the journey, in case there were unexpected problems. That would mean at least one change of fuse during the turnround. We couldn't predict if any more stops might be necessary, just as we couldn't guarantee to find any knowledgeable, Jaguar-trained assistance from the French air force staff en route.

With the task of training the pilots firmly on my doorstep, I could not escape. As most RAF groundcrew would know, aircrew don't like to be given extra jobs and all these chaps had been trained to do, other than to fly the jet, was basic flight servicing and refuelling. This would allow them to operate the jets in locations where experienced groundcrew might not be available. I explained the battery box configuration and how to use the winching mechanism. It isn't the easiest of tasks to operate the kit on your own, and even worse when the victims are experienced aircrew who think they already know everything there is to know about the aircraft. Once the battery was lowered, I removed the fuse panel cover, showed them the relevant fuse and marked the area around it with a grease pencil so that they couldn't miss it. Removal of the fuse was self-explanatory and, although I was starting to enjoy myself, given the responsibility and importance of making sure the two chaps understood, I didn't get too carried away. I'll admit, however, I became a little overconfident and sarcastic occasionally. Having replaced the fuse and refitted the fuse panel cover, I showed them how to raise and install the battery assembly to finish the job. Now it was their turn but it was obvious they weren't particularly interested, although both had sussed it out after several goes, with the odd hint from me.

The end of the deployment was looming and decisions had to be made as to exactly how the 'not fully serviceable' jet was going to make it home to Norfolk. More conversations with Coltishall ensued, especially with the squadron commander and OC Engineering Wing back at base. I suppose to authorise the jet to take off from Gib, make a 'pit stop' at Nice, and then safely to make its way back to Coltishall, was a significant decision when made from hundreds of miles away. It became quite obvious that the powers that be wanted the aircraft back home as soon as possible.

To make matters worse, rumours began floating around about a little friction beginning 'down south'. A Falkland Islands Task Force was forming but there were comments from folk asking, "where the hell are the Falkland Islands?"

The aircrew, meanwhile, were still practising with the battery and winch, and were rapidly coming around to the idea that they were not happy about replacing the fuse themselves. I was let into a little secret that they might fly someone home in the back seat of the twin-stick Jaguar, the T2. On top of that, we were to send a small contingent of groundcrew over to Nice for a 'just in case' scenario. I was a little excited at the prospect but thought that I was unlikely to be considered, as I was lucky to be there at all being a 'Klingon', as we support personnel were known, from the lekkie bay. Other squadron groundcrew members had flown in the T2 before and would, more likely, have in-date, flight medicals which were needed to fly in the back. Of course, I was really hoping for a back-seat flight but a trip to the South of France would be brilliant too as I'd never been there. Anyway, whatever the outcome, it was time to start packing for the journey back to the UK.

Suddenly and with little warning, my dream became a reality when I was told to report to the medical centre for a 'fit to fly' medical. It turned out that, due to trade boundaries in those days, an aircraft electrician would need to deploy to Nice and that there were only three electricians available and competent to carry out the task; a sergeant, another J/T and me. The sergeant was not fit to fly and the other J/T, as a permanent squadron member, had to remain on Gib, just for eventualities that might be encountered. Off I trotted to the medical centre to be given the usual general fitness checks: ears, nose and throat, lungs and breathing, checking I could pop my ears by swallowing or blowing with my nose pinched, blood pressure checks and, for whatever reason, height and weight checks. After what felt like ages, but probably only lasted around three quarters of an hour, I walked out guarding with my life, the piece of paper with the medical officer's signature and a stamp that stated I was fit to fly in a fast jet. I would be limited to no more than Mach 1 and 1.5 g but I figured I could live with that. I felt like I'd won big money on a horse race.

Back at the sharp end, I tried to be as nonchalant and calm as possible as I knew I was bound to be in for some ridicule from the lineys and I didn't

A JAGUAR T2 SIMILAR TO THE ONE FLOWN BY CHRIS BODEN ON HIS FIRST FLIGHT.
(CHRIS BODEN)

want to wind anyone up. I'd had a good detachment and wanted to end it on good terms. As it was, I did get a bit of banter but not as bad as I expected.

Once that had calmed down and, with quite a number of comments about how much beer I'd have to buy, I was grabbed by one of the aircrew to be fitted for a flying suit and helmet. I was also fitted for an immersion suit which I hoped I would not have to wear given the warm temperatures on the Rock. Despite the careful attention, the only things that fitted properly were the flying boots and gloves. Everything else was the 'detachment spare' and didn't fit properly at all. I'm glad to say that the flight plan would not take us over water so I need not have worried about the immersion suit.

The flight was planned for the following day with an overnight stop in Nice for both crews, including me. The day after, assuming everything went according to plan, would see the single-seat jet on its way home to Coltishall with my jet staying on the ground until the other was past the point of no return. At that point it could not return to Nice. We—my pilot and I—would remain at Nice until everyone was satisfied that the faulty jet was safely en route and then launch for our return trip to Gib. There was not a great deal of time to prepare, especially on my part.

I had heard stories that the back seater operated the navigation systems. For training sorties, the instructor would normally be in the back with the pupil in the front seat but for groundcrew trips, known as 'jollies', the pilot was always in the front. Ultimately, with the rear seat set higher than the front, the groundcrew had a much better view. Many times on the flight line at Coltishall and on detachment, I had prepared a jet, including setting up the navigation and weapon-aiming sub-system (NAVWASS), and had played with the moving map. I never thought I'd end up having to do it for real and, especially, not on my first trip. I had been up in the odd Jet Provost, a jet trainer, but only on an air experience flight and had never considered them to be fast jets. As it happened, I would be flying with an experienced pilot and, in any case, we were only on a ferry trip and would be escorting the other jet into Nice. I had thought about being really cheeky and ask that I go in the front seat so that the pilot could access the navigational controls but decided not to push my luck and let nature take its course.

The next morning I was up bright and early, having gone to sleep knackered from worrying about what would happen and how much kit I needed to pack into the ammo tank bay for the trip. A paperback was needed, or so I thought, along with the obligatory packed meals from the mess. With the early morning pleasantries over and a cursory wander around the jet to make sure everything was OK, I shoved my small amount of baggage into the ammo tank bay and climbed, extremely nervously and apprehensively, into the rear cockpit. My pilot strapped me in, making sure the ejection seat pins were correctly stowed in the receptacles before being strapped in himself. I'd had a quick brief about the pins and the possibility of ejecting but it would be easy to forget such an important thing with everything else going on. This was something that I'd taken for granted working on the jets and routinely strapping in the aircrew. It was not something to think about if the seat was needed in an emergency.

Starting the microturbo auxiliary power unit and engines concentrated my

JAGUAR PILOT CREWING OUT.
(GRAHAM HAYNES)

mind but I decided to sit back, keep as calm as possible, and let my jockey finish his normal routine. It seemed strange watching the groundcrew outside talking to both jockeys, going through the routine checks and the 'Jag dance'. Folks reading this from the Jaguar and Tornado communities will know exactly what I mean. It was the operation of the flight controls by the jockey in response to hand signals from the groundcrew and vice-versa. With checks on both jets complete, we were seen off, marshalled to the taxiway and on towards the runway ready for launch.

At the end of the runway, I could hear the aircrew talking on the radio, and the single-seat jet rolled first. After about ten seconds and with a great increase in power, with the man in the front talking me through it, the brakes were off and we were thundering down the runway in the direction of Spain. As we lifted off, my bodily sensations went with it. It was absolutely wonderful and not easy to describe to anyone, apart from those that have experienced it themselves. Once airborne I was able to settle down and enjoy the ride. It was time to get the camera out, take photographs of the other jet and some scenery. Of course, I had to have a shot of myself with the helmet visors, both clear and dark, up and down.

It was just like *Top Gun* except that the film was still around four years away. Then it was head out of the clouds and back to reality. My jockey was talking to me, asking me to perform functions in the cockpit, talking me through stuff as necessary. There was plenty of time available to interact with the pilot of the other jet, mainly by hand signals, but also time to take more photos, although I had to force myself to keep these to a minimum. It was 35-mm film in those days, I'm afraid, as there were no digital cameras in 1982. I'm sure something might have been in development at the time but I couldn't afford it, whatever it was. Unbelievably for me, it was quite a boring journey once I'd got over the initial excitement and I spent most of my time looking out through the canopy at the other jet. I had hoped to have a bit of a play but this was a ferry flight after all. We had a full fuel load, internal and the droppers (drop tanks) but I was told later that we had more than enough fuel as the transit distance was well within our endurance.

We landed at Nice a few hours later and on landing, the pilot used aerodynamic braking to avoid using the brake parachute. This is where the nose is held off after touchdown, using the wings like speed brakes to slow the jet down. It was yet another fantastic experience that I wasn't prepared for and it was interesting to see and feel. By that stage, I was absolutely elated as you can imagine. Once we taxied to a halt, guided by the French marshallers, I climbed out of the cockpit but only once those red ejection seat pins were back in the seat.

The French groundcrew were doing their stuff, including refuelling both jets but I had to persuade them not to refuel the single-seater until I'd had chance to lower the battery to change the fuse. With it replaced and everything put back the way I found it, I let the French guys carry on. I seem to remember a few weird looks but I suppose they assumed I was aircrew, dressed the way I was in a flying suit. I think it eventually dawned on them when they watched me perform two after-flights on the jets with the two pilots standing around nattering. At least I didn't have to do the refuelling and I didn't really fancy that in my nice new suit. I did, however, help with seeing the aircraft towed into a hangar and, although we had no covers for the intakes and exhausts, indoors was the safest place away from the elements.

I spent the night in the officers' accommodation on base with the two aircrew, told to keep quiet if anyone asked. As it happens, no one did, especially as we were still dressed in flying suits. I had 'accidentally' forgotten to carry my beret with me. The room wasn't that great anyway and I've never insulted RAF transit blocks since.

We were up the next morning around 09:00 and I was expecting to earn my trip back to Gib by performing two before-flights but was told to stick to the basics and let the French chaps do it. In any case the aircrew would have done their normal pre-flight walk round before we climbed in. The plan for the day was to launch the single-seater on its own at 1100 and to wait for it to cross a predetermined point before we launched back to Gib. This is exactly what happened and we were airborne at around 14:00. My pilot had been to air traffic control, talking with the relevant agencies to ensure the single-seat jet was at the halfway position and that we could be on our way. All went to plan.

On the return journey I played with the controls after having dropped hints for well over 12 hours. Although I was allowed a bit of 'stick time' it was just the basics as it was again a ferry flight, and aerobatics were frowned upon in the French airways—and with droppers fitted. Landing back at Gib, using the brake chute this time, I was surprised how tired I felt. Of course, I got a load of abuse—let's call it banter—from the other groundcrew, including how much it was going to cost me in the NAAFI that night. I was thanked by the detachment commander but I seem to remember the conversation went more along the lines of me thanking him for allowing me, a Klingon, to be part of the operation.

The following day, flight operations continued as normal, albeit we were one jet down. I heard a rumour, that later turned out to be true, that the faulty jet landed safely back at Coltishall without any faults relating to the fuel transfer issue. The fuse hadn't blown. That generated more jibes in my direction as to how I'd fixed it at Nice but not in Gib. I immediately offered my professional services to fly back to Coltishall in the back seat of the T-Bird to assist with the fault replication and diagnosis. I may have used the term 'electricians' magic'. I can't repeat what was said.

CHAPTER 16

The Reds and Beyond

Chris Wilson served eight years in the Royal Air Force as an airframe engineering technician including two years as groundcrew for the Red Arrows, working first and second line maintenance as an airframe mechanic. His posting meant plenty of travel and the opportunity to fly in the back seat of Hawk jets. His last four years of service, after qualifying as an airframe fitter, were spent with XI (F) Sqn working on Tornado F3 aircraft at RAF Leeming, once again presenting the opportunity of travel with exercises in Alaska, Florida, Oman and a stint in Saudi for Operation Resinate South. He retired in 2004 and became the managing director of Jet Art Aviation.

I developed an interest in military aircraft from an early age. It began one Christmas when a Matchbox 1:72 scale model Harrier GR3 appeared under the tree. I was captivated by the artwork on the box featuring a camouflaged, dart-like machine flying along at high speed, bristling with ordnance and the background all a blur. I distinctly remember sitting at the kitchen table covered in toxic glue and paint, sticking on the rocket pods, 1,000-lb bombs and cannon pods. This planted the seed and I caught the aviation bug. At the time I must have been about five or six and I had no idea that in 30 years I would be living an aviation geek's dream; firing a Harrier up in the backyard and fitting rocket and cannon pods onto my very own Harrier.

Trips to Mildenhall Air Show in the 1980s became an annual highlight from around the age of ten. The biggest military air show in Europe really was something to behold compared to the air shows of today. The selection of aircraft on display in the static park seemed to go on for miles, and flying displays from classic British jets such as the Blackburn Buccaneer, English Electric Lightning and Canberra, Avro Vulcan as well as US aircraft like the F-117 stealth fighter, SR-71 Blackbird and F-4 Phantom gave me a real motivation that a career in military aviation was going to be something for me. I saw my very first Red Arrows display at Mildenhall and in the early 1990s, after Operation Desert Storm, I would meet some of the Gulf War pilots who seemed to have, almost, celebrity-like status.

As a teenager I wasn't overly academic at school, but I excelled in technology and practical lessons. One day, while waiting outside to go into lessons, a pair of Jet Provost T5s flew low and fast, directly over the rear of the school playing field, and it's a memory that's stayed with me ever since; "Wow! How cool was that! I want to do that." I was queuing up to go into lessons and the trainee fighter pilots were getting to play in jets, flying fast down the Warfedale Valley. *Take Off* and *Airplane Magazine* became my weekly read and, although I didn't realise it at the time, thumbing through the technical profiles and studying every detail was a form of self-education for my career ahead. This interest naturally progressed into joining the Air Training Corps at the age of 13. My very first flight in an aircraft was in a Vigilant powered-glider from RAF Linton-on-Ouse. The flight lasted only 20 minutes but it was like a roller coaster ride. The pilot, keen to make my first flight in an aircraft a memorable one, demonstrated stall turns and other similar manoeuvres. It was safe to say I really enjoyed my first experience of flight and we returned to Linton with me grinning like a Cheshire cat.

Our cadet squadron commanding officer (CO) was very good at scrounging extra flights. His cadets had air experience flights in de Havilland Chipmunks and later, in its replacement, the Scottish Aviation Bulldog, at RAF Finningley. Trips became a regular occurrence, even though it meant missing school for a day, which was no drama for someone who didn't overly enjoy being stuck in a classroom. The Air Training Corps mixed education, drill and classroom-based lessons with fun stuff like shooting and adventure training. Every summer we enjoyed an annual camp to an RAF station. My first was at RAF Boulmer where the highlight was a flight in the back of a No. 202 Squadron Sea King rescue helicopter at low level along the Northumberland coastline, with the loadmaster in the back hanging out of the door, waving to people on the beaches below. Other camps included RAF Marham with the Tornado GR1 and Canberra PR9s and

RAF Lossiemouth with Tornado GR1 and Jaguars. I had no idea, as a young and very green air cadet, that many years later, as a civilian engineer running my own company, I would return to Lossiemouth to dismantle and extract my very own Tornado GR1 having just purchased the jet as surplus equipment from the MoD.

At 16 I applied for a flying scholarship and attended the Officer and Aircrew Selection Centre at RAF Cranwell. On the back of that I was awarded a navigation scholarship which entailed going to RAF Turnhouse, now Edinburgh Airport, for two weeks intensive flying in Chipmunks. I didn't quite make the grade for the flying scholarship but the navigation course was good enough for me. The instructors were old-school RAF boys who had flown Lightnings, Hunters, Buccaneers and Phantoms and were keeping their hand in by flying the Chippies. It was clear they were massively experienced. The course was hard work but good fun, flying inverted along the Forth Road Bridge, experiencing aerobatics, finishing with a break to land. The CO of the Air Experience Flight arranged a trip for me in a Bulldog with the Turnhouse University Air Squadron (UAS). Some of the other students flew in Gazelle helicopters which were visiting the base, but my additional flight was to be with the squadron leader running the UAS. On return, when asked what we got up to by the CO of the AEF and if I had enjoyed the trip, "Yes, it was awesome," was my response. "We did practice forced-landings, simulated engine failures, aerobatics, oh and we did spinning." His eyes widened. "We're not supposed to spin with cadets in the aircraft … probably best not mention that to anyone."

After the two weeks at Turnhouse I was totally hooked on flying and as soon as I got back to Yorkshire I made the application to join the RAF as aircrew. Unfortunately—or fortunately depending how you look at it—it was not to be, and an engineering-based career path was on the horizon for me. The government policy 'Options for Change' was introduced in the early 1990s which saw a major restructuring of the UK armed forces at the end of the Cold War. That, combined with a lack of mathematic skill, sealed my fate. I passed the interviews which was surprising as I have a strong Yorkshire accent, but unless you had the aptitude of a Jedi, the chance of getting into the RAF as aircrew at that time, was pretty slim. A few weeks later, a letter arrived saying that I had been unsuccessful this time around but noted that I could re-apply in a year. Alternatively, my performance had suggested I would make a good airman. I was at a crossroads, having just finished my A levels but, as a back-up plan, I had a place secured at university to study for a BSc in Geography; or I could join the RAF now as an airman. At the time it was a bit of a downer, I was working full-time in a pub and I didn't really understand that not every career in aviation involves being a pilot. However, being an airman was the next best thing and it meant I could work with aircraft instead of pulling pints. In reality it was the path I needed to be on. The bottom line was that I was better at fixing my bike than riding it, and the same applied to aircraft.

After basic training at Halton, it was off to No. 1 School of Technical Training at the Air Frame Training Squadron (AFTS) at RAF Cosford for an airframe mechanics course. I knuckled down, got my head in the books and found it really interesting as well as great fun. I was living and working with a great bunch of people, pushing the boundaries and always up to mischief. The golden rule we lived by was not getting caught. The banter was always fierce. My course lasted a year and ended with training on live Jet Provosts being taxied around by instructors with the students doing the marshalling and working the flight line. This I found exciting in comparison to the previous classroom activities. These JP5s were the exact type of aircraft that I had seen fly over my school playing field a few years earlier. Nothing prepared a student for going onto a front-line squadron like standing in front of a fast-taxiing aircraft which was making lots of noise, the jet wash coming out from the back. Twelve months later, I had to marshal a C-130 Hercules, in-close, next to a hangar and then marshal the aircraft backwards with the props in reverse pitch so that the 'movers' could load lots of kit into the rear ramp. To this day, that is still one of the most daunting things I have had to do, and without the training I received on the airfield at Cosford, I wouldn't have been prepared adequately for that experience when it eventually arrived. Fast forward 20 years later and I ended up back at Cosford as a civilian, having bought nine of the very Jet Provosts I was trained on.

I graduated from my course as 'top trainee' with a certificate of merit for displaying outstanding ability. I was called into the boss's office along with the other top-scoring student and informed that we had been chosen to be posted to the Red Arrows. Normally groundcrew must apply for 'the Reds' but due to a shortage of suitable applicants from the airframe mechanics trade, the personnel management agency—the human resources department of the RAF—asked Cosford to pick the best, most suitable candidates. I was excited beyond words. This was the first time a mechanic had been posted straight from trade training onto the Red Arrows. It was also the first time a female engineer was to be on the team. Lisa Walker, who was picked alongside me, went on to be the first female 'Circus team' member. She would be one of the engineers who flew to the air shows in the back of the Hawk jets.

My two-year tour as groundcrew on the Reds went by so quickly yet look-ing back, it was the perfect apprenticeship for the career that was to lie ahead. There were far too many adventures and experiences to cover in this chapter, but the posting got off to an amazing start. Immediately, after completion of a very rapid Hawk line training course, came a detachment to Cyprus within the first few weeks of arriving on the team. The Cyprus detachment, known as Exercise Spring Hawk was to take advantage of the good flying weather in the Mediterranean so the pilots could get up to speed before the display season. Cyprus was to be just one of the many international trips to come over the next two years with the pinnacle being the 1999 Far East tour, country-hopping all the way to Malaysia and back with visits to Italy, Germany, Jordan, Egypt, Saudi Arabia, Qatar, the United Arab Emirates, India, Thailand and Malaysia. The furthest point on the tour was the holiday island of Penang and finally Langkawi for LIMA '99 (Langkawi International Maritime & Aerospace exhibition). It was there where an international military trade show gave the pilots the opportunity to show off the BAe Systems Hawk to potential buyers, predominantly foreign government officials. Other air show participants that year in Langkawi were parked just at the end of the Red Arrows line: a pair of Russian Sukhoi SU-27P 'Flankers'.

It became very clear to me that the main purpose of the 1999 tour was to showcase the best of British, with the pilots and groundcrew being ambassa-dors for British industry, flying the flag for 'UK PLC'. A lot of the tour had been funded by BAe Systems, hopefully to win international orders. To be fair, it was an incredible way of demonstrating how good the Hawk is by flying 11 single-en-gined aircraft, including two spare jets, halfway around the world with mini-mal failures, and then being able to put up nine jets for a display, time and time again. I later found out on my next posting that Tornados were far less reliable. The Hawk in comparison, was mechanically bulletproof.

The biggest eye opener for me on tour was on Langkawi Island. At the end of one display, a group of foreign dignitaries came to the flight line to see the aircraft, escorted by the company representatives and the UK ambassador who was one of the visitors. We later found out that another of the group was a foreign defence minister. He cut the tour guide dead and marched over to the ground-crew, picking out a liney at random, taking him to the far end of the flight line for a private viewing of a Hawk, totally out of ear shot of the entourage. The look of sheer panic on the BAe Systems rep's face, knowing that a potential multi-million-pound sales deal was now in the hands of a junior technician, was priceless. I learnt a lot about business from that small incident. Firstly, the person on the shop floor, putting in the oil and cleaning the windscreen, is just as important as the person wearing the smart suit in charge of sales. They can have the same, if not bigger, influence on a sale than anyone in the marketing department getting paid rock star wages to try and sell a product. Secondly, as a buyer of aircraft and parts, I always speak to the mechanics and back-room staff wherever possible. That way I get the real facts and an honest appraisal as the pushy salespeople never really give you a true representation of what's on offer.

On the Far East tour, I was a member of the support crew flying in the back of a C-130, doing a mix of flight servicing and fixing snags. I was also on the Dye Team whenever necessary. We were responsible for the equipment that produced the coloured smoke, so reminiscent of the Reds. The groundcrew members who were members of the Circus looked after their dedicated aircraft, flying in the back cockpit to every show with their pilot and on the transit flights. On tour, once we had landed, I predominantly looked after Red 1's aircraft because the Circus leader, a chief technician who normally flew in the rear seat of the lead aircraft, took care of all the paperwork, coordinating the books and raising job cards for all nine aeroplanes. Occasionally, I looked after Red 9's aircraft as the JEngO flew in the back of this jet and generally did not service his own aircraft unless he really had to. My role for the rest of the 1999 season was as 'reserve Circus'. That meant I flew in the back of the Hawk and that was something that I loved.

Without doubt, the best thing about a posting to the Reds was the opportunity to fly. With a little bit of lady luck and some hard work, I had been posted to the only place in the air force where a very junior, and let's be honest, inexperienced, airframe mechanic would actually get to fly in the back of a fast jet, not just occasionally, but on a regular basis. My first flight in a Hawk was as a 20-year-old leading aircraftman not long after arriving. At the time, and it's done rather differently now, the management were keen to get any potential Circus candidates up in a jet for a bit of a shakedown flight to see if you actually liked flying in a jet. The g force and being turned upside down didn't suit everyone. It also made sure that you didn't get air sick. If you liked it, you could then ask to be considered for the Circus who were picked by the groundcrew senior management with the pilots having a big say. Obviously, the pilots didn't want to be stuck for a season with somebody who wasn't suitable, or in a situation where there could be a personality clash. If you were lucky enough to be picked you received extra training, had medical examinations and tests to ensure you were fit to fly in a fast jet on a regular basis.

My first flight in a Hawk was in XX306, which now stands as the gate guard for the Reds at RAF Scampton. Nothing makes you feel old quite like an aircraft you worked on in the service being put out to pasture on a gate. After a Category Two medical, a trip to the medical centre at Cranwell—which is where the Reds were based in the late 1990s—confirmed I was fit to fly. A further trip to the survival equipment section followed where I was fitted with a helmet, mask and g suit, before reporting to flight operations to watch a video, describing how to eject—just in case the need arose. Straight after that, it was out onto the flight line to be strapped into the jet by my fellow lineys.

My pilot for the trip was team supervisor Wing Commander Johnston and our task of the day was a pod-handling test. Smoke pods were, occasionally, changed if there was a leak or if scheduled maintenance required that a pod be replaced. The Red Arrows' Hawks carry a smoke pod which was similar in profile to the Aden cannon gun pod carried by training aircraft. It was fitted to the centre-line station under the Hawk's belly and was filled with diesel which produced the white smoke. Dye produced the red and blue smoke. The dye/derv mixture was pumped, under pressure, from engine bleed air and, when the pilot selected buttons on the stick, smoke cocks opened in the tail cone allowing the mixture to emerge from the back of the aircraft into the jet efflux where it instantly vaporised to form the famous red, white and blue smoke. Each time a pod was fitted to another jet or replaced, a handling test was required to ensure the jet flew in a straight line and that the smoke system worked as advertised. Smoke pods were handmade and each aircraft might handle differently so pods were sometimes changed from one aircraft to another if handling considerations dictated it was necessary.

My flight lasted 40 minutes and having got the pod-handling test part out the way, acrobatics was the order of the day. Loops, rolls, high g turns followed and I even got to take control of the aircraft on what turned out to be an extreme flying lesson, with a very experienced fast-jet pilot as my instructor. Flying in a fast jet was something that I had always wanted to do and my first experience of the Hawk did not disappoint. I flew with the wing commander on multiple occasions thereafter, on air tests and on a trip to RAF Valley and back for his simulator slot. On one occasion, when I really wanted to go on the post-primary servicing air test, he seemed genuinely disappointed that I was not joining him.

"How come you are not joining me this time," he asked.

"Not enough manpower sir. I wanted to go but they wouldn't let me."

I saw off his jet for the solo air test.

The roles for the 1999 display season were announced at a Thursday night beer-call in 'The Bowl', the bowling alley at RAF Cranwell. I was, at first, a little disappointed to have been chosen as a reserve, rather than having my own dedicated pilot and aircraft to look after. In reality, it ended up providing a more varied experience, flying in different positions rather than just the one. During the 1999 season I flew as a passenger in the back of Red 2, 5, 7, and 8 as well as on air tests, engine tests, ferry flights and for a practice display in Cyprus in the back of Red 5's jet. What a phenomenal experience. Sometimes, you would get to fly three or four times during a week, especially in the display season and that is more flights than many front-line squadron pilots get today. In between the flying was a lot of hard work on the ground including flight servicing, pulling early morning shifts, late nights and, not forgetting, lots of partying when the working day was over.

My last trip in a Hawk was a ferry flight to St Athan in South Wales which, at the time, was the RAF's major servicing hub. The flight was with Flight Lieutenant Jas Hawker who was new to the team as the 'FNG'—I'll leave the translation to you. He was new for the 2000 season, flying the Red 2 slot. The task for the day was to take a Hawk back to 'Saints' as the paint was coming off after a post-major servicing respray. Looking back, it was quite a responsibility for a young airframe mechanic. Once landed, I turned and refuelled the jet, showed the civilian painters and a mass of officers around the aircraft, highlighting all the paint defects. Once done, I conducted the pilot's walk round. The only place I have ever heard of the pilot not doing a walk round themselves was on the Reds. This was incredibly trusting of the aircrew who just turned up and climbed into their jet, having entrusted the groundcrew to complete their checks, including taking the miniature detonation cord (MDC) pins out! I then coordinated the paperwork and the Form 700 which was normally done by a senior NCO, and handed the Form 725, flight servicing certificate, to the SNCO in charge of Visiting Aircraft Squadron (VAS) so it could be posted on to RAF Cranwell. Strange this might seem but it was in case the aircraft crashed on the way back to base so that we could prove the work had been done. The rest of the Form 700 was carried in a canvas stowage behind the ejection seat in the rear cockpit. All in all, it was a huge responsibility for a 21-year-old, being trusted to work on his own with no supervision.

Talking to the lads on VAS who saw in the jet, they didn't know that groundcrew flew in the back of the Hawks. It turned out we had all been through

Cosford at similar times but they had been posted to Saints which they viewed as a jail sentence. I felt very humbled and incredibly privileged to be doing what was, in comparison, a dream job. We took off heading back to Cranwell for an uneventful transit flight. Jas Hawker was very keen to practise his break-to-land on return to Cranwell and I got the impression that getting that just right, was more difficult than it looked. He had been the youngest ever pilot to fly a Tornado and went on to fly in the synchro pair before becoming the leader in 2007, as a wing commander, taking the Red Arrows on overseas tours to the USA, the Middle and Far East and completing over 500 public displays.

Eighteen years later, the office phone rang at Jet Art and Jas Hawker was on the line. Having recently left the air force, one of his business ventures was as an aircraft broker and he had a client wanting a Harrier to join a private collection in the USA. It just so happened that we had such an aircraft in stock having spent the last three years lovingly restoring the jet to ground-running condition. We discussed the aircraft and everything sounded promising. He didn't remember me at all but faintly remembered the trip to Saints. His logbook was at hand, and he checked while we were on the phone and there was my name from back in 1999. What a small world. Impressed with my set-up, he was very complimentary. Two weeks later, the client bought the aircraft thanks to Jas's introduction. I still owe him a beer for that!

My time on the Reds set me up for the career path ahead. The flying experience made me a better engineer as it provided a better understanding of how an aircraft operated and what it was capable of. For example, on air tests, I saw how fast and how high it could go, the stresses and strains an aircraft went through in the air, (+8.5 g to -3.5 g), including experiencing first hand, why all the rivets came loose on the tailplane of a jet. It was obvious when pilots flew regular sustained 8 g breaks pulling so hard that the jet buffeted violently. It was great fun to experience these lessons in the hot seat and to realise the ordeal the aircraft we were maintaining, suffered daily.

It was not all glamorous though, some of it was indeed character building. Cleaning somebody else's vomit—normally VIPs—from the rear cockpit side consoles was a good example. The Dye Team was a tough job and the members are still considered by those in the know, to be the unsung heroes of the Red Arrows. In one incident in Cairo, I was covered in diesel having been 'dicked' to hand-pump derv from 45-gallon drums. I was teamed up with an Egyptian conscript who had far less individual protection equipment (IPE) than me. We had to manually replenish the dye rig in 30-degree plus heat. It was messy. It was really messy, so much so, that I got covered in diesel to the extent that I had to 'sky wipe' my balls on the Herc and throw away my overalls. The flight sergeant caught me in the act, but luckily found it quite amusing. After all, no smoke equals no show. Nowadays, health and safety regulations insist that the Dye Team wear full IPE making the task even more uncomfortable, especially in hot climates. In comparison, in the late 1990s, a pair of marigolds and sunglasses were deemed acceptable. A stint in the pod bay was also an interesting engineering experience making me feel sympathy for my former course colleagues who had been posted direct from training to fuel tank bays. Enduring a two- to three-year stint, sniffing AVTUR day-in day-out, was not good for the body or the mind.

During the winter maintenance periods I was part of a second-line servicing team doing primary and minor servicing for six weeks at a time. This was highly educational comprising good old-fashioned heavy rigging. It was fin off, tail plane off, wing removal and refitting and undercarriage removal and refitting. This was later to become my bread and butter at Jet Art Aviation and, for this trade experience that I received on the Reds, I was so thankful. My mentors were old-school Hawk boys who had worked second line at RAF Chivenor and RAF Brawdy and their experience was priceless. Nothing educates an apprentice more than completing a task next to somebody who has done it hundreds of times and has the experience to share.

With the Reds I got to experience the best of both worlds. I got to fly, be an engineer, travel the world and to learn about a wide variety of things outside my normal trade experience. This included an understanding of flying clothing, helmets, g suits and ejection seats. I undertook parachute drills, survival training and dinghy drills, including firing flares. I was exposed to the type of social occasions that young airmen just don't experience, where being on your best behaviour is paramount. I attended cocktail parties in the High Commission in Delhi and was a VIP guest at the British Grand Prix, flown in aboard a Puma helicopter. The highlight was enjoying the display from seats in the 'Jonathan Palmer Hospitality Suite' with a champagne lunch while watching the race. Safe to say, there are not many jobs in the RAF where groundcrew work so closely, as well as socialising with, aircrew.

On one of my final trips to Cyprus, the last four bodies left standing in the famous Aki Arms on the Akrotiri strip, that Friday night, was me, still an SAC, a J/T, a squadron leader and an air commodore. Looking back, it was the best job in the world for a young, single bloke with lots of travel, seeing the world and meeting great people. It was an epic start to my aviation adventure.

Early 2000 saw me back at AFTS at RAF Cosford for a fitters course. I had been very tempted to turn the course down for another year on the Reds, as had one of my colleagues, sacrificing her course for another year on the Circus. After a chat with my SEngO, who was an ex-airman, he strongly advised me to take the course as, in his words, he could see my potential and thought I would go a long way. Without the course I wouldn't be able to progress through the ranks which, at the time, was what I wanted to do. In hindsight, taking the course was the right thing to do and I wouldn't be where I am today if I hadn't taken the plunge. It also meant a pay rise at the end of the course and promotion to the greatest rank in the air force, that of junior technician. It gave maximum pay for minimal responsibility. As I went back to technical school, most of my civilian friends were leaving university with a massive debt. I had three years of life experience that money could never buy. I had travelled halfway around the world, experienced things that I look back on today as far more valuable than any university course could provide, and the best part: I was getting paid to do it.

My course started in the dreaded Fulton Block with six solid weeks of maths. Once again, I knuckled down and studied. It was very much a case of work hard during the week and play hard at the weekends. The course covered in-depth technical theory to enhance what was taught on the mechanics course, whilst consolidating what had been learned on the job during my first posting. New practical skills were a big part of the course such as airframe repairs, removal of complex components and fault diagnosis.

In the hangar at AFTS was a Harrier GR3 with a very distinctive No. 4 Squadron red, yellow and black lightning flash on the fin. The name 'Capt L Y Ching' was emblazoned on the side of the cockpit just beneath the windscreen. I walked past this aircraft everyday going into the hangar and it always struck me as being the coolest aircraft in the building. Ever since making my model Harrier as a young child the aircraft captivated me but I wondered why the name of a non-RAF pilot was on the side of the aircraft. Fifteen years later I, quite randomly, became the owner of this very Harrier, XZ130. Sometime around 2005, the airframe had left Cosford to become a gate guard at an air cadet unit near Surbiton in London, not far from the Hawker factory where the aircraft was made. The following ten years and the ravages of the climate had taken their toll and, by 2015, the cadets were not in a position to maintain the jet. Health and safety issues were becoming more prominent, for example, the MoD had, accidently, left a large amount of fuel in the fuselage, even though

CHRIS WILSON WITH A TORNADO F3
OF NO. 11 SQUADRON. (CHRIS WILSON)

the Form 700 said it had been drained. The fuel leaked so the aircraft was put out to tender, to be sold to the highest 'suitably qualified' bidder. That happened to be Jet Art Aviation, and in January 2015, the team collected XZ130 and brought the distinctive jet back to Yorkshire for restoration. It wasn't long before Larry Ching, whose name was on the side of the jet, was emailing the office for regular updates on 'his' aircraft. Larry was the ex-USAF exchange officer on No. 4 Squadron and, by then, a Cathay Pacific pilot.

By the end of my course, I still wanted to work on fast jets and applied for a posting to either Harriers at Wittering, Tornado F3s at Leeming, or Jaguars at Coltishall. I got my second choice and went off to Leeming to join the Yorkshire/Geordie Air Force on No. XI (Fighter) Squadron.

Moving onto Tornado F3s operating from hardened aircraft shelters, was a real eye-opener and a major change from working on Hawks. The F3 was a much more complex aircraft and relatively unreliable in comparison to a Hawk. It was also much more groundcrew dependent, requiring a lot more maintenance.

For a see-off it was normal to have a team of three lineys, although on some occasions, it could be done by one person working alone, for example, on the trail back from a detachment. Most RAF aircraft work with a 3,000-psi hydraulic system, however, the Tornado worked off 4,000 psi, the extra pressure being required for the wing-sweep system. Extra pressure meant extra leaks and fixing them was to become a regular staple for a young fitter.

On No. XI (F) Squadron we worked alternate weeks of days and nights with the occasional swing shift. The split between trade work and working the flight line was approximately 50/50. There were a lot of late nights, the lack of spares was frustrating at times but the people working with me were great, many of whom became friends for life. We very much were the 'can do' air force but got the job done, often by bending the rules just a little. Without that, things simply would not have got finished and the aircraft would not have flown.

No. XI (F) Squadron also brought travel opportunities with trips to the USA, Oman and Saudi Arabia, some better than others but all great experiences. My first detachment was for Exercise Cope Thunder, in July 2000, at Eielson Air Force Base near Fairbanks in Alaska. On this exercise, now known as Exercise

Red Flag Alaska, I worked the flight line as a liney. The true potential of the Tornado F3 was highlighted during this time. While working on the flight line, I saw in the boss's jet after it came back early from a sortie. Thinking they had a problem and coming back 'early unserviceable'—which wasn't unusual—I asked what the problem was. "Not enough missiles" was the reply from the grinning navigator. In simulated air combat flown against aggressors, they had taken nine kills, having fired all eight missiles and emptied the cannon for a final gun kill on a target at close range. The aircraft had come of age.

Working directly opposite the F3s on the same pan were the Jaguars. On one sortie on 24 July 2001, we had seen in all the Tornados and all but one Jaguar had returned. Word quickly spread around the pan that an aircraft was overdue and we heard over the line walker's radio that it had only a few minutes of fuel left.

CHRIS WILSON ON DETACHMENT AT EGLIN AFB, FLORIDA. (CHRIS WILSON)

Later that afternoon A-10 Thunderbolts took off to the area where the aircraft was last known to be flying but low cloud hampered the search. Sadly, the wreckage of the Jaguar was found six hours later. It had flown into high ground, tragically killing the pilot who was found in the wreckage still strapped into the seat. The memory of that one solitary liney, standing in the gap on the flight line, waiting to see in a jet that never came back, is an image I will never forget.

The aircrew burned a piano in the car park of the USAF officers' mess that night. For the next few days, the Americans on base were very quick to pay their condolences to the visiting Brits, very sorry to hear about the loss of the RAF pilot whilst visiting their country. They asked why the piano burning? I explained on several

CHRIS WILSON IN FRONT OF AN XI(F) SQUADRON TORNADO F3 IN OMAN 2000.

occasions, including in the Class Six liquor store and the base exchange—the supermarket—that it was a long-standing tradition, dating back to between the wars. Pianos were set alight by RAF pilots wanting to avoid piano lessons, apparently, deemed to be a suitable activity for officers to improve finesse and civility. The practice had become a traditional way of giving a send-off to a fellow, fallen aviator.

Another occurrence, on Exercise Cope Thunder, was to stop me in my tracks. Seeing an F-16 come in to land, I spotted a family of moose run directly across the runway in front of the fast-moving jet. Apparently, a regular occurrence in the wilds of Alaska, a moose would surely make a serious mess of an aircraft if they came together. It's bad enough taking a bird strike on landing but a moose strike would be on a whole new level.

Not long after my posting to RAF Leeming, in the spring of 2001, I met Melanie who would become my wife. It was a real roller coaster romance. It was love at first sight and I found myself walking around the HAS site doing 'swing snags' with a giant grin on my face, having fallen head-over-heels in love with the beautiful, blonde, primary school teacher known by her pupils, and me, as Miss Corker. We rapidly moved in together and, two years later, were married at Gretna Green, Scotland. This would be the last time I wore my dress RAF uniform; getting married in 'Number Ones' with white gloves and a dress belt. I hadn't told Melanie that I would be wearing it and the look on her face said it all as she walked down the aisle.

Being a complete petrolhead and having the massive disposable income of a J/T, plus being 'shacked up' with a teacher on a similar salary, my car at the time was a Lotus Elise. I loved parking in the aircrew car park or next to the squadron warrant officer's MGF just to stir the pot. It was the perfect vehicle for a honeymoon blast around the Scottish Highlands. Little did I know at that time, that Melanie was to become an instrumental part of the aviation adventure to follow. Without her, none of the Jet Art chapter of my life would have happened.

By this stage, my time in the RAF was coming to an end. Life outside the wire would be considerably different but just as challenging, as you will soon understand.

CHAPTER 17

The Mighty Phantom

Paul 'Maz' Beattie undertook basic training at RAF Halton in 1974 and was posted to RAF Coningsby working on the Phantom. He joined No. 54 Squadron during the transition from ground attack to air defence, retraining as an A tech propulsion in 1982. After tours on the engine test facilities at Kinloss and Brüggen, he left the RAF in 1992. Moving to BAe Systems he worked in Saudi Arabia and Brough before retiring in 2005. Since then, he has pursued his big love in life, his Harley Davidson motorcycle.

The Cold War lasted many years but was at its height in 1974 to 1976, during the time at which my story is set. The place is an airbase in Fife, Scotland that has since been handed over to the army, going the way of many RAF airfields. At that time, it had three squadrons: No. 43 (the Fighting Cocks), my squadron, 111 (Fighter) Squadron and No. 892 Naval Air Squadron. The latter was based for the main part aboard HMS *Ark Royal*, although it shared RAF Leuchars when ashore. All three squadrons were flying the F-4 Phantom with a mix of Mark 1 and Mark 2 derivations. The RAF squadrons took the lion's share of northern quick reaction alert (NQRA), ready to fly in minutes against intrusions by aircraft of the Soviet Union which tried at all times of the day and night, throughout the year, to broach the invisible boundary that we had in place around our coast. Embarked for the majority of the time, the navy squadron's participation in this tale is minimal, not that we should detract from the part it played in the defence of the realm.

I joined No. 54 Squadron at RAF Coningsby, Lincolnshire in March 1974 after basic mechanics training at RAF Halton, just as the squadron began its metamorphosis into what would become 111(Fighter) Squadron. The place was alive with the talk of our forthcoming change to air-defence duties. Our interim name would be No. 111 (Designate) Squadron until a Lightning squadron folded and we were declared operational. Once declared in November 1975, we would move 'lock stock and smoking missiles' to Fife, Scotland and RAF Leuchars. At the time, the Lightnings of No. 23 Squadron and No. 43 Squadron flying F-4 Phantoms were carrying out the NQRA duties against the Soviet 'Bear' bombers; we would be taking over from the Lightnings, joining the Fighting Cocks. The Bears would appear at any time of the day or night, often at high level but, at times, sneaking under the radar screen at low level. They would be met and escorted by the Norwegians and then, either handed over to NQRA or escorted away if they stayed to the north. Sometimes, they would penetrate further west and be picked up by the Americans, flying from their base at Keflavik in Iceland. The radius of interception was vast and shadowing could go on far out into the Atlantic, down the west coast of Ireland but just as often, be confined to the North Sea. It was dependent on where the Russian crews had been told to probe.

We, as flight line mechanics or 'flems', came from all over the UK, including one guy from the Isle of Man and even Australia. After the usual greetings we were soon getting to know each other's foibles, usually over ice-cold beer in the local pubs, which soon began to benefit from our selfless dedication to alcohol. However, after a couple of weeks of exposure to flight-line duties, we flems soon made our mark leaving the hangar guys, who had until then split their duties, to concentrate on their trades and stay in the hangar, and the flight line to us. There was little argument as it meant they would not have to work outside in the swiftly changing weather, typical of the flat terrain of Lincolnshire. We made mistakes, I am sure, but we learned from them and, with the guidance and patience of our sergeants, we established the flight line as our rightful domain and soon challenged anyone to wrest it from us.

After the first few months of 1974 we had hardened. No longer the soft wide-eyed boys who had stumbled from the bus, we had changed into experienced flems who could manage the aircraft with consummate ease and had learned how to interact with the commissioned aircrew with whom we worked every day. We had learned the ins and outs of the daily routine and how to function as part of the RAF. The change of role presented problems to the aircrew who, until then had used the Phantom mostly to drop bombs. The conversion training went a pace through that glorious hot Lincolnshire summer and, soon, we began to practise the scrambles that would become so routine over the next few years in Scotland. The aircrew also had to get to know us and how to deal with the fiery youthful spirits. We would brook no messing

A SPARROW AND SIDEWINDER MISSILE ON DISPLAY AT NEWARK AIR MUSEUM. (DAVE GLEDHILL)

about when it came to rank and, if we were upset by any of the aircrew, they soon paid for their arrogance. By working to strict rules, sorties would be cancelled when their steeds seemed to break down on start up. Magically, the sortie success rate seemed to improve when attitudes changed, although some never cottoned on. We just had to learn to live with them as I am sure mechanics through the years found. The armourers too were getting to know their new roles as they loaded missiles instead of bombs, these being the radar-guided Sparrow and the heat-seeking Sidewinder.

Along with two other flems, I was dragged across to squadron operations a couple of times a week, to discuss procedures with an ex-Lightning pilot, to make sure we had the process right for scramble starts. This routine would become the cornerstone of our activities to make certain the aircraft launched efficiently when scrambled. We flems went about learning our trade on these powerful aircraft, working on the huge, concrete area known as the pan. We shared the space with No. 41 Squadron which operated in the reconnaissance role, its F-4s specially adapted to carry the photo-recce pod with its millions of candlepower. No. 228 OCU where the aircrew 'neddies' trained to fly the Phantom and No. 6 Squadron with whom we shared nothing, also worked there. We all occupied the same low single-floor building, down at the eastern end of the pan. What I always found incongruous, in the deafening swirl of gasoline-in-fused jet exhaust and amongst the hissing, screeching aircraft, was the silent and never changing sight of the ancient church tower visible over the north-western

A NO. 41 SQUADRON F-4 PHANTOM. (TERRY SENIOR)

corner of the pan. How many years had that solid, quiet, reverent structure stood and watched the various ages of man pass by its stone and slate magnificence? How many more silent graves of aviators would it embrace in the coming years? What, I wondered, would the tower see in the next 200 years when we are all long gone and it still stands, resolute and silent in its rural majesty?

The pan was a vast area of reinforced concrete about a quarter of a mile long and about 600 feet wide, onto which the four squadrons poured their aircraft every day. For the OCU case a full day of training for the student aircrew posted

CONINGSBY CHURCH. (DAVID GLEDHILL)

188

to the Phantom ran every day. No. 41 Squadron lived in the south-western corner and the OCU jets backed onto 41 using the north-west corner. We on 'Treble One' occupied the south-eastern corner, with 'Shiny Six' lined up with their backs to us. Underneath the concrete lay a labyrinth of fuel pipes that fed the fuel bowsers we used to refuel our aircraft. Every few yards, embedded in the concrete was a small cover which hid a fuel coupling. Onto these we would connect thick hoses unwound from the bowsers and from the bowser, we would drag another hose to connect to the aircraft. The bowser acted as a mobile filter between the ground pipe work and the aircraft which supplied the pumps to drag the fuel from the underground tanks and then push it, under pressure, into the aircraft tanks.

The slots for each aircraft—the parking positions on the pan—were painted onto the concrete with a solid line to show the track each aircraft should follow, and a small 'T' to show the final parking place. Each slot had an earth point onto which the earth lead would be clamped attached, under the concrete, to an earth mat which fed any stray current to earth. This protected the aircraft from stray voltages such as lightning strikes, providing much-needed protection to the flems. Each aircraft was electrically bonded which meant every metal component was connected in series to its neighbour by thin conducting strips which made one huge circuit. Again, if say a lightning strike was to occur, the electrical path would be to earth via the earth cable. No arcing from one component to another would occur which had the potential (pun intended), to be fatal, especially around fuel, explosives, weapons, high-pressure systems, liquid or gaseous oxygen.

THE OPERATIONS BUILDING ON THE CONINGSBY FLIGHT LINE. THIS IS NOW OCCUPIED BY NO. 29 SQUADRON. (DAVID GLEDHILL)

I was shown the effect of stray voltages one day in the hangar by an 'old sweat' sergeant. One aircraft obviously had a problem with its grounding so we squatted in the nosewheel well and stroked the end of the earth cable on the metal hook where the cable was secured. A shower of blue and red sparks discharged from the attachment each time the earth cable made contact. It was a salutary lesson in reporting electrical faults and one which I ignored later in my career in the Phantom engine test bed to my cost. That's for another tale.

Back in that glorious long hot summer of 1974, we had our first spell on QRA proper as 111 (Designate) Squadron, holding Southern QRA (SQRA), responsible for the airspace over England and Wales. We were ready to reinforce NQRA if the 'zombies'—the nickname for unidentified tracks—needed an escort down

A NO. 111 SQUADRON F-4 PHANTOM LEAVING THE 'HUSH HOUSE' AFTER AN ENGINE RUN.
(TERRY SENIOR)

the North Sea. Sitting QRA meant having two armed aircraft sitting on standby, ready to launch at a moment's notice, with a crew of engineers baking on the flight line and four aircrew waiting patiently in the operations building.

During our first weekend on 'Q' we had two aircraft sitting out on the, now deserted, pan about a hundred metres from the line hut. Conditions were somewhat primitive compared to those we would find at Leuchars. Four of us slept in the same stuffy ex-storeroom lacking opening windows, just along the corridor from the line control desk. This, through the long hot days, would heat up like a sauna and cook us slowly through the nights. There was nowhere to cook so meals were sent from the mess in insulated boxes known as 'hot locks'. There was just one kettle for tea and coffee. Without showers or baths, we would stand up to wash in the ablutions used by both squadrons during the working day. I will leave the smells to your imagination but they were ripe. I do not recall being scrambled to carry out any live interceptions but, at the end of our stint, we carried out a practice scramble to keep us current in the art.

One episode almost had me shot by an overzealous military police officer who had never come across live-armed aircraft and, obviously, did not know what we were doing. He had been told to defend those two valuable assets sitting shimmering in the heat and in that task he would not fail. Every four hours, one of us had to go out to the aircraft and check the gaseous systems and replenish them if required. We would look at the Sidewinder cooling bottles installed in the missile launcher rails. The containers were reinforced, gold-coloured, fibreglass cylinders, about four feet long and about six inches in diameter, full of pressurised nitrogen gas. They were screwed into the cooling system via a threaded connection in the front end. At the rear was a small gauge that showed the nitrogen pressure. Two clamshell doors at the back end of each launcher rail were opened by a spring-loaded handle, by gripping a small ball. Pull backwards on the ball and the doors were released revealing the nitrogen bottle inside.

It so happened that a bottle needed changing so I tugged the release clamp, unscrewed the container with my plumber's tool and, with its usual loud hiss of released gas, I pulled it backwards out of the launcher rail. After plodding back into the line hut to swap the empty bottle, I trudged back out into the boiling hot but deserted pan. Due to the heat and the fact I was alone, I was wearing only a pair of shorts and working boots. With the cylinder of gas perched on my shoulder and my plumber's tool in the other hand, I wandered out to the aircraft when from behind, I heard a shouted challenge. I thought nothing of it and carried on walking. I heard the shout again but this time with an increased urgency but carried on walking thinking that it must be a mate messing about. Swapping the plumber's tool into my right hand, I gave the universal middle-finger salute but by now the shouts had gone up a pitch. I looked around at who was making the noise.

With hindsight it was ludicrous. I was working on the primary QRA aircraft which was defending the United Kingdom. At that moment, it had no cooling gas for its missiles and had been taken off state for routine servicing. Behind me was an RAF policeman who clearly had ideas other than getting it back on state as soon as possible, so I told him just that. With sweat trickling down my back and the sun burning my head, I thought of the times we had been stopped by police with dogs. We had shown our ID cards to the dogs, intimating that it was the dog that could read. We were amused, as were the dogs but not 'the plod'. My new friend said I shouldn't be working on aircraft in shorts and that he didn't believe me anyway. How could I prove who I was? I tried to tell him that only metres behind him in the line hut was my boss and that if he went in, he could check. That would let me fit this gas container and get back inside out of the heat. The impasse continued. I was standing with my hands raised with the container at my feet, with the young plod in several minds as to what to do. Luckily, he blinked first and got onto his boss via his talking brooch. Time passed as we sweated in the sun. Eventually, a police Land Rover appeared, with its lights flashing and siren sounding, screeching to a halt disgorging more plods, beer bellies flopping over trouser belts, toe caps gleaming in the bright sunshine and all looking very stern. Finally, it calmed down and an apology was made. We agreed that we wouldn't go out to the aircraft without proper denims in future—we lied. I fitted the gas container and the jet was declared back on state. What would have happened if the hooter had gone off and a scramble had been called, I wouldn't like to think.

It's summertime 1974 and it's late in the evening as we sit in the dingy snug of our favourite pub, in the village, supping brown ale and ogling the barman's very tasty wife, wondering how he could have got so lucky. Last orders came and went and we realised that the barman was in the mood for a lock-in so we fed the jukebox with ten-pence pieces and settled back to get some drinking done. Ever mindful, we kept the curtains shut and the lights down to avoid the plods trying to see who they could 'nick'. We were just getting into our stride when the door almost burst off its hinges. We dropped to the floor, hitting the lights and kicking the jukebox off knowing that it was a raid. Giggling away among the dust bunnies under the table, the barman opened the door on its burglar chain and was confronted by the military plods screaming that everyone was to report to the base immediately as it was a 'no duff' call-out. They would forget the afterhours drinking on this occasion if the airmen, they knew were in there, returned to base. We struggled to our feet saying sorry to the barman and squeezed out of the tiny door, staggering onto the street, a steady stream of similarly unsteady airmen walking with a purpose up the road. I asked what was going on and, apparently, we were going to war! The Turks had invaded the northern part of Cyprus. Blinking through the alcoholic haze, I shook my befuddled brain into wakefulness. I realised that my sister was stationed in Famagusta and hoped she was OK.

Making our way quickly to the squadron, we helped the plumbers to arm the jets with eight of Her Majesty's best weapons. Then we waited, sipping coffee, for our move onto the 'Hercs', the venerable C-130 Hercules, that were already heading for Coningsby. It would be a long flight to sunny Cyprus, albeit the sunshine would be shared with live shells, bullets, and assorted weapons that were being lobbed at the inhabitants. The Turks and the Greek Cypriots had had a hissy fit and the sun-tanned Brits would sit in the middle, sipping brandy sours, waiting for the outcome.

Our sister squadrons started up and taxied out, giving us V-signs as they went past, before taking off and rumbling off into the distance until we could hear the ever-present skylarks twittering away once more. Hours later we were still waiting, at attention, standing by for something to happen. It would be another game of volleyball or another riotous game of Uckers. Anyone who has ever spent time in an RAF crewroom will know exactly what these games entail.

In the event, we were to stay in the UK to guard our own skies while everyone else went off to war. We spent the weekend playing volleyball in the sunshine until being stood down, reverting to the normal alert state on SQRA. That was our war.

On another boiling-hot month we sweated through a four-week exercise, living on the far side of the airfield, pretending to be at war. Most of the time we lived in our 'goon suits', better known as NBC suits. In the heat this was interminable and men had begun to keel over through heat exhaustion. The exercise 'nobs' conceded that we could remove the suits unless working on aircraft or if we were on guard duty.

One of the roles during an exercise was to play as an intruder to test the station's defensive preparedness. To act as a 'goon' was the avowed aim of the more liberal-minded and creative thinkers among squadron engineers. This meant hot meals, no NBC suits, no guard duty and you got to go home at night instead of cuddling up with a sweaty armourer on the one half-decent armchair in the crewroom. You could breathe in stale farts and enough cigarette smoke to line not just your own lungs, but every lung on the squadron. To that end, enterprising people found or made a clipboard, attaching a few tatty bits of paper and adopting a studied air of indifference. Slipping into the night when challenged, the imposters would become 'exercise marshals'. However, the ruse was rumbled in just a day or so.

The flem is a wily creature and, when he finds out that marshals wear armbands, he does what every other mechanic worth his salt would do; he steals a box full and hands them out to his friends like dinner invites. Now we could go to the mess for a decent meal rather than eating a fat-congealed cold pile of unappetising goo while sitting in a cobweb-covered damp sangar in the back of beyond with no hope of being relieved before morning. Unfortunately, the

'Ruperts' in control were slippery types and they discovered the half-empty boxes of invitations, sorry, armbands. For the next exercise the role of intruder was allocated to 'commissioned basket weavers'—the OCU course students. Lo, what is this? Suddenly, our line crewroom has sprouted half-a-dozen grubby denim-wearing fight lieutenants. Someone had been rooting about in the flying clothing section, the 'squippers' paradise', and had found a little drawer filled with rank badges that fitted over shirt collar tabs and, lo, instant promotion. It was at this point the Ruperts gave up and nominated a bunch of people whose names were ticked off a list. This killed our plot in one fell swoop.

During another interminable exercise, I had just finished a coffee when the siren went, yet again. An air raid was due. Instead of taking cover, I sneaked out to a small copse and hid there, finishing my coffee, looking for the attacking aircraft. In those days, they would always attack at ultra-low level and at full power. I first saw them at the far end of the airfield looking like tiny bugs, wheeling and turning. As they drifted nearer, they resolved into a Phantom, a Lightning and a Hunter, engaged in a combat that held me entranced. They would break and split, thundering away from each other to a point beyond my vision, then reappear into yet another hard-turning fight with lots of tail chasing and vertical climbs. They broke away and the chase continued out of sight but their rumbling engines could still be heard. In a hectic finale, all three climbed above the airfield, twisting and turning until the Hunter, with his lack of power, fell out and thundered across the airfield on a plume of dirty grey exhaust smoke, its engine howling at full power. It disappeared leaving the Lightning and Phantom with burners glowing, turning hard until their airspeed also decayed and the two split up in a mini chandelle to vanish out of sight. Minutes later, all three chased each other down the runway at not much more than 100 feet, in a glorious line astern tailchase, across the bug-infested summer fields. The Lightning was first in a high-energy flickering haze just below supersonic speed, its jet pipes emitting bright diamonds of fiery energy. Close behind, the Phantom followed, with the reheat crackling and roaring, the ear-battering noise making every one of my hairs stand on end. Bringing up the rear, the Hunter was earning his name, chasing the other two across the Lincolnshire fields, the noise from his Avon un-reheated, single turbo-jet dominant even above the noise of the first two. I have never seen the like since and never will again but I was there and the sight and sounds are locked in my memory as fresh as the day itself.

November 1975 came and the move up north was underway but not before we got into some mischief that landed us in hot water with the authorities.

Of course, we pleaded innocence. Deciding to leave our mark in one form or another, we painted the squadron emblem on the roof of the barrack block for all to see. After scrounging tins of yellow and red paint, we waited for the dark of night and climbed up onto the roof which in itself was no easy feat as it was two storeys high. We were lucky as workmen had been working on the roof and we had worked out how to get their hoist working to lift our kit up onto the flat bitumen-covered roof. The 'commission' took most of the night to complete but was a work of art—even though we said so ourselves! After scrubbing hard to rid ourselves of paint, we retired for what was left of the night.

The next day was spent sorting out stuff for our move. We then went to the pub for a liquid lunch and when we returned, we knew that we had been caught out as the 'plods' were in our room, breaking into our lockers, trying to find out who had 'done the deed'. Of course, we held our tongues so, apart from one or two close confidants, we were spared the rod. Well, that was apart from, stupidly, painting our initials next to the huge yellow Maltese cross with its attendant red sabres! Rumbled. Armed with scrapers, we spent the next few hours trying to remove the, still wet, paint. At one point we were 'buzzed' by the squadron boss in a Phantom, as he took photographs using the strike pod. We heard later that at 40,000 feet, they could still see the bright yellow cross. Fame at last. The job was not easy and we hit trouble when we began to run out of paint. It had been thinned out with some methylated spirits which had caused bubbling and lifted the newly covered roof. A couple of hours later, we were called down and allowed to prepare for the move.

I travelled in a friend's black minivan with another flem, all with shocking hangovers and the back of the van taken up with a tri-wall cardboard box full of kit. There was just enough room for one of us to shimmy down alongside this box in order to get some sleep while the other two sat in relative comfort up front. At intervals, one of my mates and I would swap around for a few hours for the long haul up to RAF Leuchars. Arriving, we learned that we had a small period of grace to settle in, as the aircraft would follow a couple of days later. After the chastisement from the boss at Coningsby, albeit with a semblance of a smile, they acknowledged that they hadn't seen anything quite as amazing for a while.

RAF Leuchars sits on the eastern shore of Fife, just across the bay from the town of St Andrews and the world-famous golf course. Many on the squadron would use the course over the coming years including many visiting aircrew from all over the damned place. Aircraft from other bases would have a mysterious fault and divert to Leuchars on a Friday. This would, of course, mean that they would have to stay over the weekend and, oh by the way, there was a golf course nearby. This was fine for them, as they jumped from their steeds and wandered off to the mess looking for golf clubs. Meanwhile, we would be stuck with the aircraft, having to conduct ground runs to find what we knew was never there in the first place. Having raised a job card, we were duty bound to carry out the work. On Monday we would have extra work to see them off so that we could get on with our own work. The favourite fault for these stopovers would be 'fumes in the cockpit' as this could not be disproved by ground running the engines. It would always have magically vanished on start-up the following Monday but only after the crews had been on the lash for the weekend. The aircrew found it hilarious and would climb back into their jets, not understanding what their misuse of military resources had caused.

We lost count of the numbers of Phantoms appearing on Friday with this same fault. If there was a party locally or golf was scheduled, especially a major tournament such as The Open, it was like running a hotel with baggage pods and cockpits stuffed full with golf bags and clubs. This was annoying enough but on the return flight on Monday morning, we would have to find space for the crap the crews had been buying during their fun-filled weekends. We took great delight in scrunching packs of fags and cigars into a twisted wreckage as we stuffed them in among the golf clubs and clothes. One pilot told us to fill the airbrakes with his packs of cigars and fags once the baggage pod was full, saying that he wouldn't be using the airbrakes in flight. We followed his instructions and, of course, on final approach to his base in Germany, he popped the airbrakes open, instantly realising what he had done, as his cigars tumbled to earth.

With our accommodation sorted, we wandered down to our new home in the vast Second World War hangar where our aircraft would be housed. Our hangar sat between the two resident squadrons, but we had our own dedicated area just outside the crewroom on the western corner of the hangar. As we wandered in on the first day, there were still two Lightnings sitting in the corner. One was almost ready to go but the other was in a very sorry state. It had been used as a 'Christmas tree'; supplying parts to get the rest of the squadron away. A Christmas tree is so-called due to the number of parts that are missing. The holes in the airframe, all of which had a job card wrapped in plastic, served as a reminder to replace the parts. Over time, and as the new parts came in, they were fitted and the tags removed. Eventually the jet, now whole again, was taken out for a ground run and a systems check prior to flight. Once checked by a pilot during a shake-down flight, it would be released back onto operations.

Out on the flight line, the rest of the Lightnings were sitting ready to fly out that same day. We looked forward to seeing them off, hoping that there might be a good beat-up as they left. In those days that was still the thing to do. We helped the few remaining Lightning bods to get their pilots plugged into the jets, and after start-up, the Lightnings trundled to the end of the runway. With reheats bellowing and crackling, they rolled down the runway and into the ether.

They took off to the east straight out to sea and we thought we had been robbed of a low-level beat-up. Unconvinced, one or two of us stayed out on the pan, listening and looking. I could hear them so they were still in the vicinity and, sure enough, someone yelled, pointing to the nearby hill at Balmullo, a small quarry at the western end of the airfield about two miles away. Flitting around the hill at ultra-low level, the jets, recently departed, were going like the clappers. Within seconds they were on us and lifting their noses to clear the grass bank at the end of the runway. They passed in extended line astern, and in full burner just under supersonic speed. One after another, they screamed down the runway, in ear-shattering runs at full power, banking over in turn before straightening and riding reheated plumes in glorious vertical climbs. They turned into bright balls of flickering heated energy as they continued to climb, doubtless to find a tanker. Using reheat like that would have meant the Lightning pilots running short of fuel just short of St Andrews.

In all my time I never, ever tired of seeing powerful fighters being used like they were meant to be and I have seen some wonderful beat-ups. I flew just once but that's for another story. Sadly, the health and safety 'misery guts' were just around the corner and determined to spoil our fun. Over the years, these shows of brute power waned but, for a brief few years, I was in heaven.

Apart from the distractions of the Fighting Cocks and the Navy Boys, Leuchars was now ours.

Paul 'Maz' Beattie, K8109477, ex-RAF, Knife, Fork, Spoon.

CHAPTER 18

The Tank Trap

Martyn Mander joined the RAF in 1973 as an aircraft mechanic (weapons) and was posted to Coningsby working, initially, in the bomb dump before being posted to No. 6 Squadron on Phantoms, then 29 (F) Squadron during the build-up of air-defence squadrons. After a short tour at Laarbruch he was posted to Brize Norton, where he was involved with bomb disposal. He attended a fitters course before being posted to Gütersloh in the armoury where he deployed into the field with the Harrier Force. His final posting was at Marham, where he was involved in the build-up of the Tornado squadrons including work on a special weapon loading team. During an extensive career spanning nearly 13 years, he worked on Phantoms, Buccaneers, Jaguars, Hunters, Victors, Canberras and Tornados. Leaving the service in 1985, he worked for Martin Baker for 12 years before moving to Lockheed Martin until he decides to hang up his spurs.

This is the tale of a night shift on an RAF 'mud mover' squadron, the armourers' tenacity, ingenuity, subterfuge and success … and green paint.

It was the start of a midweek night shift on an ordinary spring evening at RAF Coningsby in early 1975. No. 6 Squadron was a night ground-attack squadron, so night flying was a usual occurrence. As was normal, the day and night shift trades got together to see what needed doing—and what jobs they didn't want to do. The trades on nights always hoped that there would be as little as possible so that we could 'stack' early; well before midnight. Usually, that was just a pipe-dream if there was night flying going on. Our beloved Phantoms always had a trick or two up their sleeves to ensure that a normal night ended around 0200, sometimes much later. The usual culprits were the inertial navigation and attack system (INAS) and the missile control system (MCS). The snags always affected the armourers, as the black boxes for these systems were in the rear cockpit and changing them meant that the rear ejection seat pan had to come out. Of course, putting it back in was one of the last jobs to make the aircraft ready for the next day's flying, so the armourers were usually the last trade working in the hangar.

There was always work on the line during the evening's flying. This was the days before the hardened aircraft shelters and all the aircraft at Coningsby operated off the aircraft servicing platform also known as the pan. This was an enormous expanse of concrete between the hangars and the runway where flight-line servicing took place, including refuelling and aircraft arming. Minor faults could be fixed which saved having to drag an aircraft back into the hangar. Each squadron had its own number of slots on the pan, grouped together for convenience.

Visiting aircraft invoked a certain amount of curiosity, and this evening, a USAF F-4D Phantom was parked on the pan on a No. 6 Squadron slot. Quite busy that evening, it was only afforded a cursory glance but maybe later, we would have a quick look if it was still there. It turned out that, indeed, it was going to be still there for some time as it had landed in emergency with engine trouble. It had been on a practice bombing sortie at one of the local coastal bombing ranges when the trouble developed, and Coningsby was the nearest diversion. Now, it always seemed to turn out that when something unusual happened at Coningsby, our SEngO would always volunteer our squadron to help and try to take care of the problem. This evening was no exception as we had been given the task of looking after this USAF aircraft until a maintenance crew from its home base in the UK could come and sort it out. After a short while, the night-shift armourers were called over to the line-control building for a briefing. We were to disarm the F-4D ready for it to be taken into our hangar, where the problem could be addressed. No problem we thought. There couldn't be that much difference in the weapon system, compared to ours. Oh yes there could. It was a lot different.

We wanted to get this extra task done as soon as possible because we still had our own jobs to do when our own jets landed. The inboard pylons were different, as the release mechanism on the USAF equipment was integral with the pylon, whereas the RAF pylon had a separate release mechanism, attached to the pylon with a weapons adapter. This presented no problem because the explosive cartridge breeches were pretty much the same, just in a different place. We disarmed the pylon when the second problem presented itself. The practice bomb carrier was a type which we in the RAF didn't use. It was a SUU-22 pod, which carried the practice bombs internally and was fitted with electrically operated bomb doors.

A SUU-22 STORES POD ON A USAF F-4 PHANTOM.

To remove the practice bombs still inside, we needed to open the doors. It was up into the front cockpit to access the weapon control panel but said panel and switches were completely different to our Phantom. Caution was essential as we were dealing with live weapons and didn't want a catastrophe. We attempted to contact the USAF crew to ask them to come over to the line to assist but it was obvious that the aircrew had already returned to their own base in Suffolk for the night; not that far away from Coningsby.

A decision was made 'up the chain' authorising us to remove the SUU-22 pod complete with practice bombs, although we were confident that this could be done in safety, providing that we moved the aircraft away from the flight line. The aircraft was defueled where it stood and moved to a spot outside our hangar, ready to remove the pod. It would then be taken to the ready-use bomb store, which was located near the pan, for overnight safekeeping.

Equipment and tools were gathered and positioned at the aircraft, the main item being the MJ4 weapon loader, affectionately known as the 'jammer', a name derived from its ability to jam everything and anything onto the bottom of an aircraft. This was a piece of American ground equipment, specifically designed for the Phantom; a self-propelled machine with a hydraulic boom, and adjustable loading head, enabling precision loading of weapons and stores.

The location wasn't the best lit on the airfield so we relied on the headlights of the jammer and a few handheld torches. Manoeuvring the jammer into place, we positioned the loading head under the SUU-22. All eyes were on the pod as it was soft-skinned and we didn't want to damage or dent it. We were relying on the driver of the jammer to make sure he was clear of the airframe as he drove into place. All was going well, and the order was given to start raising the head up to the bottom of the pod when disaster struck. The head of the jammer struck the outboard external fuel tank. This was a 370-gallon tank manufactured by Sargent Fletcher in the US, and just referred to as a 'fletcher'. The effect was to rip the nose cone of the fletcher, forcing the skin against the internal baffle plate of the main tank. Nothing else on the tank was damaged, just the nose cone but, of course, fuel leaked out. At least the aircraft had been defueled prior to moving it into the hangar, as was normal practice. Operations were halted immediately to assess the situation. The jammer was withdrawn from underneath the aircraft, and the fuel leak was mopped up using Sorbsil; a grained material not unlike cat litter used for pets. This stuff was universally known as 'chicken shit' in the RAF. That was the easy bit. Next was the problem of what to do about the damaged tank. Should a disaster flag be raised to alert everyone—causing heads to roll—or did we just get on with it and make the problem go away? Somewhere along the line, the senior NCOs talked to others, and a message came back to us lowly airmen; could we fix it on base?

Luckily, a member of our squadron was friendly with one of the guys who worked in the tank bay attached to the Aircraft Servicing Flight (ASF). All we hoped for now was that they were working a night shift. A quick trip over to the ASF hangar confirmed that they were still working, and with appropriate liquid bribery, they could put a new nose cone on for us and keep everything quiet. It was a much different RAF in the mid-1970s, still governed by rules, but not by the overpowering bureaucracy of today. There was a Cold War going on for goodness sake. Ingenuity was encouraged to get the job done.

It was a straightforward, quick job to remove the fletcher, as the USAF version was exactly the same as ours and we had the specialised tools. Loading the tank onto an S-type trolley and transporting it to the tank bay, we received the occasional odd look from passers-by. RAF fletchers were painted mid-grey on the top surfaces, with a white under surface and a crisp, straight line separated the two colours. The USAF tank was painted dark green on the top, with a more cream-coloured under surface, separated by a diffuse, wavy line. Unlike ours, there was no inspection window on the USAF tank. No problem we said, they probably won't notice.

On arrival, the tank was removed from the S-type, put onto a small mainte-nance trolley and it dis-appeared into the tank bay. 'Terms of brib-ery' were settled and we left the fletcher in their capable hands.

When we arrived back at the hangar, the SUU-22 had been removed and had been taken to the ready-use bomb store for safe keeping. We were on tenterhooks. All we could do was go about our normal work until the call from the tank bay. We went about our work as if nothing was wrong. Well, noth-ing was wrong, everything would be fine … wouldn't it?

AN RAF SARGENT FLETCHER FUEL TANK ON A BRITISH PHANTOM. THIS TANK HAS BEEN REPAIRED SIMILAR TO THE WAY DESCRIBED IN MARTYN MANDER'S STORY. (DAVID GLEDHILL)

The night shift progressed with flight-line work, the odd turnround or af-ter-flight servicing. We would be one of the last trades to finish night shift be-cause after flying ended at around 2200, that's when the real work started. The mighty Phantom had a habit of finishing night flying with some sort of snag and this night was no exception. The armourers started the ball rolling but then had to hang around until the snags were fixed and tested before we could get in again to refit the ejection seat. Normally, it was off to the airmen's mess for duty supper, the equivalent of our lunchtime, providing time to recharge our batteries ready for the long night ahead. But on this evening, we had thoughts about our poorly fletcher, undergoing major surgery in the tank bay. Would they come across any unexpected problems? Would the USAF tank have some subtle difference meaning that the new nose cone wouldn't fit? Of course, there would be no problems we thought; a fletcher is the same whichever air force is using it.

With supper finished, it was back to work but there was still no news of our tank. What were we going to tell the day shift and, more importantly, the USAF when there was no tank on their jet the next day? I suppose we could tell them that it had accidently been lost and that we had no idea where it was.

Deep down we knew that the tank bay would come up trumps and, sure enough, at around 2300, the phone rang in the armourers' annexe in the hangar. Great news. The fletcher had a new nose, had been leak and pressure tested, and was good to go. Deep joy!

Off we went over to the tank bay to collect our wayward fletcher. There she was, resplendent with a shiny new nose cone, all ready to go. Not quite. … There was the small matter of the differing paint schemes. No problem, we thought. We can sort that out, we thought. We had a well-equipped paint locker over on the squadron. It was quiet now on camp, and not a soul was encountered as the fletcher made its way back to our hangar.

We positioned the tank in a quiet corner of the hangar, and raided the paint locker, finding a suitable paint to complete the masterpiece. There was plenty of NATO green; we assumed that the USAF would use that on their aircraft, but the cream was going to take a bit of trial and error to get right. We had white and we had yellow so we figured that we could make up a convincing shade of cream to match the rest of the tank. Preparation of the surface was vital, and we gave the entire nose cone a light sanding to make sure that our new paint scheme would be authentic. Our NATO green was not the perfect match that we thought it would be. Gloom! It was too dark. We added some white, and with a bit of delicate colour balancing we, eventually, had a shade of green that would pass muster. The nose cone at this stage looked a bit like Picasso's pallet, but that would all soon disappear under our self-help USAF green. The paint went on very smoothly, even though we were brush-painting.

Standing back to admire our work, the tiny inspection window on the nose cone had now disappeared—well almost. With it sufficiently disguised, next came the challenging bit of matching the cream paint on the underside of the tank. This proved a bit more awkward and took some time to achieve a convincing shade. Constantly standing back to make sure that the pattern was the same, the most exacting part of the whole job was matching the wavy line separating the two colours. We triumphed, eventually, producing a true masterpiece of which Picasso would have been proud. The remaining problem was that it looked a bit too new but with a bit of weathering, it finally looked as if it had endured of few flights.

It was time to get our priorities right and we headed off to the crewroom for a well-earned cuppa. In those days we had the luxury of abundant manpower so the usual tasks on our own aircraft were taken care of by our fellow armourers. The other trades working in the hangar were in the dark as they had their own work to finish before going home. As always, we were the last to finish but, eventually, the final jobs were signed off and the jets were ready for the morning.

With the hangar quiet, we emerged from the crewroom to finish the job; the weathering. With a perfect example to follow on the other side of the aircraft, we began rubbing with a dirty cloth to tone down the new paint. With no obvious line between the nose and the main tank, peppering the paint on the nose tip replicated the erosion caused by blasting through the air at great speed. Proud of our work, we had every confidence that no one would notice the fact that we had reproduced a perfect USAF Sargent Fletcher tank. Our masterpiece was finished.

It was time to refit the tank to the aircraft, a routine job for squadron armourers and one that all of us had carried out many times before. Perfectly straightforward, it went without a hitch and the aircraft looked complete once more, with a not-so-shiny new nose on the tank. The paperwork was completed to sign off the work, carefully worded by our SNCOs to disguise the night's activities. It was enough to satisfy the documentation requirements. Everything was fit for flight, to the extent that brand new seals had been fitted where the fuel lines connected the tank to the wing. There might have been a bit of subterfuge but the work was to our usual high standard and we had every confidence in the quality. I know that there was a huge sigh of relief in the hangar from everyone, at every level. Well, at least from those who were in on the covert work that went on that night.

With our own work wrapped up we finished at a reasonable time and headed home, although a little apprehensive about events. We had come on shift expecting a routine night, working on our own squadron aircraft, the same as every other shift. We could never have expected to have been working on an aircraft from another air force—and then breaking it.

Although as a courtesy, our SNCO let the day-shift armament trade manager know what had happened, I think the episode was kept on a need-to-know basis. Certainly, the USAF didn't need to know! On my own part, it had been an odd night shift. I suspect that many of us lost sleep that day.

Returning to work at around 16.45, ready for shift handover, nothing was mentioned about our visitor from the USAF. The aircraft was on the flight line, prepared and ready to return to its own unit. Groundcrew from its home base had arrived that morning, worked on the aircraft all day, and had fixed whatever had been the trouble. They had even remembered to refit the SUU-22 practice bomb carrier which was a pity as we were rather hoping that they would forget it because it would have made a great squadron souvenir. They had then returned to their home base, leaving their aircrew behind, asking us to oversee the engine start, and to marshal them out. The American aircrew emerged from the aircrew briefing room, crewed in, and departed. We were so glad to see the back of that visiting Phantom. There it went, roaring into the night sky, trailing the black smoke that was a feature of J79-engined Phantoms.

That was the last we knew of it. If the new nose had been discovered, we never heard about it. If they did, they were probably impressed with the RAF workmanship. In the USAF at that time, there were so many specialist trades that they might have thought that the nose of the tank had been changed by their own personnel in some dark corner of their own airfield.

A lot of time has passed since that incident, so long ago, at the height of the Cold War. Phantoms in both the RAF and the USAF are now but a distant memory, fondly remembered by all who were associated with them. There is still a strong following from enthusiasts who have never had the pleasure of seeing the 'Mighty Phantom' roaring down the runway in full afterburner, or streaking low over the airfield, making everyone's internal organs vibrate from the sheer power.

Happy days indeed, but, sadly, I imagine 'our' USAF F-4D Phantom has long gone to that great scrapyard in the sky.

CHAPTER 19

Winging It

In 2004 Chris Wilson set up in business trading as Jet Art Aviation and is now the managing director. Initially the company built bespoke aviation-inspired furniture, but quickly evolved into the supply of collectibles, cockpits and engines. The major leap in 2007, saw the acquisition of the first full-sized aircraft in the form of a Sea Harrier. By 2008, the partnership with his wife Melanie had grown into an accomplished limited company. Today, Jet Art Aviation Ltd is renowned as being a supplier of some of the most interesting and exciting ex-military aircraft in the world for museum display and for preservation within the private collectors' market.

In 2004 I left the RAF. I had applied for premature voluntary release (PVR) in 2003 and ended up working 18 months' notice so that the RAF could get its money's worth out of me as payback for the fitters course at Cosford. The wording I used on my application was along the lines that I had become disillusioned with the RAF and felt I could better myself as a civilian. I always had the feeling there was more for me out there and didn't want to get stuck in the pension trap, having to serve 22 years. I know that if I had stayed in, I would probably have been promoted as my assessments were always excellent but I always had the feeling that my real potential was being suppressed. The RAF at the time, had no real talent-spotting process and the only way to progress was to stay in and keep your nose clean, normally by keeping opinions to yourself. By doing so, you might advance through the ranks.

A number of other J/Ts on No. XI (F) Squadron 'PVR'd' around the same time, many for the same reasons; a feeling of disillusionment and being hampered in fulfilment of their potential. We had all joined as 'mech techs' in the fast-track scheme and had higher qualifications than a lot of people joining the RAF as airmen. Most had A levels, some had degrees but having finished university and struggling to find work, ended up in armed forces careers offices. Some of the lineys on the squadron at the time were better qualified than the aircrew they were strapping into the jets.

In part, the mass of PVR applications was due to an announcement around the same time that No. XI (F) Squadron would be disbanding the following year when the Typhoon entered service. As a consequence, squadron morale was really low and, looking back, the air force lost a lot of bright engineers. Some of my peers went on to be airline pilots, one to run a power station, others went into high managerial posts and I ended up as a managing director of my own business with a small, but excellent, team of staff.

Originally, I left the RAF with the intention of renovating houses. Sarah Beeny was on TV and my intention was to make a few quid 'flipping' houses. Mel and I had already bought our home together and had renovated it while I was based at RAF Leeming, so this was something of which I already had experience.

I completed a resettlement course learning how to lay bricks, plaster, plumb and be a painter and decorator. These were the trades that would help me to become a successful property developer. We bought a house in a bad state of repair and whilst on resettlement, I grafted every hour God sent, stripping the place out. During this time Mel became pregnant with our son, Oliver, who was born at Halloween in 2004, just over halfway into the house renovation. The two weeks of self-given, (read: Mel put her foot down), 'paternity leave' was my first real break from the house project. Going back to it afterwards was a struggle. I missed the RAF; not the work, but the craic and camaraderie of service life. In the space of less than a year, I had gone from a carefree life with no real responsibilities and a disposable income, to working in solitary, out of the RAF, with no monthly income, a new baby and my wife's salary being our only income. The weight of responsibility was heavy and almost too much but having taken out a very sizable financial loan against a house, I had to sell. I had no option but to work until the job was done.

It was character building but extremely tough. However, after selling the house for a small but acceptable profit, I gradually saw the positives and began to see it as an extreme lesson in project management and business, which, unbeknownst to me at the time, would assist in the next chapter of my life. We noticed that the housing market had started to slow down and so decided not to buy another house once the first had sold. Instead, I used what I had learned during resettlement and found myself fitting kitchens and bathrooms. This was not something that held any passion for me; disillusionment set in completely.

One day, after taking out a toilet and getting covered in s**t, I had somewhat of an epiphany. I came home to Mel with the bombshell that I wasn't going to do this anymore and was going to make furniture out of aircraft parts. I would sell aircraft parts and gauges. I wanted to get back into working with aircraft and doing something I loved but, bearing in mind Melanie was still on maternity leave, being a parent was still quite new to both of us and money, or lack thereof, was quite an issue. Mel, unbelievably, backed me 100 per cent.

I tested the market with some 'gizzits' (souvenirs) that I had collected during my air force days and I quickly realised there was a market for old aircraft parts. Using online auction sites as the selling medium, we found that parts were being shipped across the world. The business quickly escalated, and I found myself doing something I loved once again; something that I had a real passion for.

I went on weekly 'picking' trips around the UK, often covering over 1,000 miles visiting scrapyards and dealers all over the country. My very first buying trip was in my battered, green ex-Yorkshire Electricity Board van to Hanningfield Metals. I had £200 in my back pocket that we couldn't afford to lose but spent it wisely on items that I recognised as being from Harriers, Hawks and Tornados. In those days £200 bought a lot of stock and being able to accurately recognise parts from aircraft I had worked on in service was a massive advantage. Putting in the miles in the van and doing a mixture of air shows and aero-jumbles, I quickly grew a network of aviation contacts. The internet sales scene was just taking off and on eBay we had approximately 50 per cent of the market in the UK; as one of the first companies selling surplus aircraft parts to collectors. Within a few months we had a huge cowling behind the shed, a garage full of aircraft parts and random things like ejection seats in the shed and propeller blades in the living room. The front room of our three-bedroom semi became a pseudo showroom for the aircraft furniture I had started to make. Coffee tables were fashioned from Tornado armoured windscreens, a Handley Page Herald pilot's seat became an office chair, Canberra air intakes transformed into coffee tables and mirrors were crafted from Tornado RB199 engine components. At the time, this was all new in the UK and we were the only people doing aviation furniture, putting the finished product on the internet. It quickly got out of control and Melanie drew the line at having "half a plane in the bloody garden". It was time to move somewhere bigger.

Over the next few years in the new house, the business grew. Instruments and gauges led to ejection seats, then engines, then to the nose section of an English Electric Lightning; a Mach 2 interceptor. Finally, in 2007, two years down the line from starting the business, we acquired a complete Harrier 'jump jet'. The work was hard; a lot of graft, stress, blood, sweat and tears. I had not only an understanding wife but one that was onside with this crazy adventure and, at many points, actively encouraged the craziness, as well as providing the motivation to go for it and take the risk.

In 2007, on one of my trips around the UK, I found not one but six Harriers, which were up for sale. All heavily stripped with the spares recovered for reuse, it seemed that they could be rebuilt and made into museum exhibits. The Harrier we eventually bought was from a company south of London, which supplied Sea Harrier spares to the Indian navy. They had bought numerous surplus Harriers from the MoD when the Sea Harrier fleet had been retired in 2006 and then stripped them of spares. We were, basically, buying their waste; an empty gutted shell of what ended up being the last all-British fighter. I knew that this was the direction we needed to take the business and I came home excited, discussing the possibility with Melanie. The reality was that buying a full aircraft was a huge leap and a significant risk. I could see the potential, had the skill set to turn the project around but had no way to fund a project like that. I talked myself out of it and persuaded myself to do it ten years down the line when the business had become more established. Mel, however, had different ideas and she could see the time was, indeed, ripe. I take my hat off to her for grabbing the moment.

There was no way a bank would offer a loan to buy a 'war plane', so Mel went online and got a home improvement loan for the new house. It wasn't really 'lying' as the money we made from the onward sale of the Harrier, did indeed pay for home improvements, like a new kitchen and a reliable family car. We, actually, had to hire a car to go to the meeting to buy the Harrier as ours wouldn't have got us anywhere near Gatwick.

It was very much a case of all in or bust. It was really ballsy stuff for a couple with a two-year-old child. This was pre-recession UK when getting funding was reasonably simple but I will never forget when Mel walked into the kitchen and presented me with a piece of A4 paper (the Loan Agreement). "There you go," she said, "put your money where your mouth is."

Things got real very quickly. Our first Harrier was a Sea Harrier FA2, a first-generation ex-Royal Navy example of the iconic British fighter jet. That alone would be a massive selling point. I spent hours doing my research and of the choice of six stripped-out hulks, I picked the one in the worst condition. Adrian who sold us the jet must have thought I was mad, picking the most battered example from his line-up. It had missing windscreens, panels and sections of de-riveted skin. However, I had picked a Falklands veteran, XZ459. This aircraft had flown 53 combat missions in the Falklands War, including the legendary raid on Port Stanley airfield on 1 May 1982 when BBC reporter Brian Hanrahan said, "Counted them all out and counted them back again". We had not just invested in a piece of scrap metal but in a piece of history with a story to tell. It was the best thing we ever did.

Collecting the aircraft in its stripped-down form was something else. I picked it up with Barry Parkhouse, the bloke who famously put the Lightning in Jeremy Clarkson's garden. It was a real eye-opener coming from an RAF background but in true Fred Dibnah, old-school, Brit fashion the job was done with minimal equipment and at a low cost. Since then, health and safety regulations have changed things massively and we just couldn't get away with what we did on the first aircraft … and rightly so! We had no ground equipment, no manuals, no insurance for the aircraft on the lorry and we got the complete aircraft, including the wing assembly, on one load. There was, however, some rather ingenious loading by Barry.

The rebuild project was finished in six weeks and involved me calling in a few favours from old RAF mates who were more than willing to lend a hand. I spent many hours on the phone, tracking down parts and then driving all over the country to collect them; panels, pylons and items like an ejection seat. The jet, once complete, sold quickly and there was lots of press interest, so much so that on the first day we unloaded it, the local papers turned up to film and photograph the 'nutter who had bought a fighter jet'. We put it in a neighbour's field next to the A644, high up on the moors overlooking Bradford. This was in the heart of Bronte country, 1,200 feet above sea level, just outside the village of Queensbury, one of the highest villages in England. It was not the ideal place to rebuild a Harrier 'jump jet' but the views and backdrop were spectacular. The aircraft quickly became a local landmark and put the business on the map. That was the start of the Jet Art aircraft adventure and was to be the first of many Harriers to follow.

The turning point that brought us into the public eye involved a Harrier T2, our very first two-seat Harrier. When we bought the incomplete, heavily stripped-out wreck, we had no idea of the amount of fuss it would create which in turn generated a monumental amount of press coverage. This was a pivotal point for the business but at the time, it was an emotional roller coaster. In hindsight, it was a massive, totally unplanned, public relations coup that enabled us to move to the next level. I was live on BBC National Lunchtime News with Ed Thomas. A week later, as the aircraft and the story went viral, Mel, Oliver and I ended up being whisked down to London to BBC headquarters.

The Harrier in question was XW269; a 1971 built T-Bird that entered service as a T2 and was later upgraded to T4 specification. The jet spent its early life out in Germany but ended its days on the Strike Attack Operational Evaluation Unit at Boscombe Down, doing the 'Nightbird' trials. It had a modified nose to house a forward-looking infra-red sensor and the trials led to a low-level, lights-out, night-flying capability for the RAF front-line ground-attack force. After its useful trials life was over, the jet was stripped down to support the famous vectored-thrust aircraft advanced-flight control (VAAC) Harrier before being put out to pasture in the open air at Boscombe Down. Fast forward ten years and the VAAC Harrier would become part of the Jet Art stable too, although if you

HARRIER XW269 PRIOR TO RESTORATION ARRIVING AT JET ART. (CHRIS WILSON)

had told me at the time, I would never have believed you. We bought XW269 in 2009 and, after dismantling and collecting the derelict hulk, we craned it into our field, high up in Bronte country, ready for the restoration process to begin.

With our small team, we restored the aircraft over the next 18 months. It was rebuilt, the cockpit re-equipped, the airframe repainted and we put it back to the earlier T2 specification, creating something unique. We even armed it up with replica SNEB rocket pods made from glass reinforced plastic. SNEB rocket pods were built by the French company Matra and were used by the RAF during the Cold War. With a pair of cannon pods—empty of course—and a set of drop tanks, the result was as if it had just landed and was ready to take off to complete a mission.

As we had done with many Harriers previously, we advertised XW269 on the internet on different selling platforms, including our own website and on eBay. The local media quickly took an interest and came along to photograph the aircraft and to write a piece. Word quickly spread and it wasn't long before there was, literally, a queue of journalists waiting for an interview. The interest was not just from the UK but TV crews from as far afield as Turkey, were running stories entitled 'British man sells warplane on internet'. My favourite was *The Sun* with 'plane nutter rebuilt fighter jet in garden!'

Mike McCarthy from Sky News came to see the aircraft and to interview me about the restoration and my RAF background. Whilst he was visiting, we got a sale. Somebody hit the £70,000 'Buy it now' option on the eBay listing and I could immediately tell by Mike's reaction, that this was going to make the perfect end to his news piece. I envisaged another headline: 'Restored Harrier finds new owner'. An hour went by and the phone rang in the office. It was the gentleman who had bought the Harrier, however, things were not as they seemed. It turned out that his seven-year-old son had been using his computer and couldn't help himself by taking the plunge and committing to buy the jet on his father's eBay account! His dad was devastated and, naturally, reluctant to re-mortgage the house to buy a jet, so rang the office as soon as the email invoice appeared in his inbox asking him to pay for a fighter jet. The chap begged for forgiveness on his child's behalf, explaining that they didn't have the funds in their piggy bank to cover the purchase. It was, initially, disappointing, but we saw the funny side. The press, on the other hand, loved it. This was a solid gold, tabloid-style press story and it went viral; 'Seven-year-old boy buys war plane on the internet'. It made newspaper headlines all over the world.

Having missed out on a £70,000 sale, we decided to relist the Harrier on eBay as an auction. The mass of press interest was driving so much internet traffic our way that the situation just had to be exploited. Such was the interest, that our website crashed from the volume of traffic. The phone constantly rung off the hook. The line of press and TV crews waiting to see the jet and to interview me just kept expanding. Then just as the press coverage of the seven-year-old buyer had rocketed the price skywards to a dizzying £94,000 from over 80 bids, eBay ended the listing without trace. It was like it was never there as they had totally removed it from the site. It just so happened that the press had, once again, been visiting us when the auction vanished. If the press coverage wasn't enough, eBay banning the legitimate sale of a decommissioned, non-airworthy, historic aircraft, citing the fact that it was a weapons delivery system and that it contravened their firearms, weapons and knives policy, really stirred the hornets' nest. It turned out that both the British media and the public quite like the Harrier, its history and the fact that, in the UK you can legitimately own a decommissioned aircraft. Nobody liked the fact that eBay, a large American corporation, were telling the Brits what they could or could not sell. This ruffled a lot of feathers, especially given the policy coming from a country where you can go into any major supermarket and buy an assault rifle.

Word spread quickly that eBay had removed a Harrier from sale over a weapons ban. An eBay spokesperson said in a press release: "We have strict policies in regards to the sale of military weaponry, meaning the jet should not have been listed for sale. We would like to apologise to the seller concerned for the inconvenience this has caused him."

What they failed to mention was that we had previously listed a few Harrier aircraft on the site, the sales of which eBay had 'creamed off' a healthy commission. We had no way of fighting it and no platform on which to sell the Harrier. If the aircraft didn't sell, we would go bust as we had put everything into the restoration. We just had to have faith that, with all the press coverage, someone out there would see the Harrier and want to buy it.

The next morning began with early morning radio interviews. Reporters, one after another, called on the phone and it seemed that everyone wanted to speak to me about the Harrier. In one interview for BBC Radio Sheffield, I said: "It's a perfectly legitimate item to sell. It's not capable of 'delivering weapons'. It's not even capable of delivering a pizza. This is a piece of aviation heritage which needs to be preserved, and we need to be allowed to restore and sell it." The press really liked the pizza line. An hour later, Moira Stuart was reading out my pizza quotation live on the BBC Radio 2 Breakfast News to an audience of millions: "Chris Wilson, 33, from Leeds said the aircraft wasn't even capable of delivering pizza, let alone weapons."

The BBC liked the story so much that they summoned us to London, all expenses paid. Me, Melanie and Ollie, who at the time was six, boarded a train to King's Cross, where we were met by a chauffeur-driven Mercedes. We were put up in a nice London hotel ready for our appearance, live on the BBC Saturday Morning Breakfast Show with Susanna Reid and Charlie Stayt. They were loving the fact that this was a family business, run by an RAF veteran who started a business from scratch, restoring historic, iconic, classic British aircraft. The eBay saga and the youthful buyer just enhanced the whole story. Although it was incredibly nerve-racking going out on live TV to an audience of millions, we told our story and the reaction was phenomenal. The real star was Ollie, who at the age of six had no nerves at all and stole the limelight. Hidden in the desk in front of the presenters were TV monitors so they can see which angle is going out on air. The viewers can't see this but the people in the studio can. This was all too much for a six-year-old who was really into his superheroes. He proceeded to practise a Spiderman impersonation, firing webs into the camera so that he could watch it on the monitors. Adjusting this jacket to show off his brand-new shirt, he stole the show. They do say never work with children but Charlie had no option but to say: " … and yes Oliver, we have noticed that you have a very nice shirt on."

On the back of the press coverage, we sold the aircraft a few days later. The buyer had seen the aircraft in the papers and then again when we were on BBC Breakfast. They got in touch, came to see the aircraft and bought it as an investment portfolio piece. Better still, it stayed in the UK and the restored Harrier was placed on long-term loan in a UK museum, the Caernarfon Airworld Aviation Museum in North Wales where it still resides to this day, preserved and undercover. It was a fitting end to the project and from a preservation perspective, a fantastic result. The money from the sale funded the move from Bradford to Selby, into bigger premises so we could expand the business and take on bigger and better projects.

In the last decade, Jet Art Aviation has gone from strength-to-strength and taken on larger and more high-profile projects. If it wasn't for the adventure with the T-Bird Harrier, XW269, and the subsequent press coverage which generated a sale at just the right time, the next chapter of the journey may never have begun. Since then, we have achieved a number of milestones:

- Restored the Transatlantic Air Race-winning Harrier, XV741, the aircraft that won the London to New York leg of the air race. We brought it back to its 1969 specification, reuniting the pilots who flew her in 1969 with their aircraft for the 50th Anniversary of the race. The aircraft is now on public display in the Brooklands Museum.
- Took on nine Jet Provosts in a job lot.
- Bought then restored Harrier, XZ130, an aircraft that I had trained on at Cosford—this was the one with Larry Ching's name on the side—and brought it back to ground-running condition. The project culminated in firing up the aircraft for the first time in 25 years followed by a complete repaint. (*See chapter 16*)
- Restored the world's only surviving Supermarine Swift F Mark 4 after it spent 50 years outside at the mercy of the elements, then once finished, installing it on display next to Vulcan XH558 at the Vulcan to The Sky Trust.
- Bought an F-104 Starfighter. It was a case of buying with the heart rather than with one's head as it was in poor condition. Nevertheless, we restored the 'widow maker' and sent it to a collector in Taiwan.
- Saved and restored eight Tornados—more than anyone else in the world and more than the RAF allocated for preservation in museums. This included a GR1 Desert Storm veteran, a Tornado F3 now on display in the National Aviation Museum of Estonia and the world's only Tornado F2A which, at the time of publication, was still on our books and preserved in a heated hangar.
- Acquired the unique, red, white and blue VAAC Harrier trials aircraft which is the oldest-surviving two-seat Harrier in the world and the longest-serving Harrier, resplendent in its unique 'raspberry ripple' paint scheme.

HARRIER XZ130 DURING ITS FIRST RUN IN 25 YEARS. (CHRIS WILSON)

SUPERMARINE SWIFT, WK275, BEFORE
RESTORATION. (DAVID GLEDHILL)

THE RESTORED SWIFT DISPLAYED AT
THE VULCAN TO THE SKY TRUST, NEXT
TO VULCAN XH558. (CHRIS WILSON)

- Took on seven Jaguars, almost having enough in the yard at one point to form our own squadron. These have since been either restored to go into a museum or are on display in private locations.
- Acquired our very first BAe Systems Hawk in the shape of the unique ASTRA Hawk, formerly of the Empire Test Pilot School, an aircraft so special that there have been limited-edition die-cast models produced.
- Taken on a mass of logistical and engineering work; difficult jobs that no one wanted to do, such as extracting Jaguar XX747 from the Engineering Officers' School at Cranwell. It had arrived before the invention of health and safety so getting it out through a tiny doorway, within the confines of a classroom, was extremely challenging. The station warrant officer at Cranwell, on his last working day in the air force, came to watch the extraction. After ten minutes he said: "I can't watch this. There's a CO's inspection in here tomorrow, so don't f**k this up!" We didn't and by the end of the day you wouldn't have even known there had ever been an aircraft inside the building.
- Supplied the undercarriage, wheels, ground locks and towing equipment for the BAe Systems Tempest, sixth-generation combat aircraft concept model that was launched to the world at Farnborough and the Royal International Air Tattoo in 2018. It was phenomenal to see that when BAe Systems needed something doing at short notice, they came to Jet Art Aviation to get the job done. We delivered, on-time and on-budget.

It's safe to say that my aviation journey, so far, has been phenomenal; a real adventure. I've worked with some amazing people and have been involved with fantastic projects. I've had the opportunity to travel and see the world, grow into a forward-thinking engineer, learn to problem-solve, think out of the box and to come up with solutions that just don't appear in manuals. My motto is if you can't get a tool or piece of ground equipment, then make it. I've had the opportunity to fly in various aircraft types from gliders, Chipmunk, Bulldog, Jet Provost, Strikemaster, Folland Gnat, Hawk and Tornado F3 and from helicopters to transport types. As groundcrew that's the icing on the cake. After all the hard work and long night shifts, to really appreciate how an aircraft works, and the stresses and strains a pilot can put an airframe through in normal flight, has to be experienced to be understood from an engineering perspective.

Squadron commanding officers today should continue giving groundcrew that experience as nothing gives an appreciation and an understanding of a flying machine like flying in one. Aircrew need to hang out with the groundcrew, getting down and dirty occasionally, getting covered in AVTUR and engine oil, to

JAGUAR XX747 EXTRACTION FROM RAF CRANWELL.
(CHRIS WILSON)

get a real appreciation of man (or woman) and machine and what is involved in engineering and maintaining an aircraft. A squadron with an 'us and them' attitude doesn't work and becomes counter-productive and abrasive. A squadron like the Red Arrows, where aircrew and groundcrew work together in unison, is certainly the way forward.

I've been lucky to have had an interesting and exciting groundcrew journey with happy stories to tell. However, I take my hat off to the groundcrew whose journeys have not been told. Those who turn up day-in, day-out and serve. Chaps from my mechs course who went onto the Hercules C-130 roll change. Guys posted to the drop tank, hydraulics or tyre bays doing the same job in, often, unpleasant conditions. To all those, like a good friend of mine who ended up doing six tours in Afghanistan. They saw him recovering downed helicopters in enemy territory whilst being shot at and washing blood and guts out of the back of Chinooks. These guys struggle to sleep at night because of the difficult things they have seen. These are the guys I raise a glass to. These are the guys whose stories need to be told.

To the top groundcrew boys; one and all!

Appendix

Aircraft problems were written up in the Form 700 after every sortie so that faults could be diagnosed and rectified. Inevitably, levity intruded. Here is a selection submitted by an anonymous contributor.

AIRCREW: Left inside main tyre almost needs replacement.
DEBRIEF: Left inside main tyre almost replaced.

AIRCREW: Test flight OK, auto-land very rough.
DEBRIEF: Auto-land not installed on this aircraft.

AIRCREW: Something loose in cockpit.
DEBRIEF: Something tightened in cockpit.

AIRCREW: Dead bugs on windshield.
DEBRIEF: Live bugs on back order.

AIRCREW: Autopilot in altitude-hold mode produces a 200 feet per minute descent.
DEBRIEF: Can't reproduce problem on the ground.

AIRCREW: Evidence of leak on right main landing gear.
DEBRIEF: Evidence removed.

AIRCREW: DME volume unbelievably loud.
DEBRIEF: DME volume set to more believable level.

AIRCREW: Friction locks cause throttle levers to stick.
DEBRIEF: That's what friction locks are for.

AIRCREW: IFF inoperative in OFF mode.
DEBRIEF: IFF always inoperative in OFF mode.

AIRCREW: Suspect crack in windshield.
DEBRIEF: Suspect you're right.

AIRCREW: Number three engine missing.
DEBRIEF: Engine found on right wing after brief search.

AIRCREW: Aircraft handles funny.
DEBRIEF: Aircraft warned to straighten up, fly right and be serious.

AIRCREW: Target radar hums.
DEBRIEF: Reprogrammed target radar with lyrics.

AIRCREW: Mouse in cockpit.
DEBRIEF: Cat installed in cockpit.

AIRCREW: Noise coming from under instrument panel. Sounds like a midget pounding on something with a hammer.
DEBRIEF: Took hammer away from midget.

AIRCREW: Unfamiliar noise from number two engine.
DEBRIEF: 30-minute ground run completed. Noise now familiar.

Glossary

'X' line Each level of servicing was numbered with first line completed at squadron level, second line on station and third line at a maintenance unit.

ABDR Aircraft Battle Damage Repair.

ACC Air Component Commander.

ADF Acceptable Deferred Fault. A known problem noted as a limitation.

AEF Air Experience Flight.

AFTS Air Frame Training Squadron.

APO Acting Pilot Officer.

APT Air Publication.

ASC Aircraft Servicing Chief.

ASF Aircraft Servicing Flight.

ASP Aircraft Servicing Platform.

AWACS Airborne Warning and Control System.

BF Before-flight servicing.

CFS Central Flying School.

CND Campaign for Nuclear Disarmament.

DME Distance-measuring equipment.

D-state A priority demand for a replacement component for an aircraft. Often, it will be unavailable to fly until the spare is fitted, unless another similar item can be 'robbed' from an unserviceable aircraft.

EAW Expeditionary Air Wing.

EES Electrical Engineering Squadron.

Fairy Avionics tradesman.

Form 700 The aircraft logbook recording all flight and servicing activity.

Gizzits A slang term for souvenirs or free gifts.

HAS Hardened aircraft shelter.

HLWSCU High-lift wing-sweep control unit. The box that controls wing sweep functions on a Tornado.

HP Handling party.

IPE Individual protective equipment.

ISO container A standard shipping container often used for storage and even accommodation in the military.

JFH Joint Force Harrier.

J/T Junior Technician.

Jockey Groundcrew slang for aircrew.

Lekkie Aircraft electrician.

Lekkie Bay Electrical bay.

Liney Flight-line mechanic.

MU Maintenance Unit.

MoD Ministry of Defence.

NAAFI Navy, Army and Air Force Institute. The service provider for military supplies such as food and beer.

NAPS Nerve Agent Pre-Treatment Set. A drug to combat nerve agent poisoning.

NBC Nuclear, Biological and Chemical.

NBS Navigation and bombing system fitted to V-Force aircraft.

OCU Operational Conversion Unit.

ORP Operational Readiness Platform. Used to park aircraft holding high-readiness states, located adjacent to the runway threshold.

PCS Personal Combat System. Combat clothing.

Plumber An armourer.

POB Persons on Board.

PSI Pounds per square inch.

PVR Premature voluntary release or retirement. A means to retire early from the armed forces. Normally a wait of 18 months.

Primary or Primary Star A second-line servicing.

QFI Qualified Flying Instructor.

QRA Quick Reaction Alert: V-bombers were held on high-readiness states armed with nuclear weapons and ready to scramble if ordered. Air-defence aircraft held higher states of alert as short as two minutes readiness.

Rates A Rate 1 was a subsistence allowance for staying in commercial accommodation.

Rigger An airframe technician.

RHAG The Rotary Hydraulic Arrestor Gear. A cable stretched across the runway which stops an aircraft, fitted with a tail hook, under certain emergency conditions.

Rupert A groundcrew term for an officer.

SATCO Senior Air Traffic Control Officer, normally of squadron leader rank.

Scaley Brat A service child.

SDSR Strategic Defence and Security Review. A regular review of defence posture and spending.

SEngO Senior Engineering Officer.

SIB Special Investigations Branch. The detectives of the RAF Police Force.

SNCO Senior Non-Commissioned Officer.

Sooties Engine technicians.

Squadron Duty Authoriser The supervisor of flying on the Squadron.

SSM Squadron Sergeant Major.

Squipper A survival equipment fitter.

'Stack' A slang term for to finish work. It was thought to derive from the name of a former air officer, Sir Neville Stack and was sometimes called a 'Sir Neville'.

Storno radio A type of radio used for ground communications.

SWO Station Warrant Officer. Responsible for discipline on a station. A much-feared figure to all ranks, including officers.

TASF Tornado Aircraft Servicing Flight.

Trolley-acc A battery unit used to provide external power.

UAS University Air Squadron.

VAS Visiting Aircraft Squadron. Non-resident aircraft and crews would be assisted with the turnround by VASF personnel when landing at an RAF base.

VASF Visiting Aircraft Servicing Flight.

Zulu A letter denoting a time zone. Alpha is normally continental time with Zulu denoting Greenwich Mean Time. Aircraft on operations use Zulu as the time reference.

Index

Index